THE
THREAT

THE
THREAT

**HOW THE FBI PROTECTS AMERICA
IN THE AGE OF TERROR AND TRUMP**

Andrew G. McCabe

St. Martin's Press
New York

www.stmartins.com

The Library of Congress Cataloging-in-Publication Data is available upon request.

ISBN 978-1-250-20757-9 (hardcover)
ISBN 978-1-250-20759-3 (ebook)

Our books may be purchased in bulk for promotional, educational, or business use.
Please contact your local bookseller or the Macmillan Corporate and Premium
Sales Department at 1-800-221-7945, extension 5442, or by email at
MacmillanSpecialMarkets@macmillan.com.

First Edition: February 2019

10 9 8 7 6 5 4 3 2 1

To Jill: my best friend, my inspiration, my strength, and my center.
Your love and support made this adventure possible.

Contents

Author's Note

Between the world of chaos and the world of order stands the rule of law. Every person in the United States, from a murderer to the president, is subject to the rule of law. This has been true since the founding of the country. Yet now the rule of law is under attack, including from the president himself. Organized criminal networks from other countries target the United States. Hackers steal our data, violate our privacy, and undermine our institutions. Terrorists target the innocent. Dirty money corrupts business and politics. Our own government officials use the power of public office to undermine legal authority and to denigrate law enforcement.

The Federal Bureau of Investigation is the principal law-enforcement agency in America. To uncover crime, and even to prevent it, the FBI combines shoe-leather investigation with modern intelligence gathering. The FBI's official mission is "to protect the American people and uphold the Constitution of the United States."

This book is one agent's story—my own. My first days in the FBI were spent investigating organized crime that traced its origins to Russia, a place where no distinction between crime and government exists. More than twenty years later, my last days in the FBI were spent investigating the Russian government's interference in our 2016 presidential election, possibly with the knowledge and involvement of that election's winning candidate. In between, I took part in the ongoing fight against terrorist threats: plots to bomb airplanes, subways, the Boston Marathon.

The FBI has always been the nemesis of criminals. Today, the FBI is under attack by the president of the United States. The president assails the FBI because he resents or fears the Bureau's independence, its fairness, its professionalism, its competence, and above all its values. This confrontation is part of my story, too.

—A.G.M.

THE
THREAT

FD-302

Application. Interview. Background check. The Bureau cherishes its procedures and lives by them. The pathway into the Federal Bureau of Investigation starts the same way for everyone. The official write-up on my own
application interview, conducted in Philadelphia more than two decades
ago, can be found somewhere in the personnel files at the J. Edgar Hoover
FBI Building, the Bureau's headquarters. It's on a form known as an FD-
302. Every interview conducted by an FBI agent is reported or summarized
on a 302. This form is the most basic building block of an investigation.
The FD-302 on me sits among write-ups on tens of thousands of other ap-
plicants over the years. I don't have access to it—I'm no longer with the
Bureau, a story for later—but my FD-302 would look something like this:

FBI EMPLOYMENT APPLICATION INTERVIEW,
ANDREW G. MCCABE

On September 14, 1995, ANDREW G. McCABE, dob 03/18/1968, address 208
Haddon Avenue, Haddonfield, NJ, was interviewed in the FBI Philadelphia

field office regarding his application for a Special Agent position. After being advised of the identity of the interviewing agent and the purpose of the interview, and after providing the interviewing agent with a completed copy of his FD-140, McCABE provided the following information:

McCABE was born in Flushing, New York. His parents, GEORGE J. McCABE and ELLEN E. McCABE, were also born in New York. In 1978 the family moved to Jacksonville, Florida, where McCABE completed high school at the Bolles School. The Bolles School registrar confirmed the dates of McCABE's attendance and graduation. McCABE's parents confirm that he is a person of high integrity. They are not aware of any significant legal or disciplinary problems in his past. They believe he is financially responsible and has not engaged in any conduct that would make him vulnerable to influence or extortion. They were surprised by McCABE's decision to become an FBI agent and do not understand why he would leave his law practice. McCABE's additional family members include one brother, PATRICK ANDREW McCABE, dob 05/25/1965, of Irvine, California. PATRICK McCABE is currently employed by Mazda Motor of America. PATRICK McCABE did not respond to repeated contacts and will be interviewed in person by FBI Los Angeles, Santa Ana RA. McCABE does not have any additional family.

McCABE is married to BARBRA JILL McCABE, dob 05/26/1968, same address. BARBRA McCABE is employed as a physician at the Children's Hospital of Philadelphia. She confirms the two met at Duke University in 1987 and were wed in Monterey, California, on 03/04/95. BARBRA McCABE's family includes DAVID McFARLAND (father), SUSAN McFARLAND (mother), both of Laguna Beach, California, and KIM MARQUARDT (sister) of Salt Lake City, Utah. Criminal records, NCIC, Triple I, and FBI Indices checks were negative on all these McFARLAND family members. BARBRA McCABE confirmed her knowledge and support of McCABE's interest in joining the FBI. BARBRA McCABE further indicated her willingness to relocate to any FBI duty station, as determined by the FBI, at the McCABES' cost.

McCABE completed college at Duke University in Durham, North Carolina, where he graduated with an A.B. in political science in May 1990. As a freshman, he was placed on social probation after being caught in possession of alcohol as a minor. In his junior year, McCABE was arrested by the North Carolina Alcoholic Beverage Control for purchasing alcohol as a minor while possessing false identification. The charges were dropped and later expunged after McCABE performed 40 hours of community service. Duke University confirmed the details of McCABE's enrollment, disciplinary record, and graduation. No professors with independent recollections of McCABE were identified.

In 1993, McCABE received his J.D. from Washington University School of Law, in St. Louis, Missouri. Several professors at Washington University described McCABE as an average student but also noted that he displayed a strong interest in criminal law. Two indicated they expected he would seek employment as a prosecutor following graduation. Washington University School of Law confirmed the details of McCABE's attendance and graduation. McCABE passed the New Jersey and Pennsylvania bars in the fall of 1993.

From November 1993 through April 1995 McCABE was employed as an associate attorney in the law firm of Greenberg, Shmerelson, Weinroth and Miller in Camden, New Jersey. He engaged in civil litigation, criminal defense, real estate transactions, and financial matters. McCABE's former supervisor, JAMES GREENBERG, ESQ., described McCABE as hardworking, intelligent, and careful. GREENBERG further stated that McCABE showed a willingness to take on new, hard assignments that pushed him beyond the scope of his experience. GREENBERG did not know McCABE to have ever abused alcohol, prescription drugs, or illegal narcotics.

McCABE is currently employed as an associate attorney at the law firm of Epstein, Becker and Green in Newark, New Jersey. McCABE concentrates on defending corporations in labor and employment litigation. McCABE's current supervisor, ROBERT H. BERNSTEIN, ESQ., described McCABE as diligent, resourceful, and easygoing. BERNSTEIN had no knowledge of McCABE's financial situation and could provide no information about McCABE's friends and associates. BERNSTEIN doubted that McCABE would join the FBI due to the lucrative future he had at the law firm. McCABE requested that BERNSTEIN not/NOT be further contacted as a part of this inquiry.

McCABE provided the names and addresses of five additional employers over the preceding ten years. Each was contacted and interviewed. Each confirmed the details of McCABE's employment but provided negative results to all other inquiries. McCABE further provided adequate explanations for all periods of unemployment, most of which occurred while he was in school.

McCABE provided the locations of each of his residences over the preceding ten years. Each location was confirmed through physical investigation and interviews of landlords and three neighbors at each location. None of those contacted could provide any specific information about McCABE beyond the details of his habitation. None were aware of behavior or actions by McCABE or others at the residences during the time in question that would cast doubt on McCABE's fitness for a position of trust with the government.

McCABE provided the names, addresses, contact numbers, and occupations for three references and three social acquaintances. Each was interviewed in person. All those interviewed described McCABE as honest, diligent, hardworking, and intelligent. Each described McCABE as patriotic and a supporter of the United States. None had ever seen or heard McCABE advocate for the overthrow of the United States, or support any group or organization opposed to the government of the United States.

None of the contacts reported ever seeing McCABE abuse alcohol, pre-scription drugs, or illegal narcotics. None could provide any insight into McCABE's financial status. Each person recommended McCABE for a po-sition of trust with the government.

McCABE provided his passport number and indicated prior foreign travel to France, Italy, Greece, and the Bahamas. This travel was confirmed through US Customs Service records. McCABE denied having any contact with for-eign intelligence officers, representatives of foreign governments, or sus-picious contacts during any of the reported travel. McCABE further indicated that his father, GEORGE McCABE, has had extensive travel to Japan due to his prior employment with Mazda Motor of America.

McCABE provided his selective service registration number, which was confirmed by the US Department of Defense. McCABE has no prior military service.

McCABE volunteered that he had "experimented" with marijuana in the past, but not in the past three years and not on more than 15 occasions to-tal. McCABE denied ever using or experimenting with any other illegal narcotics. Other than the previously noted alcohol possession arrest and subsequent dismissal, criminal records, NCIC, Interstate Identification In-dex, and FBI Indices checks all returned negative results.

McCABE denied ever having been a member of any group or organization that advocates for the overthrow of the United States government. McCABE denied being a member of any communist, fascist, or totalitarian organ-izations or groups. McCABE is not engaged in any activity that would have the effect of denying any individual their constitutional rights. He is not now and has never been engaged in any activity or behavior that could be used to influence, extort, or blackmail him.

Inquiries to TRW, EXPERIAN, and EQUIFAX revealed McCABE to be of sound financial status. His significant monthly expenditures include his rent, the lease on his vehicle (1993 Mazda Protege, NJ tag XYY-12344), and student loan debt. McCABE is not currently delinquent on any debt and has not declared bankruptcy. He has no significant credit card debt and he appears to live within his means.

McCABE acknowledged that he could be assigned by the FBI to work in Washington, DC, or in any other FBI duty station, and that he may be reassigned at any time at his own cost. McCABE indicated he fully understood that all FBI employees are assigned according to the needs of the FBI.

Following the interview, McCABE submitted to a full scope polygraph examination. Preliminary results showed no indicators of deception.

Height	5'11"
Weight	160
Hair	Brown
Eyes	Brown
Scars/Marks/Tattoos	None

1

Up for Grabs

A CONVERSATION WITH THE PRESIDENT— AND WHAT IT MEANT

Tuesday, May 9, 2017

Whenever James Comey, the director of the Federal Bureau of Investigation, was gone from the office for an extended period, my position as deputy director effectively cast me in the role of acting director. On this Tuesday morning in May, Jim was in the middle of a trip that would take him to field offices in Jacksonville and Los Angeles. I hustled through a challenging day, right up to the last block on the schedule, what we called the wrap meeting—a 5 P.M. gathering of the heads of each division. About twenty minutes later, my secretary pulled me out of that meeting and informed me that Attorney General Jeff Sessions wanted to talk to me. Immediately I thought there must be a problem—the attorney general did not call routinely. I asked, What line is he on? The secretary answered, He's not on the phone, he wants to see you in person. That meant it wasn't just a problem—something was really wrong.

I grabbed my coat, threw my notebook in a lock bag—a black bag with a key lock on the zipper for transporting classified documents—and left with my security detail, a longtime FBI agent. The walk from my office to the attorney general's took less than ten minutes: down the elevator, through the courtyard, left onto Tenth Street, and across Pennsylvania Avenue. At the corner, I noticed a couple of news trucks, which was odd. There had been a press conference about a big criminal case earlier that day, but the news trucks should have been gone.

The attorney general's office is a complex of several rooms, with a bedroom and shower upstairs. The attorney general even has his own dining room, across a hallway from the inner office, which, like most places in the Robert F. Kennedy Department of Justice Building, is elegantly appointed. The building itself—classical exterior, art deco interior—stands in contrast to the brutalist architecture of the FBI building, and the contrast captures something of the reality. The J. Edgar Hoover Building represents the instrumental aspects of justice, the Robert F. Kennedy building represents the ideal.

A secretary walked me to the door of the attorney general's private office and we waited for another ten minutes or so, making small talk—awkward, pleasant—about Alabama. She, like Sessions, came from there. I walked into an oddly formal scene. Sessions was standing up, in front of his desk. He wore his suit coat. Rod Rosenstein, the deputy attorney general, and his chief of staff, James Crowell, stood there, too, both also wearing suit coats. The three of them looked at me with expressions of wariness or expectancy—it was hard to tell. For an instant it felt even like suspicion. Whatever was on their minds, their demeanor elevated my concern: What the hell was going on?

Lock bag in hand, I said, Good afternoon, and Sessions said, Thanks for coming over. I don't know if you've heard, but we've had to fire the director of the FBI.

Time stopped for a moment. I should not have been shocked, but I was. One moment you are in an environment that you understand and know how to navigate. Then the lights turn off and turn back on in half a second, and you're standing in a completely different place. What do you do now?

You go back to what you know. What I know, from years of experience interviewing people, is that in situations of massive reorientation, you never show concern or make hasty judgments. You accept the facts that have been disclosed. You keep your feelings about those facts to yourself. In the moment, you act like a professional.

I answered the attorney general: No, I had not heard that.

He said, So we're going to need you to be the acting director for some period of time.

Yes, sir, I said, I'll do that.

He said that an interim director might be appointed during the administration's search for a new director, but for now they wanted me to run the FBI. He said, The FBI is a wonderful institution, and we're going to need you to continue to run it effectively and make sure the mission is accomplished.

I said I would do exactly that. I would await his guidance, and I would do whatever it took to ensure that we continued moving forward. I would assist the new director, interim or permanent, in any way necessary to help that person get off to a good start. I remember using words that come from the FBI's mission statement: I said we would carry on and protect the American people and uphold the Constitution.

He said, Thank you, and then asked, Do you have any questions?

Yes, I had questions. Starting with, Why did this happen? I also needed time to think. I answered, I do have questions, but I'm not prepared to ask them now. And the meeting was done, it seemed. A very short conversation.

As I was about to leave, I started reviewing all the things I would have to do. The first was to communicate with people in the Bureau. I said, I should probably send out some sort of an announcement to our workforce. Sessions and Rosenstein looked at each other, as if they hadn't thought of that. Rosenstein said, We don't want you to put out anything until we hear what the White House has to say. That was fine, I said, but I would need to say something internally. Rosenstein said, Don't do anything until you hear from us, and do not say anything about this to anyone, not even to your wife, until we get back to you.

The news of Comey's firing was on TV by the time I got back to the Hoover building, at about 6 p.m. So much for confidentiality. Listening to the news was how Comey found out about his dismissal—not in a phone call from the attorney general but from a CNN report that aired while he was speaking with FBI agents in Los Angeles. Everything about the decision to fire Comey had come across as improvised and slapdash. I walked back into the deputy director's conference room. The people at the meeting I had left were still sitting there. Obviously they knew what had happened. They looked at me. The expression on their faces said, What do we do now?

I told them exactly what I had heard. I knew that people would be anxious, scared, or upset during this period, and I sought to confront those emotions with candor. If I kept people in the loop about what was happening, it would limit the amount of time they spent wondering and worrying about what was happening. At least on the margins.

The director's secretary brought me an envelope for Jim Comey that had been delivered from the White House earlier that day. It had not been opened, and I opened it. Inside the envelope was Rod Rosenstein's three-page memo that purported to explain the cause for Comey's termination—his alleged mishandling of the investigation into Hillary Clinton's emails. The memo came with a letter of transmittal from the attorney general to the president, and the president's letter to the director, firing him. I remember holding the letter from the president in my hand and reading that conspicuous line in the middle—"While I greatly appreciate you informing me, on three separate occasions, that I am not under investigation, I nevertheless concur with the judgment of the Department of Justice that you are not able to effectively lead the Bureau." I wondered, Why would you put *that* in there? The answer would become clear as the weeks unfolded. The firing of Jim Comey gave new urgency to the FBI's investigation of Russian interference in the 2016 elections—that interference was a fact, not a supposition—and into possible collusion by the Russians with the Trump campaign. Comey's firing would lead directly to the appointment of a special counsel, Robert Mueller, to oversee that investigation.

In the conference room I told the team that we needed to figure out what to do in the next hour. After figuring that out, we would need to figure out what to do in the following hour. And then we would figure out the following twelve hours, and then the following twenty-four hours. That was my automatic response to the situation. It was a response that grew out of the cumulative experience of handling crises through my years in the Bureau: all the times I had overseen a course of action in situations with high stakes, where people's emotions and responses were highly charged and volatile. So I handled this as I had handled all those other crises. I jumped in with my team to build a plan. We had to start by identifying the most important things to do.

The first task was communication. We set a mandatory SVTC that night—a secure video teleconference. This one would connect all of the Bureau's SACs—the special agents in charge of our fifty-six field offices—so I could tell them this: There are a lot of things going through your heads right now. The absolute most important thing is that you keep your folks focused on their jobs and not on the firing of the director. Every one of you needs to get physically in front of every one of your employees first thing tomorrow morning and stress to them that we all need to stay the course. As we were sketching all this out, I got the message that the president wanted to see me at six thirty—in less than half an hour.

Whose Side Are You On?

I had been to the White House for meetings hundreds of times, and during my two decades of service to the FBI had met two presidents, Barack Obama and George W. Bush, in the course of official business. I had not yet met Donald J. Trump. Before I went over, and while I was in my office, Jim Comey called me from his cell phone. His voice was easy and unhurried as always, with a faintly *Fawlty Towers* inflection on the final vowel of his Hello! Classic Comey: Never let them see you sweat. The first thing I said to him was, What did you do now? He laughed. He said, I have no idea, but I must've really hosed something up.

The situation felt so crazy that the only correct response was to say, This is crazy. We're spinning here, I told him, trying to figure this out. He answered with equanimity, as if nothing unusual had happened. He said, You'll be fine, you will get through this. With an almost biblical intonation, he added, Have no worries.

Immediately upon becoming acting director, I was given a twenty-four-hour security detail—I was no longer allowed to drive anywhere by myself and could only ride around in the back of a fully armored black Suburban. At the White House, I bailed out of the Suburban at the little portico on the side of the West Wing, a door I'd passed through many times for meetings in the Situation Room. But I had never been inside the Oval Office.

A uniformed Secret Service officer made a phone call, and before long President Trump's longtime bodyguard, Keith Schiller, came down to meet me. Schiller, a big guy from the Bronx, has a résumé that's pretty well written in his buzz cut—Navy, New York Police Department, Trump Organization security director. Earlier that day, Schiller had been the one who had hand-delivered Comey's termination letter to the Hoover building. He introduced himself and walked me to the door of the Oval Office, then handed me his business card. Hey, he said, if you ever need anything, give me a call. I thanked him, puzzled—what did he think I might need from him?—and took his card. I stood there for a second, and then they let me in.

The president was behind the massive *Resolute* desk, built from the timbers of a nineteenth-century British vessel that American sailors had rescued from the Arctic ice and returned to Britain. He stood up and came around to the side. We shook hands. The White House counsel, Don McGahn, was there, and the chief of staff at the time, Reince Priebus, and Vice President Mike Pence. None of them said a word. No one was sitting comfortably in couches or armchairs. A row of little wooden chairs was lined up in front of the president's desk, and the three men were seated in the chairs like schoolboys who'd been called to the principal's office. One chair was empty, and I took it.

The president was sitting on the front edge of his desk chair, leaning forward, with his arms in front of him on the desk. He is tall, and very large, and when he spoke he started to make blunt gestures with his hands—kinetic, coming at you. He started off by telling me, We fired the director, and we want you to be the acting director now. We had to fire him—and people are very happy about it. I think people are very happy that we finally got rid of him. I think there's a lot of people in the FBI who are glad he's gone. We had to do it because of all that—you know, the Clinton thing last summer and all his statements and everything, he really mishandled that. He had to go, because of those decisions he made, and for a lot of other reasons.

The president was referring to the FBI investigation of Hillary Clinton's use of a private email server while she was secretary of state, and whether any of her thousands of emails had contained classified material. In July 2016, Comey had announced that criminal charges were not warranted and that no reasonable prosecutor would have pressed charges, but he had also chided Clinton for being "extremely careless." Then, in late October, he had sent a letter to Congress saying that new emails had turned up and would have to be examined—only to conclude a week later, once again, that criminal charges were not warranted. That was a few days before the election, and the controversy in all likelihood contributed to Hillary Clinton's loss. In his termination letter to Comey, which I had just seen, the president had pointed to Rosenstein's three-page memo and (as Sessions put it in his own letter) "the reasons expressed by the Deputy"—specifically, the director's handling of the email investigation—to explain the dismissal. I had been involved in that investigation and in Comey's decisions. Was the president's rationale just a pretext? I didn't quite know what to say.

The president asked if I knew that Comey had told him three times that he himself was not under investigation. I said I was aware of that—meaning, I was aware that Director Comey had told the president he was not under investigation. I could not remember exactly how many times the director had said that to the president. And at the forefront of my mind was the president's termination letter to Director Comey, which I had just read—I kept thinking about that oddly prominent mention of this concern the president was now raising, again, about whether he was being investigated.

A question was in the air: had I disagreed with Comey's decisions on the Clinton case—mainly, Comey's conclusion that Hillary Clinton should not be charged with a crime.

I said, No, sir, I didn't. Jim and I worked together very closely, and I was a part of those decisions.

The president claimed there had been a rebellion inside the FBI and asked me if it was true that people disliked Director Comey. I replied that some people were frustrated with the outcome of the Clinton investigation last summer, but the general feeling in the FBI about this director seemed positive. He looked at me, with a tilt of the head, an expression of dismay or disagreement, or both. I had not given the answers he expected or wanted. The subtext of everything that he was saying to me, clearly, came down to this: Whose side are you on?

Later I often thought about how much stronger my responses to the president could have been. But I was making my best efforts in the moment to say things that were accurate and reflective of my thoughts without flatly contradicting him. I felt it would be unhelpful in this traumatic moment to tell the president that I expected a fair proportion of our workforce to have feelings that verged on hysteria the next day, when all thirty-seven thousand of them came to work and had no idea what was going on because the director had been fired. In any case, my candor would have been irrelevant in this conversation, because we were not having a conversation. He was not really asking me questions. He was probing me, to find out whether I was on board with him or not. This was my loyalty test.

I knew that loyalty tests were important to him. Jim Comey had been pressed the same way in the same office by the same man on more than one occasion, as Comey himself had told me. And the loyalty that was demanded was personal loyalty, not loyalty to an office or a set of ideals.

The president asked me to tell him a little bit about my background in the FBI, and I gave him a brief overview of my assignments. He took this as a segue back to monologue: about searching for a new director, talking to great people, it was going to be great, they were going to get somebody great, the FBI was going to be great again, and now here I was, and wasn't it great? He said he was interested in Joe Lieberman—a great guy. They were also talking to other FBI people, he said. He loved law enforcement and the FBI. He thought police people loved him . . .

I found myself looking at the desk—baroque and bulky, intricately carved. Sitting there, I wanted to touch it, wanted to feel the nooks and crannies, the bas-reliefs, the little portraits. There's a hinged door in the front, which Franklin Roosevelt had installed to close off the opening in the desk that is left for a person's knees—so people in front couldn't see his leg braces. I remember having to tell myself: Pay attention. Stay in the moment. Don't be looking at the furniture.

The president's thoughts were frenetic. It's a disconcerting experience to attempt a conversation with him because he talks the whole time. He asks questions but then immediately starts to say something else. Almost everything he says he subsequently rephrases two or three times, as if he's stuck in some holding pattern waiting for an impulse to arrive that kicks off the next thing he wants to say. It all adds up to a bizarre encounter.

Toward the end, he said to me, So now you are acting director, and we have great hopes for you, you are going to do a good job. We may bring in somebody else to serve as interim director until the permanent director is confirmed. But we don't know. But we're going to look. We're going to get somebody great—it might even be you. It's going to be terrific. We're going to turn that place around.

The embedded assumption of all these superlatives piled up in the future tense seemed to be: The Bureau was a mess. If he believed that to be true—and it was not—then I bore a good part of the responsibility. Why, then, was he flattering me? He spent most of this meeting spewing stock phrases he often uses—You're great, you're terrific—all of which rang hollow. I knew that he had been aware of me since 2016, when he referred to me in terms that were not flattering at all. My wife, Jill, had run unsuccessfully for a seat in the Virginia state senate back in 2015, and she had received money, as other candidates did, from the state Democratic Party and from a political action committee run by the Democratic governor at the time, Terry McAuliffe, a friend of Bill and Hillary Clinton's. Because the following year I was involved in the FBI's email investigation, the president during the campaign decided to allege that I had been bribed to look the other way. He tweeted a headline from *The Wall Street Journal* that insinuated as much—CLINTON ALLY AIDED CAMPAIGN OF FBI OFFICIAL'S WIFE—and on the campaign stump expanded the insinuation into a conspiracy theory, in which Clinton directed McAuliffe to make campaign donations to Jill as a quid pro quo. So I was disregarding all of his You're great, You're terrific verbiage, letting it flow past, like the blather it was.

Then he said, Your only problem is that one mistake you made. That thing with your wife. That one mistake.

I understood that he was referring to the fact that my wife ran for office.

He said, Yes, that was the only problem with you. You know, I was very hard on you during my campaign. That money, from the Clinton friend—I was very hard, I said a lot of tough things about your wife in the campaign.

I know, I told him. We heard what you said. My wife is a wonderful, dedicated, brilliant physician, and she decided to enter public life because she felt deeply about trying to help her community. I completely supported that decision at the time, and I support it today.

He looked slightly uncomfortable. His tone shifted. Oh, yeah, yeah, yeah, he said. She's great. Everybody I know says she's great. You were right to support her in that. Everybody tells me she's a terrific person.

Good luck to you, he said at last. He got up and slapped me on the back, and I assured him I would continue to lead the FBI in the best way possible. Before I left, Mike Pence stepped forward and shook my hand, and he said something nice. Mike Pence always says something nice. Whatever else might be said about the vice president, I will say this: Every time I have met him, he has conducted himself as a gentleman. And manners count for a lot.

The Threat

I started my life in the FBI in New York in 1996, chasing Russian mobsters as a member of the Organized Crime Task Force. As soon as I became part of my first squad—from the first day—I thought, I'm never leaving this. I never lost that feeling. In a twenty-one-year career, I had just about every job an agent could have, and I always held on to a belief that this organization is unique. Its capabilities are incomparable. Today's FBI is the combined strength, knowledge, experience, and dedication of tens of thousands of people in five hundred offices across the country and around the world. They serve in war zones and other hostile environments with partners from the Defense Department and the Department of Justice. They are men and women of every race, religion, national origin, and sexual orientation. They are agents, analysts, scientists, forensic accountants, medics, auto mechanics, bomb technicians, linguists, locksmiths, hackers, ballistics experts, security specialists, administrative specialists, and secretaries. Some of them fly, some of them go underwater, and some of them know how to drive very, very fast. More than a few of them could be making a lot of money in Silicon Valley. The range, quality, and difficulty of the jobs they do would be hard to overstate. They perform feats of immense exactitude, such as recovering wreckage of a downed airliner from the sea off Long Island and reconstructing the plane in a hangar. They keep company with Americans who are coping with incalculable losses, as when, after a mass shooting, the FBI brings trained comfort dogs to sit quietly with family members of the victims. As deputy director, I had the ability to put agents on any doorstep in America in about two hours.

In the course of my career, the Bureau has undergone one of the more significant shifts of emphasis in its 110-year history. The mandate to investigate remains bedrock. But after the attacks of September 11, 2001, the FBI's number-one priority became preventing acts of terrorism in the United States or against Americans anywhere. The FBI's fundamental mission has never changed: to protect the American people and uphold the Constitution. That is its mission statement—those very words. To see the full force of the FBI deployed, as I did on 9/11, as I did after the Benghazi attack, as I did after the Boston Marathon bombing, and as I did in countless ways from the perch of deputy director, is to be astonished by this institution's mastery. It's not all hearts and flowers. We don't always get everything right. Many types of thought and action converge to serve the FBI's main purpose: investigation.

FBI investigations are predictable and orderly. FBI investigations are also fraught with surprise and wrought by improvisation. Special agents do a lot of listening and a lot of open-ended exploration. They also do a lot of strictly organized documentation, assessment, briefing, and negotiation. Investigations gather facts. Then investigators use legal techniques to discern patterns in these facts—stories about human behavior. Stories of the things that people do, how and why they choose to do those things, and the consequences of their actions. When these stories suggest that people may have broken laws, agents work with prosecutors to build cases. Cases go to court. Judges make decisions. People are found guilty or innocent, they are punished or they go free, and the rest of us go about our lives in peace.

The process of law enforcement helps to hold society together. The place of FBI investigations in this process is fundamental. Along with state and local law enforcement, we do the investigations that the rest of the system uses as the basis for the bigger decisions. The role of agents is to say, Here are the facts, here is what we found. Not, This guy's good and that guy's bad, but rather: This guy's dead, that guy had a gun, here's a list of phone calls that guy made, and here's a money transfer from this one to that one the day before the death. That's the agent's role. That's the job that I have loved.

In the scheme of things, it's easy to solve a crime involving one live guy and one dead guy—or at least, it's usually easier than much else the FBI has done in recent years. During my time as an agent, the FBI applied this country's legal investigative techniques to fight new forms of organized crime, terrorism, and online criminal activity, including cyber threats to national security. It has also been called upon to investigate matters that are unprecedented and pose existential dangers to our life as a democratic nation—most significantly, Russian interference in our elections. This interference is ongoing, and it is not conjecture. The evidence is incontrovertible: hacks of voting systems and databases; the release of private communications into public view in order to favor a particular candidate; widespread manipulation of social media in order to poison public debate. All of the country's intelligence agencies are in agreement about this. The occupant of the Oval Office resists this assessment, calling it a "hoax." Whether that man or his campaign solicited or cooperated with Russia's activities remains the focus of intense scrutiny by the FBI and a special counsel.

This book will tell how some of these investigations have worked, in a way that is faithful to both aspects of investigation I mentioned above: exploratory and procedural, open-ended and exacting, driven by individual curiosity and executed to the institution's strict legal standards. I will tell the human story of how it looked and felt and smelled to do the work I did, alongside the men and women I have been honored to work with. I will also highlight a few specific elements of how we work as an institution that, in my view, more citizens should be aware of: the FBI's investigative techniques; the way it gathers and presents intelligence; and the set of ironclad authorities on which FBI investigations are based.

It is a point of urgency for Americans to understand what the FBI really does, and why it matters, so that the citizens of this country can join together for the common good, to protect our common interests and our common concerns against very real and rising threats by those in foreign governments, and in our own, who intend to unravel the rule of law in the United States.

Let me state the proposition openly: The work of the FBI is being undermined by the current president. He and his partisan supporters have become corrosive to the organization. In public remarks and on social media, he has continued to beat the drum about the "lies and corruption going on at the highest levels of the FBI!" On Twitter alone, Trump has identified the FBI with the "Deep State," the pejorative term he uses to refer to professional public servants who conduct the nation's business without regard to politics; he has called Jim Comey "a terrible and corrupt leader"; he has called the investigation of Russian interference in the elections and possible ties with his campaign "perhaps the most tainted and corrupt case EVER!"; and he has referred to two of the investigators on the Russia case, themselves, as "a fraud against our Nation," "hating frauds," and "incompetent and corrupt." His insults have emboldened legions of goons to push further. Even mainstream news outlets have been unable to refrain from trafficking in destructive clickbait, juxtaposing the terms "FBI" and "corruption" in headlines over stories ostensibly covering "both sides" of the brawl that now passes for argument. TRUMP SUPPORTERS SAY MCCABE FIRING EXPOSES FBI CORRUPTION—that's not Breitbart, it's *USA Today*.

I knew this administration would be different from the last one. What I did not expect was the suspicion that so many members of this administration would train on those involved in intelligence gathering. The president has compared the intelligence community to Nazi Germany. He has asserted the essential equivalence of the U.S. government and the regime in Russia, proclaiming that "we have a lot of killers. . . . You think our country is so innocent?" He has stated in a press conference before the world, walking it back only under duress, and even then without conviction, that he values the word of the Russian president more highly than the collective opinion of his own intelligence services. When the president of the United States attacks the intelligence community and demeans the people who have been charged with keeping the country safe—and when he embraces conspiracy theories that politicize the FBI's most critical work—it has a direct impact on our ability to collect, analyze, and present intelligence that is essential to the security of the United States.

The FBI must perform a balancing act. To keep the American people safe, the FBI must be independent of the White House. At the same time, it must maintain a close functional relationship with the White House. Since the start of the Trump administration, that relationship has been in profound jeopardy. The president has stepped over bright ethical and moral lines wherever he has encountered them. His unpredictable, often draconian behavior is dangerous—a threat to both the Bureau and the nation.

2

Answering the Call

TRAINING DAYS, AND THE FIRST BIG CASE

The Road to Quantico

That first meeting with President Trump, in the spring of 2017, was my first time inside the Oval Office, but it wasn't my first time at the Oval Office door. In 1992, while I was in law school, I spent the summer working as an unpaid intern at the Department of Justice. One evening, a small group was given a White House tour. When we passed by the Oval Office, I remember, there was a velvet rope across the frame of the open door, as if in an old house that had been turned into a museum—which, considered from a certain angle, the White House was. We peeked in. The main thing my memory retained from that moment was the flash of the gold drapes.

That Justice Department internship turned out to be a turning point in my life. I was not a kid who watched *The F.B.I.*—the TV show starring Efrem Zimbalist Jr. as agent Lewis Erskine. The call to be an agent did not come to me early in a clear and direct way. It was indirect and slow to emerge. I did things that did not connect, and then by a process of elimination, which distilled into conviction, ended up gravitating to the Bureau.

I had grown up in the suburbs, and my dad was a corporate executive. Like a lot of kids on my block, I imagine, I looked forward to a life that was a grown-up version of the one I was already living. In college, at Duke, I took the required courses and the ones I thought I should take, eventually making my way to art history and political science. I was drawn to stories of real people—people in pursuit of love, advantage, power, salvation. In law school, at Washington University in St. Louis, I was again drawn to stories of human drama, now in the context of crime and punishment. My summer internship at the Department of Justice, in the criminal-fraud section, involved a lot of scut work—research, modest writing assignments. But I also got to read the case files and, most important, a type of document called a 302.

Those three digits are almost a magic number for me: 302. After FBI agents go out and interview subjects in an investigation, they come back and, within five days—while memory is fresh—they have to write up the results of the interview on a form called the FD-302. I caught the 302 bug reading interview reports from a public corruption case involving a pugnacious U.S. senator, his brother, and some questionable interactions they had with a defense contractor. It was a complicated business that would go on for a long time, and now it seems like ancient history. But when I read the 302s from that case, I thought, This is it. This is the marrow of law enforcement. This is the record of a conversation: people whose job it is to enforce the law actually sitting down and talking with people suspected of breaking the law, or with witnesses to a crime, or with victims of a crime, or with those who simply might have some relevant information.

Coming out of that summer, I knew what I wanted to do. I wanted to be part of the conversations that I'd been reading about. I wanted to go out and find evidence and talk with people about the times they had crossed those invisible lines of law that structure our society, or with people who had information about others who had crossed those lines. But when I came out of law school, the Bureau wasn't hiring. I became a small-town lawyer in New Jersey, waiting for a chance. On April 19, 1995, the bombing of the Alfred P. Murrah Federal Building in Oklahoma City took the lives of 168 people. The tragedy weighed heavily on me and reinforced my determination to continue seeking entry into the FBI.

Becoming an agent would mean that I'd make a lot less money than I could have made if I had taken a different path, but my wife, Jill—we had just gotten married—supported my ambitions and never counted the cost. When I told her I wanted to join the FBI, she said I should do it, because she saw how much I *wanted* to do it. I worked from then on with a sense that something was calling me to service, even as it gradually dawned on me that this job would entail risk and the sacrifice of much more than money.

On the Box

In 1996, the Bureau's doors reopened. At the time, the path to becoming a special agent started with a single page. To begin the process, you filled out a simple application and submitted it to your local field office. Anyone who failed to meet certain basic qualifications—such as having a college degree or being a U.S. citizen—was weeded out. If you made that first cut, your local field office began coordinating your background investigation and Phase One testing.

Phase One was a series of standardized exercises meant to evaluate your intelligence and computational skills. It also included a personality evaluation. If you made it through Phase One, you would be recontacted by your field office and asked to submit an FD-140—an official Application for Employment in the Federal Bureau of Investigation.

Every FBI employee, by virtue of being an employee in good standing, holds a top secret (or "TS") clearance. A TS clearance requires passing a stringent background investigation and polygraph examination. The FD-140 was the beginning, and the foundation, of the FBI's background investigation. At ten pages long, the FD-140 required you to give the FBI information about every aspect of your life. Not just your name and address, but every name you had ever used and every place you had lived in the previous ten years. It asked not just where you currently worked but every place you had ever worked. In between those periods of work, the FBI wanted to know when and why you were unemployed. It wanted the name and address of every school you attended and the grades and degrees you received at each. If you were ever disciplined at school, the FBI wanted to know when and why, and what punishment you received.

The FD-140 required you to give the FBI the names and addresses of all your family members and your spouse's family members. If any of them had lived or worked overseas, the Bureau needed that information as well. The FBI asked you to provide three references, defined as "responsible adults of reputable standing" who had known you well for at least five years. In addition, they requested contact information for three "social acquaintances," who could be your own age, and were presumably less reputable than your references, but who also had to have known you for five years.

The application required that you list every foreign country you had ever visited and any contact you might have had while there with representatives of foreign governments. The FBI wanted the details of your military service and whether you were licensed to practice law. They asked about any run-ins you might have had with the authorities, and whether you owed money to any person or business.

The FD-140 gave the Bureau a view into some aspects of your lifestyle. The FBI wanted to know if you had smoked marijuana during the previous three years or more than fifteen times total in your life, and whether you had used any other illegal drugs more than five times in the past decade. It sought to determine whether you were a communist, a fascist, or a subversive. Additionally, it wanted to know if you had ever supported the use of force to deny anyone his or her constitutional rights or had ever advocated the overthrow of the U.S. government. Before signing the application, the FBI let you know, and required you to acknowledge, that if hired you were expected to serve a minimum of three years and to move anywhere the Bureau ordered you to move at your own expense.

With this information, the background investigation was officially under way. Your field office set about sending messages to other field offices to investigate and confirm every fact you presented on the FD-140. For instance, I was living in southern New Jersey when I applied to the FBI, so my application was processed by the Philadelphia field office. It included the facts that I had worked in Cherry Hill, New Jersey; Newark, New Jersey; and Washington, D.C. Philadelphia sent requests for follow-up investigation (referred to internally as "setting leads") to themselves—for Cherry Hill—and to the Newark field office and the Washington field office. Their leads required agents and background investigators in those offices to contact and interview my former supervisors and confirm every aspect of my work history. This same tedious, labor-intensive effort would be directed at every fact on my FD-140, no matter where the work took place.

After vetting the information in the FD-140, you would be called into a field office for a polygraph examination. The exam would begin benignly—with the polygraph turned off—as an FBI agent reviewed the information on your FD-140. She would ask you questions and give you a chance to clarify inconsistencies or explain things that might have come out during the background investigation. The agent would try to eliminate any ambiguity or confusion in advance of the questions that would follow.

With questions prepared and issues clarified, the agent would set up the polygraph machine and, in FBI speak, "put you on the box." It goes like this: You are sitting in a chair with wide, flat armrests. The agent tells you to place your arms flat on the rests. Forcefully, she admonishes you not to move. At all. She places a blood-pressure cuff on your upper arm and inflates it uncomfortably. She wraps a sensor around your chest. She attaches an additional sensor to a finger. Each of these sensors is attached by wire to a box on the desk next to you. The box has multiple needles on top and a roll of graph paper that stretches beneath the needles.

When the exam begins, the agent asks you to provide yes or no answers only—the time for explanation and discussion is over. She starts by asking easy questions that call for obvious answers, such as, Are we in Philadelphia? or, Is your name Andrew McCabe? You answer Yes or No, and you don't move. Between the questions, you can hear the dull scratch of a needle dragging across paper. You wonder what it is saying about you.

Then she asks the real questions, which are derived from the information on your FD-140. The questions about drug use eliminate the largest number of candidates. People frequently minimize their history with drugs or lie about it altogether. Getting caught lying on the polygraph means you can't pass the background investigation. Your dream of working for the FBI is over.

I passed the polygraph, which meant I was officially "out of background" and still moving forward. There were still hurdles left—medical testing, Phase Two testing—but I was a giant step closer to the FBI Academy at Quantico.

I rehearsed how I would quit my job—how I'd tell my boss—working out the phrasing to eliminate any room for objection. I have spent a lot of time thinking about this, I'd say, and I've decided to leave this law practice and to join the FBI. That's what I did say, and my boss tried to talk me out of it. As had my parents. Not Jill. I took a 50 percent pay cut. To save money, we had to leave our apartment, in Haddonfield, New Jersey, and Jill moved in with a roommate. We had to be apart for the sixteen weeks of my special-agent training. I'd be in Quantico, Virginia, where the FBI Academy is located, and Jill would be almost two hundred miles away, doing her residency at Children's Hospital, in Philadelphia. I started getting up early in the morning and running, so I'd be ready for the physical fitness tests. I rigged a pull-up bar, and I'd do a couple of pull-ups on the way out and a couple more on the way back.

Hogan's Alley

Arriving at Quantico was like driving off a cliff. I had no idea what to expect. I was certainly excited, but I was stepping into a different world from the one I had known.

It was a hot Sunday night when I drove from Philadelphia to Quantico. After getting out of the car and stretching my legs, I walked in the main entrance and immediately passed through the Hall of Heroes, surrounded by the faces and names and stories of those agents who had made the ultimate sacrifice. Then I went to my dorm. Two to a bedroom, four to a bathroom—just like college, even though most of us were almost ten years older than college students. The man I shared a room with was a former Army captain from Rhode Island.

At that time, a new class of forty started at Quantico every other week. My class, NA9618—"NA" stands for "new agents"—was the year's eighteenth class. All forty of us got sworn in as special agents that night. We swore an oath to protect and defend the Constitution against all enemies, foreign and domestic. From that moment on, we were special agents in training.

The next day we picked up our uniforms—hiking shoes, tan Royal Robbins cargo pants, and a dark blue FBI Academy polo shirt. We wore the uniform everywhere. No gym clothes were allowed on campus except at the gym. No jeans were allowed anywhere at the academy, ever.

Then the classes started, covering the law and techniques of investigation: how to conduct an interview; how to write up a 302; how to handle all the different kinds of documents an agent has to handle; how to dust for fingerprints. The difference between the valedictorian and the person who came in second in our class was a wrong answer on a single fingerprint ID question on a single test. Our forensics teacher was one of the agents who had searched the cabin of Theodore Kaczynski, the "Unabomber."

The classes weren't all brain work. Agents get a full-on physical education. Taking people into custody, defensive maneuvers, hand-to-hand combat. Everybody does some boxing. Everybody learns to clear a room. Everybody learns how to plan an arrest and how to make an arrest. An agent learns how to do all these things in many kinds of environments where you can imagine an arrest being made. A restaurant, a bar, a bank, a trailer park, a motel, a school. Those environments are packed into the most famous part of the campus at Quantico—Hogan's Alley, a fake town, a full-sized replica community made up of all the kinds of places I just mentioned, and more, populated and run by character actors who live nearby. Every special agent in training learns the ropes in these false environments—figures out how to react and adapt in different situations.

The third big piece of training is firearms. Some in our class had never fired a gun before. Some had been marksmen in the military. No matter what their past experience, agents in training all start at the same level, learning the basic nomenclature, how to break a weapon down, and what every part and piece is called and how they work together. On the firing range, they learn sight alignment and trigger control. All forty of us shot thousands of rounds. By the end of sixteen weeks, we could all shoot very well.

The schedule at Quantico changed constantly. We moved rapidly from one thing to another. We were acquiring a sense of discipline, a paramilitary sense of order. I recognized the flaws of this system. Prioritizing obedience to process could create a type of groupthink that stifles creativity, independence, and critical thinking. But the Bureau is bureaucratic. It is a law-enforcement agency. It is paramilitary in nature. It also depends for its success on keeping records. It is run according to a clear and distinct chain of command. So there is a set of very basic concepts that lead to an understanding of where you stand in this big organization. You start learning those concepts at Quantico, when you're told on the first night that punctuality is not optional. If you're not early, you're late. If class starts at eight, you're there at seven fifty. Anyone who isn't early is noticed and marked as being out of step with the program. Quickly it becomes the case that no one is ever late under any circumstances. If you have only twenty minutes between your physical education class and your law class, and you have to shower, get dressed, and cross the campus to get there—you figure it out. You make it work. Those words could almost be an agent's motto: Make it work.

I embraced every bit of this culture, even the most arbitrary aspects of the discipline. Who I am fit with what this was. I wanted to look the way they wanted me to look. Loved wearing the same style of polo shirt every day for weeks on end. Loved the fact that everybody around me wore the same polo shirt, too. That polo shirt was a symbol of dedication. It announced your priorities. The more detailed the requirements of the academy experience, the more I responded to it. I wasn't just acclimating to a place, I was joining a life. I felt like every quirky, inconvenient thing about this experience was necessary and important, and, in a way, even cool.

The biggest shift entailed in learning to see the world like an agent is the shift toward altruism. It's a huge change of mind-set to go from being Joe Private Citizen, where your worries are mainly about yourself—your own safety and happiness and health—to putting all that aside and saying, I'm going to worry about everybody else first. Mortal stakes help this shift along. In one class, the instructor talked about lethal force—the times when you put yourself in harm's way to eliminate a threat to other people. There was never a doubt in my mind that this was the best thing a person could do. It's not that I ever wished to be in that situation, but I did feel on some level a desire to live on the visceral edge.

That desire inflects a thousand little shifts in perspective and technique, altering the way you see the world and make your way through it. You start to think of your whole life, almost every minute of every day, in terms of readiness. One example: In the car, when you unbuckle your seat belt, you slip the back of your hand inside the belt across your chest, you slide your hand down along the inside of that strap, and then you release the belt and push away with the back of your hand. You have to do it this way, because if you unbuckle it the way normal people do—reaching across your chest, overhand, and clicking the buckle with your thumb—then your arm is inside the triangle of the belt. And if you have to jump out of that car in a lethal situation, that could be the thing that costs you a tenth of a second and gets somebody killed.

Part of our firearms training was running shoot/don't-shoot scenarios in a video-training module, to gain practice in making split-second decisions. You knock on a guy's front door, maybe he answers and then runs back into the house: What do you do? Do you go in by yourself? Do you call your partner? You hit these decision points, and depending on how you react, the video plays differently. This is not exclusive to Quantico—police agencies all over the world use some version of it now. It's called Firearms Training Simulation—FATS, for short. In training we would all sit there in a line, dressed in our gear, and it was nerve-racking—I could hear screaming and gunfire in the video booth where the person ahead of me was training. For all I knew, the trainee had just lost his virtual life. And I was next.

In the twenty-two years since I graduated from Quantico, FATS technology has improved. It's all digital now, and the fake guns palpably re-coil, which realistically messes with your ability to recapture your sight picture—the way you frame a shot with your gunsight. It tells you when your shot is lethal. But the best part of the whole session, as it's run today, is the conversation after it's all over, between the trainee and a lawyer. The lawyer asks, Why did you shoot at this point? And the trainee says, I thought I was going to die. The lawyer says, What did you see that led you to believe that your life or the lives of others were in danger? The trainee better have a good answer. Hard conversations like these teach agents to articulate every decision they make. A decision that you can't articulate is probably a wrong decision.

'I'm Being Racketeered'

After months of learning in a fake city populated by fake characters, FBI Academy training culminates with the trumpet-blaring pomp of gradu-ation, as if we're all becoming knights of the Round Table. Then we get plunked down in field offices all over the country. When you go to Quan-tico, one thing you give up is any control over where you're going to live after you leave. Here I am. Send me where you need me. That's the deal. You get your chance to say where you'd like to go, but the three monkeys throwing darts at the map to make your assignments do not, typically, read your preferences. You get what you get, and it's all to satisfy "the needs of the Bureau"—the infamous tagline that explains all manner of offense, real or perceived.

I got New York City—lower Manhattan. It was a rude awakening, going from one end of the spectrum to the other. Quantico was regi-mented. The New York field office was a free-for-all. Where were the people handing me my new uniforms and cooking my meals?

No one would tell me what to do. There were no supplies anywhere.

They gave me a car, but no place to park it. The only parking place I could find was ten blocks away, and then I got to the office in a sweat because I was late—and realized that nobody cared. I came out of Quantico's perfectly structured world, flush with idealism, and into a world where the bosses say, Don't give me any of that Quantico bullshit, kid.

Struggle and deprivation can be gifts. In the New York field office— the biggest of the Bureau's field offices, with about eleven hundred agents and as many staff—you're limited only by your imagination and energy. If you're willing to work your tail off, even a new agent can take down the top guy in a crime family. I would spend the first ten years of my career focused on cases that grew out of two interlocking narratives: the evolution of organized crime in Russia and the export of Russian organized crime to the United States. These narratives traced a complex and inexorable process that would, despite the best efforts of the FBI as a whole, become only more dangerous. Russian organized crime today has deep ties to the Russian government. It saturates the internet. As most people are aware, the combination of crime, computers, and the Kremlin has in recent years taken aim at electoral politics—at American democracy itself.

My first big case started with a phone call. I picked up the receiver— these were the days of landlines—and heard an old guy's voice say, I think I'm being racketeered. It was February 1998. I had come to work early, because I was eager. It took a while for me to figure out that real work started late in the day. So when the switchboard for the main New York field office number put a call through to our squad, I was the only agent around to answer it. The old man on the phone spoke with a thick Russian accent. His voice was shaky and fearful. To protect his identity, I'll call him Felix. Felix ran a furniture store in Brooklyn. When I went to talk to him, he told me that a Russian thug was forcing him to pay one hundred dollars a week in "protection money"—this at a time when

Felix's business couldn't have been pulling in much more than a thousand dollars a week. Felix needed genuine protection: protection of the law, provided by the Bureau. I would be the case agent.

After Felix told his story, I went back to the office and wrote up a 302. I realized, now, that I was part of the conversation I'd been longing to join ever since my summer internship at Justice. With this case, my squad would take the playbook the Bureau had used to crack La Cosa Nostra, the Mafia's five families, and turn it against the Russian mobsters whose activities had moved Felix to call. Before the end of that year, my squad became one of the first to use the RICO statute against a Russian-organized-crime group when we indicted the Gufield-Kutsenko Brigade, a gang that extorted not only furniture stores but also restaurants and jewelry stores; sold fake Medicaid cards and green cards; kidnapped businessmen; and burned down buildings. They played rough.

Right when I was going after these guys, one of my New York colleagues was translating a fatwa issued in Arabic by a radical jihadist who was then all but unknown: Osama bin Laden. At the time, neither the Russian Mafia nor radical Islam had been getting much attention because the country was distracted by politics: the unfolding Bill Clinton–Monica Lewinsky scandal, which ultimately led to impeachment proceedings and, along the way, jacked up tensions between President Bill Clinton and FBI Director Louis Freeh. That episode was just the latest in a series of struggles, such as those involving the Khobar Towers and "Filegate," between the director and the president that had all but alienated the FBI from the White House. It is striking that this moment in the late 1990s, when radical Islamic extremism and Russian organized crime were emerging with new clarity, was also one when the poisonous personalization of politics deflected attention from those very threats. In the present moment, as I write, both of these phenomena—foreign terrorism and foreign organized crime—represent two of the greatest threats we face.

The Bureau had a long tradition of ignoring organized crime. Old-school law enforcement was all about statistics, or "stats"—that is, measuring the numbers of arrests, indictments, and convictions. Those numbers proved the Bureau's worth, at least in the eyes of presidents and of Congress, and justified our funding. Mob investigations, which are complicated and lengthy, tend to produce a low yield of favorable stats. Under J. Edgar Hoover, who ran the Bureau for almost fifty years, starting in 1924, the FBI paid scant attention to the problem.

After Hoover's death, in 1972, the FBI put some manpower on La Cosa Nostra. For these investigations, the Bureau mastered new ways of doing business. It learned to reckon with complicated international criminal structures, to collect and process evidence in other countries, and to overcome language barriers in order to navigate foreign courtrooms. By the end of the 1980s, the Bureau had built competence in all these areas, and the mob's reign in New York was coming to an end. Louis Freeh helped make that happen, first as an FBI agent and later as a federal prosecutor. When Freeh became the FBI's director in 1993, he brought this experience to the Bureau.

Freeh had a personal authenticity that immediately won the respect of agents. Everyone referred to him as Louie, whether you knew him or not. He had been one of us. He became the kind of prosecutor we all wanted to work with. Time as a federal judge gave him an imprimatur of knowledge and authority. I traveled with Freeh on several overseas trips—to Budapest, Hungary; Almaty and Astana, Kazakhstan; Moscow and St. Petersburg, Russia—as part of his security detail.

Though naturally quiet, Freeh was a superb diplomat. In Russia, he drank vodka shots with officials of the MVD, the interior ministry. In Central Asia, he ate the eyeball from a barbecued goat. No matter where he was, he liked to get up early and go for a run. This meant that his advance team had to plan the running routes and run them ourselves at the exact time Freeh would, so that we could gauge lighting conditions, access routes, traffic, and crowds. Freeh held a strong seven-and-a-half-minute-mile pace. He always invited the cops or agents from the local service to join him. At every location, some local cop would want to race the FBI director to show what he was made of. Somehow, the local stallion always won. On the last night of each trip, Freeh would invite the entire team up to his room for drinks.

Under Freeh's leadership, the Bureau developed a more international perspective. Freeh opened many legal-attaché offices—called legats—overseas, including one in Moscow. He built relationships with law enforcement in Russia and in Armenia, Ukraine, Lithuania, and throughout the Caucasus. These relationships fed Freeh's awareness of organized-crime networks in Eurasia and how they operated in the U.S., mainly in the Russian-immigrant communities of New York, Philadelphia, Chicago, and Miami.

This work got little support from the Clinton administration. In the heady first years after Soviet communism fell, President Clinton and Vice President Al Gore wanted to see democracy and free-market capitalism take root in Russia. Who didn't? But they wanted so badly to see this that they failed to understand how firmly organized crime had taken hold in all of the former Soviet republics. You have to wonder what might have happened if the U.S. government had taken Russian organized crime more seriously during those years—but beyond a certain point, it's also pointless to wonder. Nobody can see everything.

In 1996, the New York field office had the largest organized-crime operation in the country. There were several Italian-organized-crime squads. There were Asian-organized-crime squads. And there was a new one, just started in 1994, for organized crime in Eurasia, including Russia. As shorthand, we used the terms "Russian organized crime" and "Eurasian organized crime" interchangeably.

My first assignment had been Italian. The Colombo family. The first thing you do, on any assignment, is your homework. You read the binders.

I started plowing through the whole history of investigations of the Colombo crime family, and before long I found a surprise: the names of a couple of people I knew. One had been to my wedding and given me a wedding gift. This seemed like a problem. I asked my supervisor. My supervisor said, Stop reading the binders. I was given another assignment.

This turned out to be the best possible bad luck. I got moved to squad C24, Eurasian organized crime. At the time, Russian mobsters were seen as the junior varsity when compared to the Italians. Both kinds of gangsters were interested in the same targets of opportunity—drugs, human trafficking, money laundering, and financial fraud—but if the Italians got involved, the Russians would go running.

The criminals' hierarchy also applied to cops who chased them. New York City loves its Mafia. It's part of the culture there. So those of us who worked Russian organized crime were like redheaded stepchildren. The Cosa Nostra squads had twenty-five years of intelligence collection to draw on. They knew who was in what family, who was affiliated, who was at war, who had cooperated, and they had a deep bench of grand old men. We had nothing like that.

Second fiddle suited me fine. And like a lot of underdog teams, our squad had the best coach. In style, Raymond Kerr was a G-man's G-man: rock-square jaw, purse-lipped smile, steel-gray hair, pants creased, shirt tucked. He must have had a suit coat or blazer around somewhere, but you never saw it. He wore gold-rimmed glasses for reading. Every two years, Kerr would trade in his immaculate Bureau car—his Bu-ride, a Ford Crown Victoria, the legendary Crown Vic preferred by old-school cops and taxi drivers everywhere—and get an even more pristine new model. I can still hear the soft whoosh of the SWAT-issued Gore-Tex raincoat, sleeves sliding on side panels, as Ray walked into the office. But what I remember most is his voice.

Kerr was the ultimate agent's supervisor. He was completely focused on cases and operations, and on throwing bad guys in jail. He would sit in his office for hours and talk to us about the people we were chasing, the informants we were using, and the prosecutors who were building cases with us. He was our strategist, our sage, our cheerleader, and our conscience. He pushed us to meet aggressive goals and helped manage our expectations when things didn't quite measure up. After a colossal mistake on a case where my partner and I arrested the wrong person, Kerr told us that if we made the best decision we could with the information we had at the time, we had nothing to worry about. Then he made sure we had our professional liability insurance paid up. Even though we were federal government employees and theoretically protected by the Justice Department, you never knew when you'd need a backup policy. Kerr taught us to be prepared, always do our best to get things right, and not take it out on ourselves if things didn't go our way. The only sin was to do nothing at all.

When Kerr was angry, you knew it. He wasn't a screamer. Instead, he got quiet. The rock-square jaw got rockier. And before he told you what he really thought, Ray would toss a quick glance to each side, over his shoulders, as if there might be somebody standing behind him listening. It was the kind of thing you would expect an informant to do, in a dark alley, in a 1940s movie. There never was anyone listening in—it was just a tell, his way of emphasizing that the next thing he said was for you and no one else. After the side-to-side look, he'd look you straight in the eye, point his finger at your chest, and say, That guy's not just a moron. He's a *fucking* moron.

Kerr had been in charge of the first Asian-organized-crime squad, so he knew how to build from the ground up. He found people with real knowledge about Russia, like Michael McCall, to add to the team. A fluent Russian speaker who came over from counterintelligence, McCall brought an understanding of how organized crime worked in the former Soviet Union and an awareness of how it was being exported to the U.S.

The central idea of Russian organized crime is *vory v zakone.* The phrase means "thieves-in-law" and refers to the top tier of the underworld. Russian organized crime grew out of the Soviet prison system and reproduced the hierarchies of the gulags. The only law the *vory* observe is the "thieves' law," a strict code that says they will never work, never hold a legitimate job, never do what the authorities tell them to do.

To be a made man in the Italian Mafia means being accepted into a family, in a bona fide induction ceremony—we've all seen the movies. The path to becoming a made man in Russia is different. The *vor* must have been to prison, done hard time, and declared himself a thief for life. People who live like that will, as a consequence, keep going back to prison. The more times the *vor* goes in and out of prison, the higher his status, which is written on his skin. Icons are as important in Russian crime as in Russian religion, and one way to spot the *vor* is by his tattoos. The tattoos are an intricate symbolic language, inscribed with ballpoint pen ink and sewing needles, dark and rough and hittery-skittery. Crosses on the knuckles indicate the number of times a man has served time in prison. Stars on the shoulders signify authority. The real leaders who emerge from that process are the *vory v zakone*.

One of the first *vory* of stature to come to the U.S. was Vyacheslav Ivankov. From the prisons of Siberia he made his way to Brooklynski—Brighton Beach, the home base of Russian organized crime in the U.S. Spinning cycles of extortion that touched the worlds of nightlife, sports, entertainment, and investment banking, Ivankov became the first target of Kerr's squad. In late 1995, they got him. In news footage of his perp walk—with Mike McCall at one elbow and his partner, Lester McNulty, at the other—Ivankov actually spits at the camera. The month Ivankov went on trial, the *New York Daily News* alleged that he put out a murder contract on both agents. All the way to sentencing, in 1997, he refused to admit any guilt for anything. "I am not in a church," he told the judge. "I have no need to make a confession."

The Wire

After C24 caught its first big fish, the waters were calm for a while. I and a few other new agents joined the squad—Ray's Day Care, we called it. Fresh out of Quantico, full of piss and vinegar, we knew nothing. We were all eyes, all ears. A lot of the Russian gangsters were unrefined, but their behavior had its logic. One man arrested in New York for murder confessed that, back in Russia, he had carved up a few bodies with a blowtorch. A blowtorch is better than a saw, he explained, because it is so much cleaner. Dismember and cauterize, in one easy step.

At first, our investigative strategy was, basically, to walk around asking people, Are there any *vory v zakone* here? This strategy did not get us very far. Kerr taught us to take a different approach. We started asking, Who's hurting people? Who's ripping people off? And especially, Who's showing off? There's a big overlap between gangsters and people who look like gangsters—a big overlap between true *vory* and people who go to wiseguy nightclubs and flash a lot of money. We would get to know the bartenders at Russian mob clubs. A bartender at, say, Rasputin in Brighton Beach, might tell us, These five guys come in here every night, spending loads of money. There's girls all over the table. We'd ask the bartender to describe those five guys in detail.

Eventually, the victim of a crime would describe a criminal who sounded like one of the five guys at Rasputin. Now we were getting somewhere. We would poke around to see what connections might exist between this person and that person, build up a trove of what's called association evidence.

It's great to have a tape recording of a thug threatening a victim. But that's rare. It's also great when you execute a search warrant and find a shoebox full of happy-snap pictures in their house. That shoebox is a gold mine of association evidence. Oh, really? You don't know the guy? That's funny, because here's a picture of you and him at the beach. That can be valuable not just in building the case against your subject, but also in building your knowledge of the organized-crime networks in the area. Look, here's that guy Leo is investigating. I didn't know Leo's guy knew my guy. Then I go talk to Leo, and it turns out that both of our guys went to St. Barts for Easter break.

Where is all this going? As an agent, you don't know at first. You probably won't know for a long while. And the starting point can seem innocuous, like that call from Felix, the furniture-store owner.

Kerr said I had to go out and interview the guy. Felix lived in a predominantly Russian part of Brooklyn, but his store was in Flatbush, a very different neighborhood. Imagine a five-foot-eleven-inch whippet, so excited: That was me. I told a salty old New York detective who had been assigned to the squad where I was going, and he said, Whoa, whoa, you can't go out to that neighborhood by yourself. One white guy in that neighborhood in the middle of the day: victim. Two white guys together in the middle of the day: cops. Then he asked, What are you driving? Light blue Chevy Caprice, I said—classic bubble cruiser. You're good, he said. You're fine, you're gonna be fine.

Kerr said, Who are you going to take with you? I rattled off the names of the most senior people on the squad. Kerr said, Let me see . . . He looked out his door and saw Greg Sheehy. He said, Take Sheehy.

Sheehy? Sheehy was more junior even than me. Didn't even know the almost-nothing that I knew. But again, best possible bad luck. Sheehy proved to be a great agent and an even better friend. From that day forward we were partners. So we drove out to Flatbush. Met with Felix in his store. Raw space, wallboard, almost like a warehouse storefront, stacked to the ceiling with bargain furniture, priced to move. The clientele appeared to be all working people from the neighborhood, without a lot of money to spare. Felix told us a story.

The story was about a guy named Dimitri Gufield, who had been

Felix's partner in a different furniture store years earlier. Then Dimitri moved back to Russia for a year. When Dimitri returned, he reintroduced himself to Felix. Dimitri was a gangster now, and he expected Felix to start paying him protection money. Felix was deeply offended by this. Offended to be treated as a stooge by someone he thought was a peer, an equal. We're the same, we're furniture guys! Who are you to think you're some tough gangster?

Dimitri lived in a nice colonial house out on Long Island. Had a nice family—wife, kids—and they lived what seemed to be a respectable middle-class life. But Dimitri's dream, the thing he wanted most in life, was to be a big-time gangster. He gathered a little crew around himself, and every young punk in this crew had to go out and identify businesses to extort for protection money. Dimitri's own focus was on furniture stores, because that was what he knew.

Krysha is the Russian word for roof. The word can be used literally or figuratively. *Krysha* refers to the exterior top surface of something, such as a building or a car. Or *krysha* can refer to a person who provides the same kind of protection as a roof. "I'll be your *krysha*"—I'll be your roof—means that I will stop things from falling on you. Since the early 1990s, most businesses in Russia have had to operate with the protection of a *krysha*. Even if provided by the police or other government officials, the *krysha* is ultimately tied to organized crime. There is no effective distinction, in Russia, between organized crime and government, so *kryshas* have proliferated to where they block out the sky. Everyone lives under protection. The transformation has been systemic. It cannot be attributed exclusively to the actions of any one individual. But under the presidency of Vladimir Putin, the cohabitation of crime and government became the norm. Crime is the central and most stable force in Russian society.

Dimitri pitched guys like Felix, and Felix agreed to pay right off the bat. Felix was irate, he felt humiliated, but he was susceptible because he had a family, too. Then Dimitri wanted more. He went back to Felix and said, The other owners, they look up to you. I need you to bring them together. We'll have a meeting. Call in half a dozen of them. I'll be there. You'll tell them you've decided to start paying me, and you'll tell them they should follow your lead and pay me also. That's when Felix called the FBI. He didn't want to go through with this meeting. He hoped we could protect him from the protection racket.

A phone call and a story like Felix's are uncommon. An agent does not often get tipped off to an extortion demand as it's happening. So Sheehy and I were keyed up. We went back to Kerr's office, wondering what we should do, and Kerr asked if Felix would wear a wire. I said, I think so—this guy seems all in.

Felix was all in. In our first meeting with him, he said, I shouldn't have to pay, because this is America. Nobody has to pay for protection here. He looked at us, two fledgling FBI agents, and he said, about the thug who was trying to rule that neighborhood by fear and force, I don't need *him*—I have *you*. Felix was a tax-paying, green card–holding, law-abiding citizen, and his calculus was just that simple. Hearing what he said, I experienced again what I had first felt at Quantico: a shift in the most basic sense of who I was and of my purpose in the world.

Two days later, we went back to Felix's store, and in his little office he took off his shirt so I could put the wire on him. The recording device was a metal box about the size of a pack of cigarettes, with wire leads connected to microphones coming out of it. Putting the microphone up high on the chest catches the sound best, but on a hairy guy—and Felix was hairy as a bear—you can get a lot of scratching sounds. The device itself has to be hidden somewhere that won't be found on a typical pat-down, so we tucked it into a pocket designed to hang in the groin area from an elastic waistband.

Felix's street nickname, which was accurate, if not imaginative, was Big Felix. He was so large that the Velcro ends of the elastic waistband were never going to meet. He leaned over a table and I stood behind him, trying to pull the thing together—like a lady's maid tightening the strings on a whalebone corset. Then Felix had an inspiration: We could make the waistband stick with packing tape. We wrapped it around and around him and then sent him in. I remember wondering what it was going to feel like when the tape was peeled off.

The meeting was at another furniture store. Dimitri Gufield and his number two, Alexander Kutsenko, along with a man named Mani Chul-payev, who turned out to be in many ways the brains of the gang, rolled up in tricked-out Benzes and BMWs and swaggered onto the sidewalk wearing three-quarter-length black leather jackets. Nothing subtle about this scene. Sheehy and I were staked out up the block in a car. We took a lot of pictures.

Later, when the meeting was over, Dimitri went out on the sidewalk and talked to his guys in front of Felix, and talked to Felix alone a little more. Felix was chain-smoking, gray faced, perspiring heavily. We met up with him later and went to his store. By now he was drenched, looked like he was having a heart attack, fumbling with his keys, couldn't unlock his own front door. We got the wire off. Then Felix described what had happened. One of the older people in the meeting, Pavel, who was in his late seventies, allegedly owed Dimitri money on a separate debt, so Dimitri made Pavel sit in the middle of the group. Dimitri berated him and slapped him around as he told the rest of the furniture-store owners about the payments he wanted them to make. When a woman told Dimitri, No, she wasn't going to pay, Dimitri started beating Pavel, as if to show, This is what's at stake. By the end of the meeting, everyone there—except for the woman and her business partner—agreed to pay. Back outside, Dimitri told his guys, I want the woman beaten, I want her put into the hospital so she stays there for at least two weeks. That's what Felix heard him say at the end, when he was melting in sweat. We took off the wire and listened. It was all there.

On our instructions, Felix called another meeting with Gufield,

Kutsenko, and Chulpayev, and he asked them not to beat the woman. He said he would pay for her. We paid Felix, Felix paid them, and from then on it was a steady cash flow. We spent the next few months collecting as much information about the gang as we could. The first step in the collection stage of an investigation is to figure out who all the targets are. Once you know who they are, you figure out where they live, whether they're married, what they drive, what their phone numbers are. Who else do they hang around with? What else are they doing? Who else are they extorting? Are they running drugs? Sheehy and I followed the members of the gang, doing surveillance, nights and weekends. We found a guy on the Upper East Side who hooked them up with stolen cars. We found a connection to a gun supplier in South Carolina who sold them semiautomatic weapons, including a MAC-10.

We went to a federal prosecutor, Judith Lieb, who put the whole case together under the Racketeer Influenced and Corrupt Organizations Act—the RICO statute. Passed by Congress in 1970, RICO is the law that made it possible for the U.S. government to prosecute the Mafia—and the law that deters organized crime from infiltrating legitimate businesses. RICO allows the leaders of a racket to be tried for the crimes they ordered others to commit, or assisted others in committing, but did not carry out with their own hands. It is one of the most important laws enacted in the past half century, and it has global reach.

Every RICO charge has to go to the Department of Justice for approval because so much is at stake in the language. No one wants to bring a RICO case that gets challenged and risk an appeal that pulls the teeth out of the statute. The path to use this statute against Italian crime families is well trodden. But we found no preexisting language for a RICO case against a Russian-organized-crime group. Individuals had been arrested and indicted for the various predicate offenses that could have gone into a RICO case, offenses such as drug trafficking, extortion, and kidnapping. Apparently, the Bureau had never alleged an overall RICO con-spiracy involving a Russian-organized-crime enterprise.

We put it together, Lieb charged it, and we arrested six guys right off the top—the two leaders of the crew, three guys who were "furniture," or muscle, and the key figure in the case, Mani Chulpayev. Mani was not in New York the day we made the arrests. He was in Los Angeles. He and his partners, it turned out, were also involved in human trafficking. They would bring women from Russia and Uzbekistan to the U.S., seize their passports, and make them work as prostitutes to earn money toward getting the passports back. Mani was in Los Angeles delivering one of these women to a pair of Russian dentists who wanted their own live-in prostitute. The L.A. field office put Mani on a flight back to New York, and Ray Kerr gave us a master class in how to flip somebody.

Mani was Uzbek. He had immigrated to the U.S. as a child. His father supported the family by running food carts in downtown Manhattan. By the time of his arrest, he was five feet six of puffy hubris. In the inter-view room, Greg and I were not getting off jump street with him. Then Kerr walked in and sat down in his perfect dress slacks, perfect dress shirt, gold-rimmed glasses, tie perfectly knotted.

Ray started talking to Mani. He said, You don't have to say anything, Mani. Don't say a word. Just sit here, just listen. Listen to us. I'm gonna tell you a little bit of how this process works, what kind of system you are in now, what's going to happen after tonight, what's going to happen to-morrow morning, what's going to happen to you, what you're facing, when you'll be able to speak to your lawyer and your family. I'm just going to talk to you a little bit—just stop me and ask me questions if you'd like—but you don't have to say anything. Don't feel any pressure. We're not going to ask you any questions right now.

I could see Mani thinking, Ahhh, this is all right—I can handle this.

Kerr laid out the situation for him. Here's how it works. You've been charged by complaint. This is what that means. You're going to get to see the judge. It's an initial appearance. Ray walked him through the process and then started slowly asking a couple of questions. And Mani, being a spectacularly arrogant person and wanting to tell of his greatness, began to talk.

But Ray interrupted, rum voiced, the perfect host: Okay, before you go any further, let me just say you should probably—you know, we'll stay here as long as you want—we'll stay here all night with you if you like. We'll get you some food, we'll get you something to drink. We'd love to hear what you have to say. I'm sure you have a side of this, and we'd like to hear what that is. Before you do that, you should know that you do have the right not to speak to us.

Mani said, Yeah, yeah, yeah, I got that. Don't worry about it. And he signed the consent to be interviewed without an attorney present, and proceeded to tell stories that we had never heard before. He told us about the time the crew kidnapped a guy, took him to somebody's basement, tied him to a water heater, beat him with a tire iron, and stubbed out lit cigarettes in his ears. Told us about collection kidnappings they had been doing that we had no idea about. Guns they had bought. Stolen cars. The human trafficking.

As he spoke we could start to see how the various income streams converged. The guy on the Upper East Side who was the connection to stolen cars also had a person in the New York State Health Department who could create fraudulent Medicaid accounts. For a few hundred dollars, you could get a Medicaid card and have total access to health care. There was no operating cost for the scam. It was pure profit. We asked, Do you know who you did this for? Mani said, Yeah, I know who I did it for. It's all in my notebooks. He had kept a handwritten ledger of who brought in how much money for which job; who owed money; who had been paid. It was like the Rosetta stone of the gang's activity. We got the notebook and charged the gang. He laid it all out to us that night.

Olympic Dreams

When our squad shut down the Gufield-Kutsenko Brigade and another gang with a similar MO—rackets revolving around violence—it had a chilling effect. Wiseguy nightlife started powering down. White-collar insurance fraud started picking up. One gang set up medical mills all around the city, hustling for people who had been in car accidents. Patients came in to the mills and got pushed through a dozen doctor's appointments in an hour. The mill would bill for every bogus treatment, while insurance companies got taken for a ride. To prove the case—which resulted in fourteen arrests and the closing of several clinics—we staged a car accident on paper and wired up three NYPD detectives who went undercover as patients.

By the following year, Russian organized crime was moving further away from violence and toward the bigger prize of high finance, a realm that was more abstract but in some ways even more threatening to the country. By the end of 1999, the FBI had helped shut down a seven-billion-dollar Russian money-laundering scheme that had been operated through the Bank of New York. (The bank ended up paying thirty-eight million dollars in fines because it "did not adequately monitor or report suspect accounts.") That case, in retrospect, looks like a moment when Russian organized crime staked an early claim on the American frontier. The money laundered had come from a mixture of legal and illegal activities. The laundering itself was done by people who worked as legitimate professionals. The more that criminal money became entangled in legitimate business, and the more involved that formerly legitimate professionals became with organized crime, the more difficult it would eventually become for law enforcement to remove the criminal elements from the U.S. economy. Like the melding of organized crime and government in Russia—where each depends on the other for reinforcement and resources—the Bank of New York money-laundering case offered a glimpse of what the world can look like when the boundary between legitimate and criminal business is blurred. The Bank of New York case also signaled how much money Russians could bring to the table.

During the next few years, it became clear that Russian oligarchs—the men who, during Russia's transition from communism to kleptocracy, made billions by acquiring state-owned companies for a song—were supporting some of the *vory* outside Russia, but not yet in America. We realized that Russian criminals had so much money that if the money came here, whole institutions could be undermined. So while most of our squad continued chasing thugs around Brooklyn or figuring out the latest financial fraud schemes, Kerr made sure one guy kept watch over the big fish beyond our shores.

That kind of work could be even harder to justify than more typical organized-crime investigations, because it might never lead to indictments and stats. Kerr protected our squad's ability to do it anyway. He could see that something sinister was taking shape out there. It had spread from Moscow to Tel Aviv, and now we were seeing it in London. Globalization is not just for Google. Kerr's support for big-fish background work exemplifies one of the most important things I learned from him: If you see something that needs to be done, your whole job is to make your best effort to do it.

The fingerprints of the *vory* were turning up in America with growing frequency. We chased leads on Russian gangsters sent to New York to "organize" the rackets in the city. We followed leads about young Russian players in the National Hockey League who were being extorted by gangsters back in the homeland. One of the kingpins we were tracking, Alimzhan Tokhtakhounov, concocted a scheme to guarantee a gold medal for Russian pairs figure skaters in the 2002 Winter Olympics in Salt Lake City. The fix worked. The Russians were awarded the medal, but after the ensuing scandal about the judging, the members of the second-place team were awarded duplicate gold medals, too.

Vadim Thomas, one of the best investigators on our squad, pitched the figure-skating case to the Southern District of New York—known as the Sovereign District of New York, because the U.S. attorney's office there has a lot of power and does not shy from using it creatively. Tokhtakhounov was indicted and arrested by Italian police on charges of conspiracy to rig the competition. For months the FBI worked with the Italians and with Interpol to get him extradited. Before long, word came to the squad that a Russian oligarch had pledged two hundred million dollars to get Tokhtakhounov out of jail. Next thing we knew, his release was ordered by the Italian Supreme Court. He was gone, in the wind, back to Russia, where he has been living openly. (And from there, he allegedly continued to run criminal enterprises in the United States. In 2013, Tokhtakhounov was indicted for money laundering in connection with an illegal gambling ring that operated out of Trump Tower. Several months after this indictment, Tokhtakhounov was a VIP guest at Donald Trump's Miss Universe contest in Moscow.) We've never had a chance to get him again. In the scheme of things, the evident corruption behind a figure-skating medal may seem trivial. But for me and for a lot of guys on our squad, this was a critical turn of events.

One of our worst fears was that the top tier of the *vory v zakone* would use money to undermine Western institutions in which many millions of Americans have reflexive faith. That fear had now been realized, and we asked ourselves what institutions might be next, and we asked whether any American public official might be susceptible to a two-hundred-million-dollar bribe, and we asked whether democracy itself might become a target.

Enterprise Theory

Muddy Wingtips

Most FBI investigations are conducted by the Bureau's criminal, counterterrorism, or counterintelligence divisions. Whether they are investigating organized crime, international terrorism, or Russian involvement in the 2016 U.S. presidential campaign, all of these divisions use a technique of investigation called the enterprise theory.

Enterprise theory allows investigators to structure their understanding of crimes that once seemed too vast to understand. Enterprise theory is to investigation as grammar is to language. Without grammar, language would be a sprawling mush of verbiage. Without the enterprise theory, FBI investigators would find it practically impossible to wrap their minds around criminal activities of sprawling scope—criminal activities for which many people share responsibility.

In recent decades, enterprise theory was notably advanced by agents such as Bruce Mouw and Philip Scala, who brought down John Gotti and the Gambinos in the early 1990s. Enterprise theory was an answer to a problem that had been more than a century in the making: the problem of organized criminal activity in the United States. As far back as Reconstruction, racist groups built on hierarchical structures, such as the Ku Klux Klan, conspired to commit criminal violence against African American communities in the rural South. During the same period and with a similar discipline, Tammany Hall in New York City built a system of public corruption involving government officials. Among the immigrant throngs that passed through Ellis Island were mobsters, and La Cosa Nostra learned to do business in Queens as it had done in Palermo. All these criminal subcultures thrived. They showed that criminals working together were much more effective than criminals working alone.

Compared with these adversaries, local police and prosecutors investigating individual criminal acts in isolation were outgunned and outmatched. Organized criminal groups—with multiple members organized in hierarchies, supported by transportation and communications infrastructure—had no trouble staying one step ahead of the law. While these criminal enterprises grew and evolved over a century, American law enforcement—including the FBI, from its inception in 1908—questioned the very existence of organized crime.

That changed on November 14, 1957, when Joseph Barbara hosted a meeting at his country home in Apalachin, New York. High-ranking members from more than fifty organized-crime groups around the U.S. converged on Apalachin, about a three-hour drive northwest of Manhattan, not far from the Pennsylvania border. When townsfolk saw a bunch of luxury cars driving around with out-of-state license plates, they called the police. The police conducted surveillance on Barbara's fifty-acre estate. The gangsters quickly got wise to the cops and scattered on foot into the woods around the house. The result: lots of muddy wingtips, and irrefutable evidence of a national organized-crime syndicate.

"The Apalachin Meeting" is celebrated in FBI mythology as the event that dragged this institution out of its long period of denial of organized crime. J. Edgar Hoover, who had spent years trying to keep FBI agents out of organized-crime investigations, could no longer keep his eyes closed. During the decade that followed, politicians such as Senator John McClellan and Attorney General Robert F. Kennedy attacked the problem in very public ways. Hearings of what was then the Senate's Permanent Subcommittee on Investigations drew citizens' attention to the effects of racketeering—a series of events that culminated, in 1970, with the passage of the Organized Crime Control Act, which included the Racketeer Influenced and Corrupt Organizations provision.

The RICO Revolution

RICO created important new prosecutorial options. For the first time, the leaders of an organization could be held responsible for the crimes they had ordered others to commit. Each member of a group who participated in a pattern of racketeering activity could bear the full weight of responsibility for all the acts conducted by the organization. A conviction under RICO could carry stiff civil and criminal penalties, including up to twenty years in prison.

Now the FBI had a challenge: to develop a new model of investigation that would enable agents to take full advantage of the authority offered by the RICO statute. Criminal investigations are typically structured around proving the elements of a single criminal offense. RICO opened the door to prosecuting an entire organization. The enterprise theory was the structure by which agents learned to investigate whole organizations. Enterprise theory taught agents to identify new elements of a crime, to satisfy the new requirements of the statute, and to gather new forms of evidence. Through the lens of enterprise theory, agents could begin to see an organization as a whole, to understand the role and significance of each member, and to develop an understanding of the breadth of the group's activity.

Like national-security investigations, enterprise investigations involve extensive intelligence collection. To prove the existence of a RICO enterprise, criminal investigators conduct surveillance, talk to witnesses, and target the group with human sources—the same techniques national-security investigators use to track a foreign adversary. While collecting this intelligence, enterprise investigators look for pieces of intelligence that can be used as evidence not only to prove the enterprise exists, but also to prove that members of the enterprise committed particular crimes.

The first major requirement of the RICO statute is to prove the existence of the enterprise that is the subject of investigation. The statute defines an enterprise as "any individual, partnership, corporation, association, or other legal entity, and any union or group of individuals associated in fact although not a legal entity." If the subject of an investigation is a legal entity, proving its existence is easy. Many criminal enterprises, however, are not legal entities with a known public presence. Organized-crime families, narcotics-trafficking cartels, and terrorist groups usually don't have articles of incorporation or signs above their offices. They don't have departments of human resources or offer 401(k) plans. To satisfy RICO, the enterprise theory directs agents to collect association evidence: proof that people are associated with each other in a way that could qualify them as a criminal enterprise. Before the enterprise theory, if agents executed a search warrant at Mobster Sal's house, they were likely looking for evidence that Sal himself had committed a crime—things like stolen property or narcotics. The enterprise theory made it just as important for agents to find pictures of Mobster Sal hanging out with Mobster Vinny. Those pictures proved the two were "associates." Their association, or a larger one of which they are a part, may qualify as an enterprise under RICO. Association evidence takes many forms—bank records showing money transfers between individuals, joint names on legal documents such as contracts and leases, communication between subjects. Generally, any physical remnants of historic, legal, social, or other associations could help the investigators prove the existence of an enterprise.

In the case of a well-known organization, like the Genovese crime family, the FBI has extensive historical intelligence that makes a convincing case that the family functions as a criminal enterprise. This intelligence consists of years of interviews of witnesses and victims; informant and cooperator information; electronic intercepts of communications; evidence seized in prior Genovese cases; and records of previous convictions. In the case of new or previously unknown organizations, enterprise proof can be harder to find. This was a challenge for my squad in 1998, when we worked to prove the existence of the Gufield-Kutsenko Brigade as an organized criminal enterprise. While preparing to use the RICO statute against a Russian-organized-crime crew, we lacked historical intelligence or boilerplate language for the indictment to rely on. We used witness testimony to identify the members of the group at meetings where crimes took place. We used cooperator testimony about roles and responsibilities of the members of the group. We used audio recordings of Gufield, the enterprise leader, directing others to commit crimes. All this evidence painted a clear picture of a structured, hierarchical, criminal enterprise.

The second major RICO requirement is to prove that each member of the enterprise participated in a "pattern of racketeering activity." Investigators must prove that each subject participated in two or more of the crimes that are specifically defined in the statute. These include numerous federal crimes such as bribery, counterfeiting, and fraud, as well as offenses that are typically prosecuted by the states, such as robbery, drug trafficking, and murder. Following the enterprise theory, agents examine the full scope of criminal activity associated with the entire enterprise from the inception of the investigation. By collecting this intelligence all along, agents develop a rich picture of criminal activity and later sort out which member participated in which crime.

Establishing that rich picture can be done historically or proactively. In a historical RICO case, agents look for intelligence about past activity. Witness testimony can offer powerful evidence of past criminal behavior. Victims, informants, former criminals who cooperate to avoid incarceration, or even police officers and detectives who responded to crime scenes can serve as witnesses. With that intelligence in hand, agents look for artifacts that help to prove the crime was committed by members of the enterprise. Bank records, police reports, telephone records, documents, emails, or recorded communications are all effective proof of past crimes. Historical enterprise cases are some of the hardest to make, and their agents are some of the most capable investigators in the FBI. Each piece of evidence is like a piece of a puzzle that, when complete, forms a picture from the past. The case against Baldassare "Baldo" Amato, a soldier in the Bonanno family, is one example of a historical RICO case. In 2006, to convict Amato of racketeering and two murders, FBI agents used cooperator testimony, documents, police records, and forensic evidence. At sentencing, U.S. District Court judge Nicholas G. Garaufis called Amato a "Mafia assassin" who "used murder as a business tactic." Amato was sentenced to life in prison.

Proactive enterprise cases are focused on collecting evidence of an enterprise while criminals are still committing crimes. This means collecting intelligence and evidence in real time, from within the enterprise itself. One way to do this is through electronic surveillance. Electronic surveillance, or "technical collection," enables the investigators to collect the content of communications between members of the group. This requires specific authorization from a federal court and can involve some of the most sensitive investigative tools available. The result is usually worth the effort. Recorded communications reveal the activities of an enterprise, the leadership structure that makes the gang work, and even the personalities of its members. My squad mates and I once overheard a Russian crew talking insistently about making sure "the boots were in the car." We couldn't understand why they were so focused on footwear. It was only after a slow-minded soldier told the boss that he had made sure there was one boot for each person that we realized they were not talking about boots—they were talking about guns. Unfortunately, criminal organizations, terrorist groups, and foreign spies now routinely utilize encrypted communication platforms that put the content of their conversations beyond the reach of law-enforcement and intelligence-agency surveillance.

Proactive cases can also be built on intelligence and evidence collected by someone who is a member of the group or has unique access to the enterprise—someone like Felix, the furniture-store owner. People with this kind of access are typically confidential informants (CIs), cooperating witnesses (CWs), or undercover employees (UCs). In the FBI, a confidential informant is someone who regularly provides information to the FBI but whose role as a source can never be revealed. Exposing the informant's relationship with the FBI could place the source and his or her family in great danger. Protecting the identity of a confidential informant is one of an agent's most sacred responsibilities. Some confidential informants provide information about the activity of an enterprise and its members for many years. One drawback of relying on a confidential informant is that the sensitivity of maintaining confidentiality means the source's information cannot be used as evidence in court. It is purely intelligence.

A cooperating witness is someone who maintains informant-like access to an enterprise, but who also understands that he or she may one day be exposed as a government cooperator. Cooperating witnesses offer all the insights and intelligence of informants, but they are also available to take the stand and testify at trial. They are highly valuable for this dual role, and their testimony is often essential to convicting the leadership of a criminal enterprise. In some ways, this strength is also a weakness.

Providing testimony usually signals the end of their career. Once they are publicly revealed as government cooperators, or "burned," it becomes far too dangerous to have them continue to associate with their former criminal associates. Agents often have to relocate cooperating witnesses and their families to ensure they are not harmed.

The most sensitive and dangerous of all these efforts to penetrate a criminal enterprise comes when investigators attempt to insert one of their own into the group. Undercover employees can provide extraordinary insights into the working of an enterprise, and they can also steer conversations in order to obtain recorded statements on particular events. They are even able to alter the activities of a group to prevent acts of violence. During a trial, undercover employees provide powerful testimony. They offer both the access of an enterprise member and the credibility of a law-enforcement officer. Undercover employees are uniquely skilled and highly trained and require intense effort to support as they essentially live inside the criminal world. Their assignments are dangerous, incredibly stressful, and often crucial to the enterprise investigation.

Protecting Informants

Near the end of May 2018, the president falsely accused the FBI of having put a "spy" in his campaign and called for an investigation. The president's allies began demanding that the so-called spy's identity be unmasked. The FBI had, of course, not put anyone inside the campaign. A confidential informant with preexisting tangential ties to people associated with Trump's political operation had provided information relating to specific national-security risks, in this case involving possible Russian influence in the conduct of a presidential campaign. Reading the news of President Trump's demand to know details about the confidential informant, I wanted the leadership at Justice and the FBI to say, We will not provide any information.

We are going to protect the people who work with us, period. In the end, the deputy attorney general, Rod Rosenstein, sought to defuse the situation by referring the matter to the inspector general and giving confidential briefings to key members of Congress. To prepare for such an important briefing, it would be customary both to review the raw intelligence of 302s from interviews with the confidential informant and to work with an analyst who processed that raw intelligence into a more finished briefing product. When the information was properly prepared and presented, after various people had taken the time to understand it, even some FBI critics on Capitol Hill realized—and publicly stated—that there was no issue here.

Not giving up your people: This is important. It is crucially important not only to the FBI but to the country's safety and security. The ability to identify and develop relationships with human sources is oxygen to the FBI. The Bureau cannot live without that. It is the first step toward the activation of any of our other, more sophisticated investigative authorities. You do not get to search warrants, you don't get to subpoenas, you don't get to listen in on a subject's communications through a FISA or Title III court order, without people telling you what they know. And if you can't credibly tell them that you will protect and conceal their identity if they are willing to go out on a limb, if they are willing to risk their own and their families' lives and welfare—if they can't trust that you will protect them—then they will not cooperate with you.

Discretion allows the FBI to generate human sources. Human sources build the credibility of this institution. No other U.S. agency has a pool of human sources bigger than that of the FBI. That is the true strength of this organization: the ability of its agents to go out into any part of this country, sit down with people, and get information from them in a lawful, constitutionally protected way. A person who is willing to have an ongoing relationship of this kind with an agent is called an informant, or a source. Without those people, we're sunk—as a law-enforcement agency and as a law-abiding society.

So—hypothetically—if the FBI finds out that someone who is definitely associated with a domestic political campaign has made a comment to a high-ranking government official from another country about possibly colluding with a foreign adversary in the course of that campaign, the FBI is obligated to look into that. The foreign counterintelligence implications of this information are obvious. The Bureau would be guilty of dereliction of duty if it did not open an investigation and look into the matter.

And the Bureau's goal would be not only to find out who is responsible for working with the enemy, but also to protect the campaign from the foreign influence that might be seeping into what they are trying to do. No campaign in the U.S. would want that. And it could be illegal—the Federal Election Campaign Act strictly regulates the participation by foreign nationals in U.S. elections and specifically prohibits the provision of money or anything of value. The FBI would open an investigation to protect the people who are involved in that political activity from malicious foreign influence. We assume the campaign is operating under good faith. We assume innocence until proof of guilt. That is why, in this hypothetical situation, a case would be opened.

What would happen once that case was opened? Would agents go busting out and interviewing people willy-nilly? Would they publicly line up everybody in that campaign and ask, Did you talk to anyone from this foreign country? No, they wouldn't want to do that. If they did, they would communicate to all the world the FBI's investigative interest in this subject matter—which would have an indelibly deleterious effect on both the investigation and the campaign. The question of when to move from one stage of an investigation to another—when to move from collecting evidence to briefing any of the subjects involved—is a delicate one, involving consideration of many factors. Absent imminent threats to life and limb or the destruction of evidence, once a case is opened, agents conduct the investigation quietly and covertly.

What would agents do first? It could be a good idea to start out by talking with people who have a history with other people in the campaign. So agents might go to those people and say, What do you know about this person? And have you heard anything about that? And if, in talking to those people, agents came across someone who had exposure to and knowledge about this person or that issue, or was in a position to find out, agents might say to the person, See if they know anything about this or that, and let us know what they say.

That is the answer to a president who is worried about a nonexistent spy in his campaign and who demands that an informant be identified.

3

The Shift

SOLVING CRIME—AND PREVENTING TERRORIST ATTACKS

Ground Zero

It was a bad Monday. I'd just come back to New York from a trip to Fort Lauderdale with one of the detectives on my task force. We ran an operation there that triggered turf issues for the field office, and the local FBI supervisor screamed at me like I'd never been screamed at before: You are banned from the state of Florida! So on this Monday, I expected my boss to chew up what was left of me. I stayed at the office late, coming up on midnight, to offer my hide. The boss just made me wait, and then he left.

So I got home late—I was living in Westchester County—and I canceled plans to meet my workout buddy at the gym by the World Trade Center, where we usually met on Tuesdays. I slept in. When I was getting out of the shower, I heard Katie Couric on the TV in the bedroom say a report had just come in: A small plane had flown into the side of one of the towers at the World Trade Center. The phone rang. It was Jill, saying, Did you see what happened to the World Trade Center? You'd better get into work. I was confused. I said, I'm not a fireman. What do you want me to do about a fire at the World Trade Center? Then the newscast cut in with an update.

I floored it in the black Chevy Tahoe, tinted windows up, speeding into Manhattan. Bureau radio on, I listened to the chatter, tracking calls to rally—first at an intersection right next to the towers, then in China-town. The bridges were closed. When I got near the Triborough Bridge, the on-ramp was a parking lot. I drove on the shoulder, lights and sirens on, trying to maneuver around the cars, and there were orange construc-tion barrels in the way. When the other drivers saw the lights and sirens, a bunch of them jumped out of their cars and started lifting the barrels out of the way so I could get through. When I made it up onto the bridge and drove across, my car was the only car on the bridge. It was like that scene in *Vanilla Sky*. Southbound on the FDR, again I was practically the only car on the road. By then the first tower had fallen. I took the right-hand exit at the Brooklyn Bridge, and I saw a crowd of people walking the other way on the FDR, away from downtown. They were all white, covered in dust. Not excited, not talking. Calm, dazed, a crowd of ghosts walking along.

I made it to 26 Federal Plaza, dropped the car, and immediately the SWAT team rallied, right there: Get your gear on, get in the vehicles, get together. We're going to stage the vehicles, we're going to be ready, because no doubt we're going to get called. The SWAT team would be the ones who would arrest the people who were involved in this. Any second now—I was sure of it—we would get the order to go out to some loca-tion in Brooklyn or the Bronx or wherever, and get this guy or that guy. They moved our team over to the West Side Highway, by the heliport. The weather was absolutely gorgeous, blue sky, not a cloud, and we stood there and we waited.

And we waited, and we waited. Nothing happened. And eventually we started to realize that probably nothing was going to happen that day. There was no one to go get, because no one knew yet who had done this.

By that night, it was decided that the field office could not work from the old Federal Building. The air quality was too bad. The building had sucked in all the fumes and dust from Ground Zero. So the field office moved uptown, to the FBI garage, a huge brick building on the corner of the West Side Highway and Twenty-sixth Street. Oil-stained cement floor, debris everywhere, cars everywhere. This was the graveyard for old Bureau cars—name your style of anonymous dark sedan, they were all there, along with cars that had been seized. Ferraris and Bentleys, rusting and rotting away, going nowhere.

All that stuff got hauled out, and we put in tables, phone lines, computers. This was the command center. This was where the terrorism case squads worked their investigations. All the intelligence on the attacks was pouring in here. All decisions about deployments and investigations were made here. The SWAT team provided a perimeter of security around the building, twenty-four hours a day. Every street agent who wasn't on a terrorism squad or with the SWAT team was shagging leads for the case. The lead pool ran out of the USS *Intrepid,* the old aircraft carrier docked a few blocks up the river, and it ran around the clock. This was the rhythm: show up at the *Intrepid* at 7 A.M., grab a stack of leads, go work them, come back at 7 P.M., give your paperwork back, go home and sleep, repeat.

On and on it went, one week working days, the next week working nights. It rained, the air was freezing, and we stood there. Somebody had to stand guard, so we did it. But we wanted to do more. We wanted to find the people responsible for this—even though, very quickly after the attack, we in fact knew who they were: terrorists affiliated with al-Qaeda and directed by Osama bin Laden. We also knew that the nineteen hijackers, the ones most responsible, had all died in the attack when the airplanes they had hijacked crashed into the Twin Towers, the Pentagon, and a field in Pennsylvania.

Most of us on the SWAT team were criminal guys. Agents who do criminal work have traditionally seen themselves as the only true agents, the ones who do the real work. Everybody else could mess around sending cables back and forth, swapping "intelligence." Criminal agents did the big stuff. We arrested people. Of course, the agents who worked on terrorism thought *they* were the real thing. Each side had its own myths to deploy against the other. Being of the criminal camp, I was champing at the bit to get moving. Instead, I found myself saying, Can I see your ID, ma'am? to every twenty-five-year-old on the way into work at Martha Stewart's headquarters, upstairs in our building.

'I Am Sikh'

September 11 was the day that made everything look different from how it had looked before. This is true even in a literal way. After standing watch the night of 9/11, three of us drove downtown. By that point, everything south of Twenty-sixth Street was like a world under martial law. No private vehicles. Restaurants serving food only to first responders. I remember coming down Broadway with city hall on the left, the park in front tapering to a point. It looked like a winter morning after an eight-inch snowfall. Every surface was white. It looked peaceful. And it was quiet—the dust, like snow, muffled every sound. There were no people walking around, and there was no traffic.

We dropped the car at 26 Federal Plaza and then walked over to see Ground Zero up close. I remember reminding myself, That's not snow. That's just the buildings, and everything and everyone that was in them, a physical manifestation of violence and hatred. But also of all the people and lives and families and businesses and enterprises and hopes and plans and everything that intersected at those two tall towers, turned into dust.

The dust and debris would be hauled to Fresh Kills Landfill on Staten Island, and agents and police officers would go out there every day to sort through it. They would put on their Tyvek suits and take garden rakes in their hands and rake the dust and debris, looking for human remains, day after day. Living persisted, in all the forms living takes. My friend Michael Breslin worked at the morgue, documenting the bodies and body parts being brought in.

At another level, the wheels of national government were grinding forward. First, federal immigration services stopped all regular processes of deportation—no illegal aliens would be sent out of the country until the FBI cleared them of any connection to the 9/11 attacks. Second, at the same time, immigration enforcement became much more aggressive, particularly as it concerned Middle Easterners, than it had been on September 10. Attorney General John Ashcroft was blunt: "If you overstay your visa—even by one day—we will arrest you." And third, hundreds of agents, not only in the New York area but all over the country, were processing leads generated out of the 9/11 case files, which were known as PENTTBOM and TRADEBOM.

To show what happened when those three lines intersected, consider one scenario that might have unfolded if you'd become the subject of a lead after 9/11. Let's say you were from the Middle East, and your neighbor had called the FBI and said, The person who lives next door comes and goes at odd hours, and he hangs out with other guys with Middle Eastern names, and I think I saw him wearing a turban once. The FBI got thousands of such calls. Every call became a lead. We would get the address, and two agents would go out that same day. Once the agents arrived at your doorstep, even if you weren't there, if any of your neighbors passed by, the agents would have struck up conversations with them. If one of those neighbors, too, happened to have come from a Middle

Eastern country, the agents would have asked if he was a citizen or to see his green card. If that man wasn't a citizen and didn't have a green card, he would no longer have been your neighbor. He would have been detained.

All of a sudden, the U.S. was enforcing immigration laws in a way that it had not done for decades. Many, many people were picked up and thrown into deportation proceedings, which would not occur until they were cleared of any connections to terrorism. A massive logjam formed.

In addition to all the people who were getting picked up in the New York area, others were picked up around the country, and some of them caught the interest of the terrorism squads, so they asked for those detainees to be sent to New York. The Immigration and Naturalization Service, as it was then known, quickly blew through all of its detention space. The INS started signing contracts to house detainees in county jails in New Jersey. The Passaic County Jail, the Orange County Jail—facilities with some hard-core inmates—started to fill up with immigration detainees who had not even been accused of a crime. These detainees were virtually all Middle Eastern. They were virtually all dark skinned. They were not treated with courtesy.

As the numbers grew, it finally dawned on someone that we had to start vetting these detainees so that we could figure out whether to let them go or start deporting them. So the special agent in charge asked Ray Kerr to come up with a plan. Ray grabbed a few of us and explained the job. We were eager to do anything. None of us knew anything about terrorism. We didn't know what a vetting investigation for someone with connections to terrorism should even include. The process we set up was not efficient. Some of those first groups of detainees were in custody for a long time—six months or more—before we were finally able to build the system and then get them through it.

The program generated a lot of lawsuits and prompted my first interaction with the inspector general's office at the Department of Justice. Sometime after we had concluded the detainee clearances, the inspectors came to New York to investigate how we had handled our assignment. Ray Kerr and I sat for that interview together. They asked a lot of questions about why we had detained so many people, how we created the clearance process, and why it had taken so long. The only candid response was to point to the context: This was New York in the traumatic aftershock of 9/11. The attorney general had asked the FBI to render an opinion on every immigration detainee's possible connections to terrorism. We created a process to do that. We had never done it before. It was far from perfect.

Our group ended up processing about 550 detainees. The best thing about this job was that it got done. The detentions were incredibly hard on people. Most of the detainees had blue-collar jobs, and most of them were guilty of nothing other than violating immigration laws that typically had not been enforced. One day another agent came back from the Passaic County Jail. A man he had been interviewing had broken down in tears. Said that after 9/11 people called him horrible names and gossiped about bad things he was supposed to have done, things that he did not do. Called him a terrorist. Then he looked at the agent and said, I am Sikh. I'm not even Muslim.

Not Mr. Casual

I am continually struck by the strangeness of living in a world where many people cannot connect with 9/11 in a visceral way. It is still so much with me. Five years after the attacks, I started working on counterterrorism full-time. Having spent most of the period since 9/11 looking closely at terrorist groups and religious extremism, these things weigh differently in my perspective than in most people's. Some people see counterterrorism as essentially a political issue, even a fearmongering technique. It is sometimes both of those things. It is also very real. People who work in counterterrorism are correct in making this point: The fact that 9/11 happened once does mean that something like it could happen again. And the fact that we should have seen it coming the first time—we could have seen it, and we didn't—instills everyone involved in counterterrorism with a vigilance that manifests as dread and fear. Not a fear of bad things happening, but fear of missing something. A relentless second-guessing. People who take this threat seriously are more on edge than people who don't.

The FBI after 9/11 is a different entity from what it was before. There were agents who were working drugs on 9/10, and from the next day forward, for the rest of their careers, worked terrorism. I went back to my organized-crime squad, where we all expected that any day someone would walk in and say, Okay, C-24 is now Eurasian Terrorism. That didn't happen, but terrorism changed the way we thought even about crime. The old tribal structure of the Bureau—criminal versus counterterrorism, knuckle-draggers versus pinheads—was blown away. Now we were all in it together.

In the summer of 2006 I moved out of organized crime and into counterterrorism. My first case was the London airliner plot. A bunch of young terrorists had learned how to make bombs out of easily available household products. The airliner plot is the reason why, today, when you get on an airplane, all your liquids, aerosols, gels, creams, and pastes have to fit inside a quart-sized plastic bag. The key word for understanding this case—its plain facts and its larger significance—is "components."

The terrorists had devised a way to break down the components of explosive devices so that they could elude detection at airports by airport security and then reassemble the devices once an airliner was aloft. My unit and I gathered intelligence from the British investigation and tried to determine if any Americans were involved. Coordinating the various services—the FBI and CIA; British intelligence; and others—required learning how to share information seamlessly. This case also brought me face-to-face for the first time with the man who succeeded Louis Freeh as FBI director, Robert Mueller.

Over the next twelve years I would be fortunate to have a great deal of interaction with Mueller. He is not—and I think he would admit this, probably while feigning slight resistance for comic effect—Mr. Casual. He is not a charming communicator, the way Jim Comey can be. Mueller was a Marine lieutenant commanding a platoon in Vietnam. He achieves change through force of will. It was not a relaxing experience for me to be told, You're going to brief the director twice a day on this case, every day at 7 A.M. and 5 P.M. Mueller was also a prosecutor. He cross-examines you every time you're in front of him. Ball-busting is his way of expressing affection. If he said, Where does a person even find a tie like that? I knew things were fine: He never went out of his way to insult anyone he didn't actually like. He had strict habits and boundaries. Dress: blue suit, white shirt, red tie. His idea of relaxed attire was losing the jacket and wearing a V-neck sweater over the shirt and tie. Later, when I traveled with him, Mueller's most senior assistant said, The first rule is, Don't be late—if you're late, you will be left behind. Another rule was, Don't talk to him during the flight. He's reading and studying. If he has questions, he will get up from his seat and come back to speak with you. No matter where we were, no matter what was happening, when the day was done, he always went straight to his hotel room. Never stayed up late in the bar with the rest of us or invited people up to his room, the way Louis Freeh had when I traveled with him.

When I moved over to counterterrorism, it marked a permanent change in how I lived my life. Working in counterterrorism means approaching every holiday with an overwhelming sense of dread. Christmas is the Christmas Threat. New Year's Eve is Times Square. There is not a single joyous holiday occasion that doesn't have an undercurrent of Are we positioned correctly? Did we give the field the correct guidance? What do we know about the one hundred suspects we think are the closest to doing something violent? Work in counterterrorism means you're always at an elevated state of alert, and all personal plans, no matter how important, are subject to change. On the way to my dad's sixty-fifth birthday party, I got a call about a break in the airliner plot. I flew back to D.C. and went straight to the office. I regret having missed family celebrations like that and other parts of normal everyday life—but the choice was clear.

Operation Overt

Thursday, August 10, 2006. At Heathrow, lights are off. Doors are locked. At every other airport where flights to Heathrow were scheduled to leave from—JFK, Reagan, de Gaulle, Dublin, Schiphol, Frankfurt, and more—departure terminals are mobbed. Security lines are thousands of people long. The lines don't move. Today, nobody gets through. Traffic outside is backed up. People are bailing out of cars a mile away, trudging toward the terminal, and dragging suitcases behind them, streaming like crowds of refugees along the shoulders of highways.

On this day I woke at 4 A.M. and drove to work alone, on the toll road, listening to the radio. News reports described the bedlam at the airports. Three words drifted through my mind—*We* did this. I was connected to this chaos. My office was the place where, when we gave the word—because of something we had learned—the global transportation system went haywire. I could see the sprawling interconnectedness of what I would be doing at my desk today. I would be dealing with the consequences of an ongoing investigation into a plot to take down commercial airliners with ingeniously devised homemade bombs. Unexpectedly, an arrest had just been made, meaning that the terrorists would soon know we were onto them and maybe would launch their attack. So an alert had gone out to airline-security personnel worldwide—with results I was listening to on the radio.

The job of working counterterrorism is to prevent acts of terror. To protect people from an ambush out of nowhere. Stop them from getting hurt or killed. Foil plans of attack meant to pitch the world into a black hole of anxiety and fear. All of which can prompt, at times, a feeling of propulsion and even exhilaration, something that people in counterterrorism rarely discuss but would have to acknowledge. The intense, even addictive, feeling of priority. The sense of necessity built into the job. Necessity not just to your government but to other governments and to everyone you are responsible for protecting. Those feelings are validating—validating of the call that, in the first place, draws practically every agent to the Bureau, every officer to law enforcement.

I parked my car at Liberty Crossing 1. LX-1 is an intelligence facility on a little piece of land in McLean, Virginia. Onion layers of normality and strangeness make up the culture of this place, and it shows in the design. On the outside, LX-1 looks like a typical four-story office complex, modern and nondescript, its footprint in the shape of an X. On the inside, it contains elements of the FBI and the NCTC, the National Counterterrorism Center—since 2004, the country's main nerve center for counterterrorism intelligence collection and analysis. The NCTC includes representatives of all the U.S. intelligence agencies that work terrorism. Hallways are lined with massive, solid-oak doors. The work spaces behind those doors, known as vaults, don't look much different from the cubicles you'd find in any office. Because of all the classified material handled here, the whole building is a sensitive compartmented information facility, or SCIF, pronounced "skiff."

Face pale, eyes frozen in a thousand-yard stare: That was my ID picture, taken on my first day on the job there, in May 2006. What had I gotten myself into? I had left a tight community in New York, where I was a leader. I had jumped into a field I barely knew, with a unit of agents who were strangers, in a section known as the meat grinder: International Terrorism Operations Section I—ITOS-1. Another job, another acronym. ("ITOS" is pronounced "AYE-toss.")

Setting up ITOS-1 was one of the Bureau's first steps toward becoming an intelligence-gathering and terrorism-prevention organization. Before the Twin Towers fell, there had been just two counterterrorism units at FBI headquarters—the Osama bin Laden Unit and the Radical Fundamentalist Unit. Those units would grow and the number of units multiply. By the time I got to headquarters, the FBI had two counterterrorism sections, encompassing more than ten units. My section, ITOS-1, covering all cases involving Sunni extremists, had six units corresponding to geographic territories. Four units—called the CONUS units ("CONUS" rhymes with "bonus")—covered the continental United States. A fifth, the Arabian Peninsula Unit, also covered Iraq, Afghanistan, Pakistan, and Asia. The sixth, the Extraterritorial Investigations Unit—the ETIU—covered the rest of the world: Europe, Canada, Africa, South America, Eastern Europe, and Russia. I was the ETIU unit chief.

Counterterrorism is a tough job. The work is grueling, devouring nights and weekends. You operate with zero margin for error. Worse, merely by identifying someone as a threat, you and the FBI take responsibility for that threat. If a terror subject comes on my radar, and I investigate and find nothing, but five years later the suspect launches a deadly attack, it's on me. Why wasn't that guy stopped five years ago?

Despite those burdens, and also because of them, morale in counterterrorism units is high. I loved working there. After all their years of service, most agents look back on one division or squad or field office as having been their home in the FBI. For me, ITOS-1 was home. The section had tremendous camaraderie because everyone was toughing it out together. A huge sense of mutual respect and self-respect emerged from the job's relentless pace.

Regularity and accountability were the principles that drove our work. Meetings happened every day, rain or shine. And every day our section chief, Michael Heimbach, who ran ITOS-1, held us accountable. Mike Heimbach was the FBI's answer to George Hamilton, the actor: chestnut tan, slicing smile, extremely expressive eyebrows. Heimbach's management style involved a lot of laying down of dares. A standard Heimbach line was, It's time to step up. In the daily morning briefing, we all got our heads screwed on straight so we could march forward in the right direction. In the wrap that afternoon, we shared progress reports, answered questions from Heimbach, and spoke freely about longer-range issues. Working under such orderly management was new for me. As a supervisor in New York, I had struggled to schedule formal meetings with my squad even once a month. But I took the ITOS-1 model of orderly management into every job I had later.

Living with a daily expectation of progress reports ingrained the importance of follow-through. Heimbach would never dance around a central question. He always came right at it, always carried himself with confidence that answers would be given. Dissembling, obviously, was not acceptable in these conversations. Neither was self-delusion or trimming. Dishonesty and obfuscation are strategies that people engage in when they think the questions they've been asked will eventually just go away. ITOS-1 was a culture where everyone knew that legitimate questions always had to be answered. Where everyone knew that legitimate questions never go away.

'When Are We Going to Fix This?'

That summer we had started getting information from British intelligence about a group of young men in London. The men had come to the attention of British security services through the investigation of the London transport system attack the prior year. On July 7, 2005, four suicide bombers in London had killed fifty-two people and injured nearly eight hundred more on the Underground and a double-decker bus. A few weeks later, a man named Abdulla Ahmed Ali came to the attention of MI5, the British security service whose focus is on domestic matters. (MI6 is the service that operates overseas. The division is roughly that between the FBI and the CIA.) A tip suggested that Ali might be connected to those bombings. The Brits put him under surveillance and kept collecting intelligence on Ali for a year. Then Ali went to Pakistan.

Surveillance there found that Ali was spending time with an extremist named Rashid Rauf. Rauf had fled Britain in 2002, under suspicion for his uncle's death by stabbing in Birmingham. Now he was an operational planner for al-Qaeda in Pakistan. In cooperation with an al-Qaeda senior commander, Rauf taught Ali how to build liquid explosive devices using common chemicals—peroxide, hexamine, citric acid—that could be detonated with AA batteries.

Ali went back to England, paid cash to buy a little apartment, and started experimenting. He and his friends bought plastic bottles of a sports drink called Lucozade—a British version of Gatorade—and they worked on turning each one into a handheld bomb. They would drill a small hole through the plastic nub in the bottom of the bottle. They would let the liquid drain out from that hole. They would use a hypodermic needle to inject the empty bottle with explosive ingredients. Then they would seal the hole with epoxy. Properly assembled, each device was powerful enough to blow through the cabin wall of a commercial passenger jet.

This whole operation was being watched. By now, British investigators had cameras and microphones in the apartment where the experiments took place. Around the country, some twenty other subjects were being tracked. The conversations were sobering. After one young father took a child to play in a park on a weekend, he was overheard struggling openly with the knowledge that when he became a suicide bomber, he would never see his child again. He and his associates were forming a plan to take bombs on flights from London, we believed, to the United States, and then to kill themselves and everyone else on those flights.

The members of this terrorist cell also had connections to people in the U.S. Those connections were the FBI's big concern. Monitoring the American side of threats was traditionally the Bureau's role. To do that, we needed the best and freshest intelligence about the situation. Did we know exactly what the CIA knew? Were they giving us what we needed so that we could do the work we needed to do? It's not enough for the Brits to say, Our bad guy here in London talked to three people in New York last week. The FBI has no way of knowing what that means until we get the names. We need to open cases in order to figure out if they're just family members of some bad guy and know nothing, or if they are passive collaborators, or if they are actively doing bad stuff on their own.

The name of this case was Operation Overt. The Brits named it. I have no idea why they called it that. Counterterrorism case names were frequently obscure or awful. Kinetic Panda, Bubble Puppy, Milk Can. Mueller would always ask, Where did that name come from? The person briefing him would usually answer, We have a machine that gives us the names. It's random. It comes from the machine.

I hate it, he would say. Or—since the FBI does not in fact have a naming machine—he would say, I don't believe you.

Operation Overt fell under my aegis. As a result, I became the FBI's conduit for information flowing from several directions, formal and informal. The British provided daily written reports to the FBI legat in London, who passed them on to me. Colleagues in Pakistan did the same for our legats in Islamabad. If the legats had drinks or dinner with their local partners, they'd give me the skinny afterward. I had extensive conversations with the legat in London. At some point in the process, I started riding over to Langley every day with Art Cummings, the deputy assistant director for counterterrorism, to sit in on the secure video teleconferences with foreign counterparts at the Agency's Counterterrorism Center. My unit and I had to suck back all this information, figure out if there was a U.S. angle, and open cases—which involved surveillance on those targets from field offices and more information ricocheting back to headquarters. We had about 150 agents checking bank accounts, credit cards, communications, travel. We opened 150 or so cases. We had court-authorized electronic surveillance on the communications of a small number of subjects, which generated more information on the individuals we deemed of greatest concern.

We pulled at threads to see if something might unravel. Send me the honey, read one line of one transcript of an intercept. I'm going to the wedding in Massachusetts, read another line of another transcript. We were inclined to interpret such things in the widest possible ways. In counterterrorism, "wedding," for instance, has historically been used as a substitute word for an attack. But sometimes a wedding is only a wedding. And it's as common to ship honey back and forth in Yemen as it is to FedEx a contract in the U.S. But how can you be certain whether honey is more than honey?

Piecing all this information and insinuation into a coherent picture would have been challenging in an atmosphere of mutual confidence, honesty, and trust. International interagency relations during that time could not have been described in those terms. British and American intelligence did not have high confidence in each other. No one was sure what was happening in Pakistan. Everyone connected with this investigation spent a lot of time wondering what they weren't being told.

There was also a lot of distrust between the CIA and the Bureau in those days. The FBI was always wondering, Are they telling us everything? The CIA was always wary: Don't tell them everything because they'll screw it up. The two agencies got along better than they had prior to 9/11, but things were far from perfect. You can't repair relations with the flip of a switch. We cherished our mutual suspicions. With Overt, the FBI quickly saw that we should be working our end of this thing, and quickly moved to make the CIA cut us in and be more transparent.

One part of my job was to distill all this into a briefing for the director, twice a day, every day. Whether I briefed Mueller face-to-face or by secure videoconference, I always brought a fresh link chart. Pictures, name tags, colored string, pushpins: On TV and in movies, obsessive investigators build elaborate link charts to show connections among persons of interest. These portrayals are not far from the truth. We build charts because charts help us solve problems. Put somebody's picture on the chart, and you find yourself thinking about that person. Leave the person off, and you might not. Mueller had a lot of quirks about the link charts. He detested diagonal lines. Some colors he liked. Some he didn't. The most important rule was not to use too many colors and not to use bright colors. This wasn't an eccentricity—it was wisdom gained from experience. Sharply contrasting colors could become distracting and could also make you think that colors that were different had nothing to do with one another. Mueller did not want to be distracted, and he also wanted to be able to see the problem whole. He wanted to know everything that we knew but did not want clutter. Sometimes he would take out the chart and suddenly you would see his face fall, as if to say the kind of thing that he would rarely say: Who made this piece of crap?

The chart was always changing—names appearing and disappearing—and in each meeting I had to talk through every single element that had changed since last time. Mueller would kick back in his chair, sitting up very straight. Put his hand to his mouth. Circle his chin—really, polish it—with his knuckles. You could see him thinking, making connections, preparing questions. He might interrupt with a curveball—What happened with that guy who was going to the wedding in Massachusetts next week?—recollecting some little piece of information that I'd given him in the days before. I had to be ready for anything.

If he leaned forward, it was a very bad sign. Mueller leans forward only when frustrated. He gestures, taps his finger on the table. He points—he is a pointer. Also a hand tosser. He tosses his hands and sighs. If he leaned forward, looking at the chart, and then smacked the side of his hand against his head—then it was all over. Time to grab that stick and aim the plane back to the sky, because you are about to crash. When the hand hits the head, Mueller is not with you. Does not put faith in what you're saying. Or is just not following. You have not communicated a good position effectively.

The most memorable thing about briefing Robert Mueller, though, was the questions. Always the questions, welling up from his prosecutorial soul. Cross-examination is one of Mueller's most basic forms of human interaction, and it's the vehicle for one of his most basic traits: curiosity. He loved to get down into the details and fire off questions one after another in a firm, clear, resonant, courtroom voice.

Sometimes in briefings he would eviscerate people who did not know what they were talking about, hadn't followed up on things that he'd asked them to follow up on, or were bringing him the same problem they had brought months earlier but made no progress on. Evisceration was an occupational hazard for analysts, especially, because analysts like to chew on both sides of a question. Could be this, could be that. They are inclined to provide indirect answers to direct questions in exchanges along these lines:

Mueller: Is this guy a danger?

Analyst: He seems to have extremist beliefs, but I haven't seen him do anything illegal. I don't have access to everything the Agency has.

Mueller: Why not? We talked about this three weeks ago when we spoke about that other case. Have we made progress? Last time we talked,

I told you to get with the CIA and fix this. Make sure that we're getting what they're getting. Why are we stumbling across the same problem again? When are we going to fix this? Really. Tell me when this problem will be fixed.

I learned early on that if I didn't know something, it was infinitely better to say, I don't know the answer to that, sir, but I will get it for you—because that would end the matter. He wouldn't rub your nose in it. But if you promised to get the answer, you had to follow through and *get* the answer. You would never just make the promise as a way of making him back off. You would figure it out, put it in an email, send it to his chief of staff. And that could be as good as knowing the answer initially, because you were showing that you were thorough, you followed through, you were resolving his question—which was the most important thing. Because everyone knew, in Mueller's FBI, that legitimate questions do not go away.

By the time I got through the morning cycle of briefings and got back to my office, it seemed like I had five minutes before I had to meet Art and go to the CIA. By the time we got back from there, it was noon: time to start deciding what to say in the afternoon meeting with the director. Sometimes it seemed the briefing cycle was more important than the information—were we working the briefing or working the threat? The truth is, they're inextricably related, and you have to work both. Tension was high. I would constantly analyze every gesture Mueller made, every word he said. I watched him as closely as I watched the intelligence.

Rocks in Our Pockets

Then a man got arrested in southern Punjab, bringing a giant swath of the global air-traffic system to a halt. While the Brits had been monitoring the network of collaborators in Britain, other intelligence services had been pursuing a vigorous ground operation to locate Rauf in Pakistan. When the Pakistanis nabbed him in the city of Bahawalpur, on or around August 9, it took the Brits by surprise. It took the FBI by surprise, too. Also airport security, everywhere.

For no one was this a completely happy surprise. Arresting Rauf was like taking a card out of the bottom of a house of cards. At that point, the whole investigation came down. When Rauf was taken into custody, all the suspects in the UK had to be taken into custody, because once they got word of his arrest, they could have rushed their plot forward or taken it underground.

The timing of a takedown like this needs to be carefully choreographed. You don't want to do it suddenly. You have to be up on your surveillance to see how all the contacts respond. You have to coordinate arrests and searches—more than twenty arrests, in this case, and more than fifty searches. You have to agree on what Brits call "forms of words"—the precise wording of legal documents and of media releases, so those statements are all positioned and ready to go. Airport security has to be briefed, so they can revise their standards rationally, not in a panic.

All these processes of preparation had begun, but we were nowhere near ready. Absurd warnings got dropped on TSA and its many variants around the world: Look out for Gatorade or Lucozade bottles that might have had their bottoms drilled out. Immediately, nobody could take a carry-on bag onto an airplane. Nobody could take a liquid on any flight anywhere.

The follow-on consequences of Rauf's arrest were at the top of the news as I drove into work that morning. In the coming hours, there would be a lot of shouting inside the FBI and inside British intelligence: How the hell did this happen? I understood all too well what had happened. There's always a tension between the desire to keep collecting intelligence and the need to disrupt a plot before anyone gets hurt. Case by case, experts will often disagree over where the sweet spot is. Sometimes people will jump the gun. The jumpers see themselves as prudent. There should be no sudden jumps. I was as unnerved by the sudden move as anybody. On the highway to LX-1 in the early-morning dark, though, my momentary reaction to this turn of events was something more like wonder.

Overt was a lesson in that basic tension within counterterrorism. Is it time to take this down, or do we need to let it go a little further? We never had those conversations about Operation Overt in the way we should have, because Rauf's arrest brought the whole thing to an end so suddenly. That disruption was a radical departure from how we worked counterterrorism in the Bush administration.

One of my first bosses in counterterrorism used to tell a story. A boy walks down the beach. Sees a pretty rock lying on the sand. Squats down, picks it up. This rock is perfect for his rock collection, the boy thinks—and he puts it in his pocket—and then off to the side another rock, glinting in the sunlight, catches the boy's eye. He goes and picks up that one, too. Then another rock, and another, and the boy goes on like that until he is so weighted down with perfect rocks to take home that he can't carry them all. He plops down in the sand, paralyzed by treasure.

The FBI counterterrorism division, my boss said, was like that boy. Any shiny thing we saw, we picked it up. In those years—the years of collection—we wanted to know everything that we could possibly know about what our subjects were doing and about the networks that they might be functioning within, so that we could find out more about the threat in general.

We collected to the verge of overload because, as an organization, the FBI didn't know what we didn't know about terrorism. We did not know much about whether there were al-Qaeda operatives in this country, or what they might look like if they were here. We were trying to establish a net of collection that would show us the dangerous people and show us how those people were connected to dangerous people overseas. We opened cases, opened more cases, and then kept opening cases. We had pockets full of rocks.

That approach came with high costs. It cost human resources. We had to keep renewing FISA warrants, had to maintain and monitor electronic surveillance, had to keep translating what came off the surveillance, had to keep analyzing all the data. We weren't even sure how to identify the point of diminishing returns. In the dance of collection and disruption, the art is sensing a delicate balance: the time when you've collected enough to understand the immediate threat—the subject you're following or investigating—and also to understand the broader potential impact of that person and the person's involvements. When you feel you've hit that point, you've got to be able to disrupt.

But in the Bush years, we erred heavily on the side of collection. The pressure, in every case, was to collect. Do you have FISA up, do you have enough FISA up, are you collecting enough, who are you going to go up on next? The pressure was never to make an arrest next week. To make an arrest, you had to prove something almost impossible to prove: that you've squeezed the lemon dry, that there is no more juice in this investigation.

Collection and disruption roughly correlate with two parallel investigative approaches: muscling and targeting. Muscling drove the FBI's post-9/11 drill of running every lead. If we got thirty thousand leads in a month, so what? In those days, when agents got a counterterrorism lead, we would muscle it, hammer it, throw people and eyes and effort at every line of every spreadsheet, never sleep or stop or take days off, because we were t-crossing, i-dotting, shoe-leather-destroying beasts.

Consider, for example, the threat of the so-called California Brothers. This was a potential threat that bedeviled us the whole time I was in ITOS. It grew out of a report that suggested an al-Qaeda member had referred once to "the brothers in California."

The California Brothers became a source of unending worry, hysteria, and frustration. I can't even remember where the idea of this threat began. But I can guarantee that if you walked up behind any ITOS agent from that era, even today, and whispered the words "California Brothers," that agent would jump back, punch you, maybe shoot you, while dropping dead from a heart attack.

Once or twice a year, another agency might send a cable, continuing a series of what we came to call the Scary Cables, in which some analyst would observe that a shift in the wind had been recorded in Tajikistan at the precise moment when sixteen chickens in Alabama had simultaneously laid green speckled eggs, and then go on to suggest that the intersection of these events, in all likelihood, pointed to California—raising the ongoing concern that the California Brothers had yet to be identified.

The implication of the Scary Cables was always, What have you done about the Brothers, FBI? This would provoke such massive hysterical reactions among the ITOS leadership, me included, that we would do things like re-review every single case in every field office in California. Or go out and check for every male between the ages of X and Y who traveled to California from country Z. These were massive data-gathering exercises that consumed huge amounts of investigative and analytical resources and turned up nothing.

We were, yes, looking for a needle in a haystack. But our general attitude was: The FBI's not afraid of haystacks. We're that good, we're that strong, that is who we are—we do hard stuff better than anybody. If FBI agents have to take each stalk of hay off that stack, inspect it individually, and replace it precisely where it was before, we will goddamn do that, and for your convenience also provide you with a spreadsheet by four o'clock this afternoon that tallies all stalks of hay that were inspected in the last twelve hours. And this will be no sweat. And it will be preferable by far to taking the risk of failing to sweep up that one crucial bit of hay that we should have gotten.

That, in a nutshell, was the FBI's muscling approach to counterterrorism in 2006: If you tell me there's a terrorist in California, I will go to California and look at every human being in the state.

Muscling was driven by fear—the fear of missing something. Our biggest fear after 9/11 was that more people in the U.S. were connected to al-Qaeda or similar groups. That fear proved legitimate. Operation Overt helped make it clear that al-Qaeda was in fact metastasizing. Its members *did* want to strike us again. They *did* want to hit aviation. And they were quickly discovering the internet's power as a tool for terrorist recruitment and planning.

Just before I moved to headquarters, and just before Overt went into high gear, the FBI arrested two U.S. citizens who had been radicalized by online contact with jihadist recruiters abroad. Ehsanul Islam Sadequee and Syed Haris Ahmed lived in Georgia—in Roswell and Atlanta. Through web forums, they had been in contact with a Brit named Younis Tsouli, an early author of online propaganda for al-Qaeda in Iraq. (Online, Tsouli actually called himself "Irhabi007"—Arabic for "Terrorist 007.") Sadequee and Ahmed traveled to Washington, D.C., and made some videos, casing targets for terrorist attacks—the Capitol, the World Bank headquarters, a fuel-tank farm along I-95—and sent these videos to Tsouli and to another contact in Britain. They traveled to Canada to meet with the ringleader of the Toronto 18—a group that was planning to attack a range of targets from power grids to the Canadian Parliament building. Ahmed traveled to Pakistan and Sadequee traveled to Bangladesh, where they discussed plans that didn't get much traction—for instance, plans for the creation of an "Al-Qaeda in Northern Europe," to be based in Sweden.

These two were idiots, but they had no-kidding connections to al-Qaeda, and they were doing jihadist work. How important or threatening was that work? Unclear. They were not building bombs in their basements, with a view to blowing stuff up tomorrow. But for more than a year, they made consistent efforts to participate in preliminary planning and casing for al-Qaeda attacks here in the U.S. and abroad.

Theirs was one of the first cases with a real operational connection to the internet. The internet pervades human existence so thoroughly now that it can be hard to remember how recently life was mainly analog. When was the point of no return? Maybe around 2006. In July of that year, a microblogging platform called Twitter debuted for the public. In September, Facebook launched a new feature called "News Feed" and opened membership to all comers, where before you had to be part of a college or school network to join. In 2006, YouTube was barely a year old. The first iPhones didn't go on sale until 2007.

Terrorists were enthusiastic early adopters of every new technology. In 2006, when al-Qaeda launched a digital-media initiative, it pushed out more messages in one year than the group had released in the previous three years combined. The internet made it much, much easier for al-Qaeda, the Taliban, and susceptible Westerners to connect and share information with one another. New social media platforms in particular gave everyone, from hardened terrorists to innocent teenagers, tools to make spectacles of themselves, for good and for ill. In Operation Overt, when we saw that half a dozen of the conspirators had made "martyrdom videos"—a suicide bomber's version of a suicide note—we knew it was a harbinger of things to come. The melodrama of terrorism, always cranked to 10 on the crazy meter, was about to ratchet up even higher as technological capabilities kept growing.

DVDs were already big. As of Christmas 2006, DVD players outnumbered VHS players in American households for the first time. A lot of stores were doing good business with a run-of-the-mill job: transferring old videotapes onto new DVDs. Around this time, a video-store clerk in New Jersey was doing a transfer and could not believe what he was seeing on the screen. The tape showed ten young men shooting automatic weapons. They were yelling, "Allahu Akbar!" and talking about jihad. The clerk saw something, the clerk said something.

We put the young men under surveillance. They were Muslim. Half of them were in the country illegally. They liked to get together and watch Osama bin Laden videos, or videos of American soldiers being attacked—when they saw a Marine being blown up, they thought it was funny. They were planning to attack a military base and had their eyes on Fort Dix. We shut that down.

In June 2007, we wrapped up a sixteen-month-long sting operation on Russell Defreitas, a U.S. resident from Guyana connected to an extremist Muslim group in the Caribbean. Defreitas planned to blow up fuel lines and fuel tanks at John F. Kennedy International Airport in New York. He made some very incriminating statements, which allowed us to intervene before he could do anything. "Anytime you hit Kennedy, it is the most hurtful thing to the United States," Defreitas was heard to say in a recorded conversation. "They love John F. Kennedy like he's the man. . . . If you hit that, the whole country will be in mourning. It's like you can kill the man twice."

Disruption of plots such as these sparked two kinds of conversation. The first happened in courtrooms—the formal legal proceedings to prosecute people for breaking laws. The second happened everywhere else—the informal public conversation about law enforcement and terror.

Disruption always kicks off a three-day news cycle that opens the Bureau up to criticism. On day one, everyone is shocked at the plot that has been uncovered, riveted by the danger, and relieved to hear of the arrest. By day three, the tone has turned 180 degrees. Now the story is, These guys couldn't have pulled off a serious attack. They failed out of kindergarten and their ex-wives say they have mental disabilities. The theme of the conversation becomes, The FBI is taking advantage of goofballs who probably couldn't have blown up a balloon.

The operative word there is "probably." The FBI does not have the lux-

ury of assessing whether people are fully capable of doing what they suggest they might do. If you are inclined to film yourself firing an AK-47
while hollering about jihad, and if you are taking affirmative actions in
line with those sentiments, then you have cast the die and have set yourself up for investigation. It would not be a reasonable response to those
situations if the FBI were to say, Well, this guy, he's kind of dumb, so
we'll just leave him be—we only build cases on people who got good
grades in high school. That would not be a wise or just process. But it's
the strange way some people suggest we should operate.

From Muscling to Targeting

Some of the disruptions I've described were partly enabled by more targeted investigative techniques. Many targeting techniques are based on
access to and organization of data. In truth, targeting isn't that much easier
than muscling, but its ambitions usually fall a little bit shy of muscling's
ideal of omniscience.

A targeted approach to finding the California Brothers might have
looked like this: First, we go to all the terrorists we know in California,
around California, in states not even close to California, and then maybe
in foreign countries that have flights to California. Then we look at all
those people and see if, in their networks, we can make a connection to
California. That will give us a pretty good lead. Targeting is the Bureau's
preferred mode of counterterrorism investigation today.

To get from muscling to targeting, the Bureau had to develop a certain level of confidence in its own ability and experience, and a certain
tolerance of risk. Our overblown response to the California Brothers is a
perfect illustration of how little risk we were capable of handling during
the Bush years. By "we," I mean not just the FBI but Americans as a whole.
What do Americans do as soon as any tragedy strikes? We immediately

go back with a microscope and try to figure out which individual to hold responsible. To some degree it's an understandable reaction. But taken to an extreme, it expresses and perpetuates damaging and unrealistic expectations about how intelligence and law-enforcement services are able to function in society.

A turning point in the Bureau's shift from muscling to targeting was Bryant Neal Vinas. He was a Latino kid from Long Island who shattered some of our preconceived notions about al-Qaeda. Prior to Vinas, we thought it wasn't possible to get sources in al-Qaeda, wasn't possible to send cooperators into the Federally Administered Tribal Areas of Pakistan (FATA) to start really developing relationships. There was a notion that al-Qaeda was so expert in sniffing out spies in their ranks that all roads to the FATA were lined with the severed heads of failed infiltrators. It was too dangerous a proposition to operate the kinds of sources—cooperators or undercover—that we would do with organized-crime or terror groups in the U.S.

Vinas had converted to Islam, hopped on a plane, flown to Pakistan, and joined up with al-Qaeda. He took part in an attack on an American base, then went to Peshawar to find himself a wife. The Pakistanis arrested him and turned him over to us. He was charged with material support of terrorism—our meat-and-potatoes charge for people who become affiliated with terrorist groups—and he decided to cooperate. He let loose with all kinds of eye-opening intelligence about the process of affiliating with al-Qaeda, meetings with high-level al-Qaeda leadership, how he got there, and other Westerners he met along the way. From that we were able to take a closer look at people whom Vinas met and the people they knew. It was a giant leap in the evolution of the targeting process, much more efficient and less legally dubious than some of the earlier ideas that hypothetically might have made it onto the counterterrorism-division whiteboard—looking at every twenty-year-old who traveled to Pakistan last year, for instance.

After learning the story given to us by Vinas, a lot of people in the Bureau thought, Oh, my God, is it that easy? If a kid from Long Island could do it, why couldn't we? We proceeded cautiously. It's not like all of a sudden the floodgates opened and we sent every Joey Bagadonuts from Staten Island over to Waziristan. But Vinas did change how we thought about our options. His experience told us that al-Qaeda would talk to foreigners, as long as those foreigners were not on the radar of intelligence services as people who might be associated with terrorism. They wanted people who had "clean" passports—passports that would allow travel back to Western Europe or the U.S. without visas. For al-Qaeda or ISIS, that's the prime asset for a Western operative. To recruit a person with a clean passport, indoctrinate them, turn them around, and send them back—that's their goal, and that's our nightmare.

For the Bureau, Vinas was also a turning point in terms of confidence building. Not only did he provide more information, he helped us see the situation of recruitment from a different angle. That let us become much more aggressive in identifying people in the U.S. with potential capability to work for us on the ground. After Vinas, we developed sources that became extremely valuable to the U.S. intelligence community. He also turned us on to a number of specific people whom we began to look at with more of a targeting mentality. We saw how those people connected to one another, where they came from, where they were going.

There was never a watershed moment in the shift from muscling to targeting. The FBI never decided, Tomorrow we're going to do everything differently. The Bureau evolved over time. We learned by doing. Where we succeeded, we pursued.

We are still shadowed by expectations that we should be muscling machines. Today, when we open an investigation on U.S.-based extremists, we are thinking from day one about disruption. From the first minute of collection, we are looking for things that could be used as evidence in some kind of criminal prosecution. Constantly thinking, What do we have on this guy? Is he a felon who happens to be in possession of a firearm? Did he lie to Customs and Border Protection last time he entered on his flight from Pakistan? When he's not in the mosque, is he selling coke on the corner?

We're constantly building into the case a disruption strategy. We do that for two reasons. In case he's a serious threat, or in case he's no threat. In the first scenario, we consider disruption because flash to bang, the time between inspiration and action, tends to be quicker now. A suspect can be receiving instructions from Syria on his smartphone while he's shopping at the grocery store—so we may need to take him into custody immediately at any time. In the event that he's not a serious threat, if no plot and no immediate risk develops, there will come a time when we realize that we have collected enough. There will come a time when we see that the guy doesn't seem to have any true connections—sure, he's following propaganda, he's following Twitter feeds, but in reality he's not talking to anybody overseas. He has a small number of friends here, but none of them seem to be interested in his supposed desire to blow up a bank or a restaurant. So we will just take the case down—make an arrest if appropriate, or simply close the investigation. Because we don't want to carry it around for another five years.

Which is what we did with the 150-odd cases connected to Operation Overt. The FBI was just like the boy on the beach. We carried the load of Overt cases around for what seemed like forever. Most of those cases went nowhere: The people had no nexus to terrorism and were not engaged in any activity that was terrorist related. But some were indeed engaged in suspicious activities, and some were arrested for terrorism-related offenses.

When the stakes are high—when people feel desperate, and when they want to act with an abundance of caution—there's a real temptation to muscle it. But in the years to come, as I continued working counterterrorism and played my part in the shift to targeting, I would often consider our collaborations on Overt. The CIA, to its credit, will muscle nothing. We learned a lot about targeting from our interactions with the Agency, just developing our relationship with them and reaping the benefits of their targeting activity. Working with the Brits, who have a more realistic risk tolerance, also helped a lot. They know their population includes extremists. They accept that fact. They calmly try to focus on the people who appear to be most likely to act on those beliefs. Start with known bad guys, known bad organizations, and work out from there. Don't just look for every brother in California.

As for Rashid Rauf, whose capture took so many by surprise, he was not in confinement for long. The next year, Rauf managed to escape after an extradition hearing when he asked to stop at a mosque for afternoon prayers. Some while later he found himself in the wrong place at the wrong time and ended up dead. Which can happen when you're a high-profile terrorist in a dangerous part of the world.

4

Interrogation

ASKING THE RIGHT QUESTIONS, AND ASKING THE RIGHT WAY

A Cooler Full of Flour

In the late summer of 2009, Mike Heimbach gave me a call. He said, I need you to go to Denver to help them work on a CT case. The case was called High Rise. It involved a potential plot to attack mass transportation in a major city. I asked, When do you need me to go? He answered, Tomorrow.

High Rise was heating up. Because the Denver field office had not had much experience with counterterrorism, the case was causing some struggle. A situation like the one unfolding in Colorado creates a lot of special needs, just in terms of information flow. The director requires regular updates, and a thick stream of intelligence has to be nimbly routed among various departments at headquarters and throughout the intel community. Asking a field office to manage all that in the middle of a crisis is onerous. If they don't execute flawlessly, they're liable to get buried. Today, with the benefit of lots of counterterror crisis experience, headquarters collaborates well with the field. A decade ago, when the FBI began experimenting with sending HQ agents to the field as liaisons, agents in field offices sometimes felt they were being bigfooted by a babysitter. That was the reception I faced in Denver.

The subject of High Rise was Najibullah Zazi, a twenty-four-year-old Afghani raised in Pakistan and then in Flushing, Queens. After high school, Zazi ran a coffee cart in lower Manhattan, near Ground Zero. Along with two of his high school friends, Adis Medunjanin and Zarein Ahmedzay, Zazi became radicalized. Following his father's lead, Zazi sided with Taliban sympathizers at his local mosque. He and his friends watched hundreds of lectures by jihadist imams. They watched internet videos of American soldiers being ambushed. Zazi also fell into debt and went bankrupt.

In 2008, he and his friends traveled to Pakistan. They connected with highly placed al-Qaeda terrorists, who provided weapons training and taught them to build bombs. They went through what amounted to Terrorism 101—complete with graduation—and came back to the U.S. Together, they hatched a plan to detonate homemade explosives on the New York City subway. They planned to do this on September 11, 2009— the eighth anniversary of 9/11. Intelligence indicated they were directed by influential al-Qaeda operatives, possibly including Rashid Rauf, a key figure in the London airliner plot.

Back in the U.S., Zazi and his parents moved to Colorado, where Zazi conducted experiments in bomb building. He was following directions he'd been given in Pakistan. He would go to beauty-supply stores and buy chemicals like hydrogen peroxide in bulk. (When an employee at one of the beauty-supply stores made a comment about the volume of his purchases, Zazi said, "I have a lot of girlfriends.") He rented hotel rooms where he practiced cooking the peroxide down to potent concentrations. On Memorial Day weekend 2009, the FBI got a tip that Zazi's communications to his trainer back in Pakistan had been intercepted. That's what set us to looking at him.

By the time I got involved, Zazi had completed his experiments. He had taken the bomb-making materials he'd constructed, put them in his rental car, and started driving to New York. Along the way, he got pulled over for speeding—upward of a hundred miles per hour—but the materials were not found. On the weekend of the 9/11 anniversary, he was in New York. He and his associates were tipped off to FBI and New York Police Department surveillance by Ahmad Wais Afzali, a Queens imam who knew them and who was also serving as a source on this case for the NYPD's Intelligence Division. (The imam's double-agent work later caught up with him—he was charged with making a false statement in a terrorism investigation and, as part of a plea deal, he left the U.S. for Saudi Arabia.)

Spooked by the surveillance, Zazi hopped a flight back to Colorado. Unbeknownst to him, more than a few of his fellow passengers were undercover FBI agents. By the time I arrived, Zazi was still in Colorado, and he knew that we knew something and were investigating him vigorously.

Any major case like this is chaotic. The whole field office works on it. Everybody operates around the clock. In the FBI, the agent who opens a case or is the first assigned to a case owns that case, period. The case agent is king. Every case agent has a partner, a co–case agent, who lends a hand. But essentially the case agent is responsible for every aspect of the investigation for that case, from surveillance to warrants to evidence analysis to interviews. In a typical case, such as a onetime bank robbery, handling the details is straightforward. A massive national-security case that involves multiple field offices, multiple search warrants, mountains of evidence, and thousands of pages of handwritten notes needing to be transcribed can turn anyone into a one-armed paper hanger. It's more than any one human being can handle.

You have to run those cases in a different way: Assign discrete elements of the investigation to discrete teams and create a structure of oversight for each slice of the pie. One agent, for instance, will be in charge of phones. Whatever phones we come across, whatever phones we seize, whatever phones we're interested in, we lob them over to you, the phone person in charge of the phone bucket. The phone person should be able to say at any given moment how many phones we have, whose phones we have, what kinds of phones those are, which ones we're able to get into, which ones are encrypted and we can't get into, what we're doing to pursue access to those phones, and where the process stands on each of those phones. If we seized the main suspect's T-Mobile phone, has the warrant been served on T-Mobile? If so, did we get the results back? If so, have the results been uploaded into the system and analyzed? Even that list of questions, for multiple phones from multiple suspects, pretty quickly becomes overwhelming for any individual. So the person in charge of the phone bucket generally oversees a team of people working various aspects of the enterprise. It's a grueling job.

Physical searches aren't a whole lot simpler. And you never know when a demanding, complicated operation is going to suddenly get much more complicated. I got to Denver just before the field office executed search warrants at Zazi's apartment and at the home of his aunt and uncle. Executing such warrants involves seizing such a massive amount of potential evidence that no one person can fully keep track of what the organization has. In this case, one of the main things we were looking for was bomb-making material. During the search of one of Zazi's residences, agents opened the door to a bedroom closet and found a five-gallon Igloo cooler filled with white powder. Who keeps five gallons of white powder in a cooler on the floor of a bedroom closet? The team immediately thought it might have found enough of the peroxide-based explosive TATP to take down the entire building. So on an already full day, Denver had to cordon off the area, lock down the apartment complex, evacuate the building, and bring in bomb-recovery personnel. It turned out that the bucket the agents had left in place contained . . . five gallons of flour.

Every crisis has moments like this. A big pack of investigators can be like a bunch of very young kids playing soccer: Everybody chases the ball. In any game where everybody chases the ball, you can be sure that almost everybody is ignoring important stuff that needs doing. So in every crisis, you have to keep a kind of balance about the situation, and an inward distance, despite the fact that your mind is blowing up at all the crazy things that are happening. Effective response to chaos involves keeping meticulous order.

In the midst of all this, Zazi called the FBI field office, out of the blue, and said, I want to talk. We did not ask Zazi to be interviewed. He just volunteered and was coming in. The case agent got a heads-up about the development. He came to me and said, Zazi's coming in. What do you think I should ask him?

Inside, my response was like smothering a silent scream as I considered how, in this situation and cases like it, the Bureau should have had a whole team of people involved: those who knew everything about Zazi's life, family, and associates; those who were plugged into all of the information we'd collected from the investigation in New York; and those who could distill from this mass of information the requirements—that is, the questions and topics—that we wanted Zazi to discuss. I also wondered, for this important interview, whether the case agent was the right person to do it. If the case agent is new to the job, maybe not. If the case agent's career has been mostly focused on national security, maybe not. It has been my impression that agents who mainly work counterterrorism have conducted fewer interviews than agents who do criminal work. Zazi's was one of the more mature and better-organized domestic terrorist plots we'd encountered since 9/11. Improvising did not feel like the right way to do this. That said, I had faith in this case agent.

All right, I said. Forget about everything else. We sat down. We gamed out a little strategy for this interview. Because Zazi had called and offered to come in, the first approach would be to let him talk. About anything he wanted to talk about. From there, questions about his life, his family, and his beliefs would be productive, nonconfrontational ways to build rapport and fill in any blanks we had in terms of background information. Each question he felt comfortable answering would subtly establish a pattern: The case agent would ask a question and Zazi would answer it. Slowly the case agent would weave in facts that we knew to be true. Zazi would either admit them, incriminating himself, or he would lie about them.

Zazi came in with his attorney. The initial interview went on for many hours. We broke for dinner. Ordered pizza. The case agent did the interview. I sat in on some of it. I also observed it from another room. The interview took place across three days. In the in-between times, the case agent and I would talk.

Interviews raise all kinds of questions about technique. What should you show someone during an interview, if you want to confront them? You ask the suspect if he's done something, he denies it, and you have a document, like a transcript of an intercept, in which he admits having done it. Do you want to place that document in front of him or not? That can be a very powerful thing to do in an interview. But it can also compromise the case, because the suspect then knows what surveillance you have. In a national-security case, the question of disclosure is even more complicated, because the document you want to use—or the information contained in that document—could be classified. If it is, you can't use that document or that information before having conversations with headquarters and with lawyers, and perhaps going through a process of declassification, which is also complicated. The way that you proceed, laying bricks of an argument in the right order and direction to build a proper legal justification, determines whether the results of that interview will be effective and useful or not. Zazi made categorical denials in his interviews that we were later able to punch through, and he made statements that were absolutely devastating to him.

The Denver field office did a great job on High Rise. They stepped up, as Mike Heimbach would have said. The case agent's interview with Zazi pulled enough information that, combined with other evidence, he could write a solid complaint. Zazi was charged, presented for arraignment, and taken into custody before I left. Ultimately he pleaded guilty to conspiracy to use a weapon of mass destruction, conspiracy to commit murder in a foreign country, and providing material support to a terrorist organization. After his conviction, while incarcerated at the Metropolitan Detention Center, in Brooklyn, Zazi cooperated with the government. He testified about his terrorist experiences. Someday, when the government decides it is time, he will be sentenced for his crimes. Meanwhile, his associates were also brought to justice. Zarein Ahmedzay pleaded guilty and is cooperating. Adis Medunjanin was convicted at trial of multiple terrorist offenses and was sentenced to life in prison. For me, those two weeks in Colorado opened a wide window onto a set of problems that, at the time, I had no idea I would work on practically every waking moment for the next two years.

'You Know What *I* Like to Do?'

Those next two years started at the Denver airport. My phone rang as I was about to board my flight home. The call was from Art Cummings's office. Cummings and the director wanted to see me right away, that afternoon, after I landed in D.C.

I first met Art Cummings during Operation Overt. Art had been serving as the special agent in charge for counterterrorism at the Washington field office. We had heard that the director had pulled him out of there and thrown him back to counterterrorism at headquarters to keep an eye on us. I remember feeling as if this were Mueller's way of saying he didn't entirely trust what we were doing.

The notion that Cummings would be a force to hold us back was quickly dispelled. He was a former Navy SEAL. He spoke Mandarin fluently. He had started in the Bureau as a field agent in L.A. doing crack cases in Compton in the 1980s. The first thing that hit me about Cummings was his eyes. They are blue, but it's not the color that counts. It's the way the eyes move, the way they lock on to you, the way they look through you as you talk. Without saying anything at all, Cummings seemed to be saying, Oh yeah? You think so? That's what you got? If you gave him a good idea, he responded with a better one. If you gave him a great idea, he wanted more of them.

The entire time he worked with us at LX-1, Art lived on a friend's boat, which was docked in a marina in Annapolis. His family lived in Richmond, where his sons were in school; and rather than moving them all to D.C., he decided to sleep on this boat. It was no luxury craft. It had a bench that served as a seat during the day and as Art's bed at night. It did not have heating or air-conditioning, or a galley or bathroom. Art bathed and dressed every morning in the public restroom of the marina. At night, on his way home, he bought a tuna sandwich and ate on the boat. His austere existence added to Art's mystique.

As soon as he joined the team at LX-1, Art set his sights on the CIA. He was convinced that the agency, for whatever reason, was not sharing with us all the knowledge about Overt that it was getting from the Brits. Were there any U.S.-based plotters? Were any associates of UK suspects living in the country? He demanded a seat at the agency's secure video teleconferences with the Brits. I accompanied him as his plus-one. After the TV went dark, Art would sometimes accuse the senior CIA officer in the room of holding back. He would demand to know why we hadn't heard some of this stuff until now. It was a level of confrontation I had never seen before.

Upon arriving in Washington after receiving my summons at the Denver airport, I made my way to Art's office and asked him what was up.

He said, It's that hig thing. *Hig* thing? I didn't know what he was talking about. Hig! he repeated—and then it clicked. HIG must be an acronym, since half the words out of an agent's mouth are acronyms. He went on: HIG—the High-Value Detainee Interrogation Group. A new interagency effort. We're going to revamp the way we do interrogations and interviews of terrorism suspects.

Then we were off to the director's office—which meant, in the first instance, presenting ourselves to Wanda Siford, Mueller's secretary, assistant, and Praetorian Guard. She had spent much of her adult life serving directors in the FBI. Wanda *was* the FBI, or at least some hard-shelled part of it. Competence personified—dressed and coiffed with enormous dignity and professionalism—she sat behind a high desk in the inner reception area of the director's suite. I knew Wanda as an older woman, at the end of a long and esteemed career. She embraced her role as the director's protector and commanded the respect, and fear, of the highest ranks of the organization.

Wanda looked at us, picked up the phone, and called Mueller. She hung up and swept her hand to the left, signaling that we were to proceed. We passed through the conference room and entered the director's office. The space had been built for J. Edgar Hoover, though he died before he could move into it. The office is not opulent and does not occupy a corner. It looks across Pennsylvania Avenue to the Justice Department. Congress has set a limit on the amount of money that presidential appointees are allowed to spend on office furniture, and the limit is low—five thousand dollars per appointee during the duration of an appointment. For an FBI director, that's ten years, the period fixed in order to keep the appointment as much above politics as possible. FBI directors never do much decorating. But the office has a sense of grandeur nonetheless. These walls have seen seven FBI directors work with eight presidents and fourteen attorneys general. They have witnessed moments of triumph, such as the capture of Ramzi Yousef, one of the perpetrators of the 1993 attack on the World Trade Center, and moments of anger and disgust, as when the Bureau reckoned with the treason of agent Robert Hanssen. Since the Hoover building's dedication in 1975, thirty-nine FBI agents have died in the line of duty, and from this office the first calls went out to spouses and families.

Mueller sat behind his desk. He started by asking me questions about the Zazi case. Then he turned to the matter at hand. He asked, What's your plan next?

I said I was looking forward to continuing what I was doing. He said, Uh-huh, okay. And then he said, Well, there is this other thing that's come up. President Obama has asked the FBI to take responsibility for building and running a new group, to be called the HIG. He explained the basics. It was an effort to professionalize how the government conducted interrogations of high-value terrorist suspects detained overseas. He described it as an effort to get away from the abuses that had occurred at Abu Ghraib and in other controversial CIA programs. He said, The new president wants to do things differently. There's been a study about this, and a recommendation that came about as a result, and we've been asked to take charge. And we're going to do it. And *you're* going to do it. You're going to build it.

I had not been aware of this study. I didn't know what the recommendations were. This was not something I had much experience with.

Mueller said, Don't worry about that. You can read all that. CIA and the Department of Defense will be your partners, but they're not going to like it. There are things they don't want to do that they are going to have to do. You will be the director. Your job is to make this work. That is the whole of your job description. If you start knocking heads with the Agency and with DOD, and you can't get them to agree, then *get* them to agree. And when you absolutely can't get them to agree, I don't want you to fight with them. Come to me, and I will fight those fights for you. Because your job is to build it and make it work.

After all this, Mueller asked, Is there anything else you would like to tell me? I thought I saw an opening and tried to take it. I said, Sir, I'll do whatever you want me to do. But if you're asking my preference, what I would like to do is work counterterrorism. Mueller looked at me, cocked his head slightly to one side, and said, You know what *I* like to do?

No, sir, I said.

I like to try homicide cases. And look what I'm doing.

Developing Rapport

In Accra, Ghana, at 6 A.M. on Christmas Eve 2009, the young man checked out of the Tops Hotel and went to the airport, where he did not speak to another soul. He flew to Lagos and on to Amsterdam, and then boarded Northwest Airlines Flight 253 to Detroit. En route, he watched the video map, waiting for the plane to cross into U.S. airspace, because his teacher had instructed him, "Wait until you are in the U.S., then bring the plane down." When the airplane was over the U.S., the young man went into the restroom. He brushed his teeth. He put on perfume. He prayed. He returned to his seat and covered his lap and legs with a pillow and blanket. He reached inside his clothing and depressed the plunger to activate the bomb inside his pants. The bomb in his pants made a hissing sound and then a loud pop, as if a bottle had been uncorked—and apparently that was all. The young man thought his bomb had failed. He started thinking that he would have to wear the failed bomb in his pants as he passed through immigration before throwing it away in the men's room. Then his skin began to burn. He tried to take off his pants and underwear. The bomb and his clothes and his skin were on fire now. There was dark smoke rising from his body. There were flames. Seeing the fire, he thought maybe he had not failed. Maybe the bomb would explode, bring down the plane, and kill all the passengers, and his martyrdom mission would be complete.

I had seen a lot. I had never seen 302s like these: reports on the case of Umar Farouk Abdulmutallab—the so-called Underwear Bomber, who was being held in Michigan after his failed attempt, on Christmas Day 2009, to blow up that Northwest Airlines flight. Here was an al-Qaeda terrorist who—after a long, carefully planned process of patiently executed interviews—was divulging every detail of his radicalization and the planning of his attack. Every detail, right down to the architecture of the compound in Yemen where he trained. I read every page, every sentence, the Detroit field office pushed into the system. Read with rooting interest, though I'd already heard a lot of it. The case of the Underwear Bomber was the first deployment of elements of what would become the High-Value Detainee Interrogation Group that Mueller had assigned me to run.

At the HIG, I was in some ways more removed than I had been from the action—I never went to Detroit, never left my vault at LX-1. I was also more in charge of what was happening. I influenced the response to this case in ways known only to a small inner circle, while at the same time managing how our work would eventually be seen by the world beyond that group. Running the HIG, I crossed over to the dark side. Crossed into the realm of law enforcement where politics exerts decisive influence on outcomes in ways no honest person would deny.

I mean politics in two senses—one functional and necessary, the other toxic and obstructionist. Politics in the first sense—small-"p" politics— means the navigation of human relationships. Politics in that sense is the DNA of law enforcement. Law enforcement manages the shape of society with respect to legal parameters of acceptable behavior—parameters set by the Constitution and defined by statutes. The second kind of politics—party politics—means the execution of partisan strategy for purely political advantage. That kind of politics should have no place in American law enforcement. The only circumstance that might effectively force law enforcement to be partisan, in the two-party American political system, would be if one party unambiguously ceased to respect the laws and the Constitution.

At the HIG, I saw the first kind of politics operate in law enforcement at the highest levels. I began to know, and to some degree exercise, the inherently strange and fine-grained phenomenon of power. I also saw the second kind of politics encroach upon law enforcement—saw partisanship intensify to the point where it seemed almost to threaten the constitutional and legal system.

The HIG was born in a whirlwind, and at the center of the whirlwind stood a prison, Camp X-Ray, at the U.S. military detention facility at Guantánamo Bay. Campaigning for president in 2008, Barack Obama had promised to close Guantánamo. His Republican opponents wanted Guantánamo kept open. This was a disagreement about many things, but centrally it was a disagreement about the best way to get intelligence from suspected terrorists.

Obama believed the War on Terror had led the U.S. in the wrong direction. Like many Democrats (and many others), he believed the use of "enhanced" interrogation techniques, such as waterboarding, amounted to outright torture and had compromised our values as a nation. He also believed that forms of interrogation that fell short of "enhanced" were ultimately more effective. Many Republicans, but by no means all, saw the War on Terror from a different angle. They believed all terrorist suspects, including U.S. citizens, should be treated as enemy combatants—with no rights or constitutional protections. They believed the military and the intelligence agencies should use whatever interrogation methods they thought would get results. The ends justified the means.

Three days after Obama's inauguration, he signed Executive Order 13491—"Ensuring Lawful Interrogations"—which established a task force to evaluate the federal government's interrogation and detainee-transfer policies. The next document he signed, Executive Order 13492, ordered the closure of the detention facilities at Guantánamo Bay. The first policy documents of the new administration, these orders became choice targets for Obama's political opponents. Most congressional Republicans would not have cared if the executive orders had been blank, or filled with Holy Scripture. As Obama's first forays into counterterrorism policy, these orders were bound to be condemned for political advantage.

In August 2009, the presidential task force recommended two interrogation reforms. The first was to create an interagency group to conduct interrogations of high-value terrorist suspects—the CIA would be involved, and the Department of Defense; the FBI would run the group, and it would report to the National Security Council at the White House. The second was to ban the use of enhanced interrogation techniques by any U.S. government entity. From now on, only techniques from the U.S. Army Field Manual and those used by federal law enforcement, which had been compiled to be in conformity with the Geneva Conventions, would be allowed. The president accepted both of these recommendations and asked Director Mueller to create the High-Value Detainee Interrogation Group.

At the beginning, the only things I knew about the group were that it was supposed to exist; that it would be a three-way effort by the FBI, CIA, and Defense Department; and that whatever was not in the Army Field Manual would be off-limits. I read the Field Manual. I read the manual's breakdown of interrogation phases and its definitions and taxonomies of each: the five main ways to approach a subject; the five main kinds of questions to ask; the many subcategories of both; and the permutations of ways to combine them. The terms, when listed one after another—Fear-Up, Fear-Down, Pride and Ego, Futility, We Know All, File and Dossier, Establish Your Identity, Repetition, Rapid Fire, Silent, Change of Scene—triggered a scatter of associations: goofy, clinical, ominous. But "Developing Rapport," the foundation of all approaches and modes of questioning in the Field Manual, was already second nature to me, from all the interviews I'd done over the years.

Flashback to Quantico. A classroom. The teacher was John Hess. Hess was old—he had been around, it seemed, since J. Edgar Hoover was a kid. He had served for much of his career as an agent in Montpelier, Vermont—not an al-Qaeda hotbed. The course I took with him was called Interview and Interrogation.

In class, somebody asked, What's the difference between an interview and an interrogation? Hess answered, When you are convinced of someone's guilt to a moral certainty, it's an interrogation. I remember thinking, How am I going to know when that happens? And that was his point, I think. Moral certainty is rare.

When I became an agent, I learned that the FBI does very little interrogation. It does a lot of interviews. Here is another difference between interviews and interrogation: Interviews take place in a longer-term context. Interviews help agents build relationships. Relationships nurture informants. The job is to create in someone's mind a sense that you are worthy of trust. That you are competent. A professional. Doing the right thing. The challenge is demonstrating that your interests are in alignment—even if your ultimate goals are not the same. The agent who believes that he can take hardened criminals, show them the light of patriotism, and teach them the right way to live is the agent you will find in the back booth at O'Malley's nodding for another shot at 4:58 P.M.

In most interviews, all an agent has to do is demonstrate that talking to and working with the Bureau is a good idea—to convince a person that talking about bad things they've done is in their best interest, which often comes in the form of a reduced sentence. Some interviews become confrontational or hostile. That's necessary every once in a while—but not all that often if you've properly sized up what's important to someone in an initial conversation.

Compared to the work of the Bureau, pure intelligence efforts by the CIA and the Defense Department relied more heavily on interrogation. To start the HIG, I learned a lot about how both agencies approached the job: their goals, their strengths and weaknesses. Their approach was intelligence driven. They did well on some of those things that—for instance, in the Zazi case—I had observed the Bureau doing poorly. Analysts were central to the process. Before intelligence case officers interrogated a detained terrorist, they conferred with analysts—experts in the subject matter. The analyst with the best knowledge of the terrorist group and the terrorist activity provided requirements. In the intelligence world, a "requirement" is a need for information, prompting a question to be asked. So this was the great strength of their approach: There was nothing vague or open-ended about it. Every question was shaped by intelligence and driven to expand intelligence. The weakness of their approach was its inflexibility. Interrogations proceeded down a checklist: What do you know of Osama bin Laden? Where is Osama bin Laden located? Who did you speak to last week about Osama bin Laden? If the person didn't answer, he didn't answer. That's what the cable would report.

Defense interrogations involved slightly more in the way of rapport building than CIA interrogations did, but only as defined and allowed by the Army Field Manual. Military interrogators cannot, for instance, give a person any food or drink unless the Field Manual approach explicitly allows offers of food and drink. And in order to employ that approach, senior ranks must approve the interrogator's written plan in advance. The interrogation plan names the approaches to be used and explains precisely the ways in which they will be used.

An FBI interview flies by the seat of its pants. This is its greatest strength and biggest weakness. We don't do homework like the Agency. We don't have the meticulous organizational skills of Defense. But FBI interrogators know how to read the subject. They know how to respond to the subject's reactions to questions. They know how to borrow from and weave together various approaches. This guy looks hungry: I think I can warm him up a little bit if I give him a cup of coffee and let him smoke a cigarette.

Three agencies, three approaches. A case study of an age-old conflict: flexibility versus organization. Everybody needs some of both. I hoped the HIG could come up with a synthesis that would improve on all three approaches.

A Sweeping Portrait

Setting up the HIG, I got a crash course in establishing a government program. The president had signed executive orders, but the presidential pen is not a magic wand. I had to figure out how to get a staff. How to find office space. How to make the space secure for working with classified material. DOD sent me an experienced interrogator to work with. I hopped the Metro to Rosslyn and together we made some scratch marks on a yellow legal pad. Riveting stuff, which I will spare you.

On we limped, to Christmas. Family. Presents. Breakfast. Down to the basement for some exercise. Turned a TV on. Breaking news: Northwest Airlines Flight 253—". . . the Underwear Bomber was taken into custody . . ."

My first thought was, I am so glad to be out of counterterrorism. If I were in counterterrorism right now, I'd be on the way into the office, barking at the phone: Who is this guy, where is he from, who does he know, is there another on the way, what do we need to get out in front of here? But not today—I'm running the HIG, and I don't even have interrogators on board yet.

Cue the phone call—it was Art Cummings, asking, You got your team out there? I said, What team? Art said, Bullshit. This is the biggest thing that's happened in ages, and the HIG should be a part of this.

Fortunately, Umar Farouk Abdulmutallab was not ready to talk right away. On arrest, he went straight into surgery to treat serious burns of his groin, genitals, and legs. When he came out, he invoked his right to counsel. This gave me time to figure out what to do.

A few things happened. As soon as Abdulmutallab was taken into custody, the Detroit field office identified his family in Nigeria. His father was a prominent banker. He had many brothers and sisters. Detroit sent an agent to Nigeria to connect with them. The agent was there to explain to the family how the U.S. justice system worked and how it would be to Abdulmutallab's benefit for him to cooperate and talk—how cooperation could affect his sentence, where he served his time, and the conditions under which he served his time. He was dead-to-rights guilty of trying to destroy an airplane. But there were still ways cooperation could have a positive impact on his outcome. The agent was also there to listen. If we wanted Abdulmutallab to open up and share intelligence, we needed to know how to talk to him. We needed to know how he came to find himself on a Northwest Airlines flight with a bomb in his underwear. The agent convinced Abdulmutallab's mother and uncle to come back to Detroit, to meet with Abdulmutallab in jail, and to try to help us convince him to cooperate.

At the end of January, I sent a couple of people to Detroit. Not to take over the investigation, but to help the Detroit agents with their interviews the way I had helped Denver with Zazi. One of the people I sent was Joe Yungwirth, a former Special Forces officer and a former member of the FBI fly team—agents who deploy overseas when we need to put additional eyes and ears on the ground. If something big pops up for our legat in Abuja, for example, we'll send a fly team guy out there to help. They are prepared to dig in and stay for a while—months at a time. Joe had a lot of experience with fast, deep learning. I also sent a few subject-matter experts up there, and a reports officer to help them get the paperwork out quickly. All of these people went on to play key roles in the HIG.

It was a very low-key, low-visibility deployment. They helped design, and eventually became, the infrastructure for the conversation that the intelligence community wanted to have with Abdulmutallab. It turned out to be a very challenging interview.

Abdulmutallab was, and probably is to this day, a reticent, closed-off, quiet man. He is very pious, with a black-and-white view of the world. Everything beyond the parameters of his religious beliefs is alien and condemned. Despite the severity of his burns, he never requested or accepted a single pain pill. He wore regular clothes, stayed in his cell, ate like everybody else, and would not outwardly acknowledge what had to be great physical suffering. He spoke to no one else in the facility. He kept completely to himself.

At the heart of every good interrogation or interview is a relationship, one in which the interviewee begins to trust the interviewer and decides that talking is in his or her best interest. Here we had a young man who was isolated, injured, and profoundly devout. The Detroit agents, with assistance from our team, rightly concluded that Abdulmutallab's family were in the best position to convince him that he could trust the FBI. The agents initiated the ultimate interrogation of Abdulmutallab by getting the family to convince him to talk to us.

When he did start talking, he told us the story of how he became connected with Anwar al-Awlaki. From my first days in counterterrorism, I had been conscious of, and actively tracking, Awlaki. Born in America to Yemeni parents, Awlaki grew up to be a charismatic jihadi preacher and al-Qaeda recruiter. After 9/11, he fled from the U.S. to Yemen. By the time I came to counterterrorism, Awlaki was on his way to becoming the most effective popularizer of militant Islam in the English-speaking world. Budding terrorists hoarded Awlaki's lectures on CDs. Awlaki was connected to my very first case at ITOS-1, just before Operation Overt. When the original, core al-Qaeda began to weaken, Awlaki became a leader of that group's first and most dangerous offshoot, al-Qaeda in the

Arabian Peninsula (AQAP). His lectures influenced Najibullah Zazi. And he was a mentor to Nidal Malik Hasan, who killed thirteen and injured thirty-two more in a mass shooting at Fort Hood, Texas, one month before Abdulmutallab boarded the plane to Detroit.

Abdulmutallab told us about traveling to Yemen's Shabwah Province, where he was a guest in Awlaki's house. He described how Awlaki introduced him to the foremost terrorist bomb maker in the world, a man named Ibrahim Hassan al-Asiri, who went on to create devices such as the printer-cartridge bomb years later. It was Asiri who taught Abdulmutallab how to handle, wear, and deploy the underwear bomb. Abdulmutallab provided granular information on terrorist operations, amounting to a sweeping portrait of al-Qaeda in the Arabian Peninsula's inner workings—a portrait that helped to guide U.S. intelligence operations for some time to come.

At breaks, and after interrogation sessions, Joe would call to tell me what had happened. At the same time, interrogators were disseminating the results to reports officers—not just handing off their notes but carefully walking them through them, so that no one would get hung up on illegible handwriting or unfamiliar terms. Within the intelligence community, we disseminated this information as broadly as we could, to show other agencies the potential of an expert-assisted interrogation. The FBI has a reputation for not sharing information in a timely fashion. I wanted to change that reputation. Every gesture like this—every mechanical refinement of workflow—would help convince another person or two in the intelligence community that this collaboration was a good idea.

And to persuade the field offices that this was not a land grab, I made sure Joe worked closely with the local case agent, the Detroit agent who had gone to Nigeria. Because the goal was not just to suck the intelligence out of Abdulmutallab and leave him there. The goal was to create an ongoing relationship with the suspect. Keeping the local case agent involved through the whole process ensured that someone in Detroit would be able to keep the conversation going.

Soft on Terrorism?

Is terrorism a crime or an act of war? Should terrorists be tried in the justice system or handled by the military? Because Abdulmutallab was a direct agent of AQAP, and because he exercised his right to remain silent for some time after being given his *Miranda* warning, this case—and involvement in this case by some of us who later made up the HIG—immediately became an easy way for both Republicans and Democrats to express their views on the U.S. government's appropriate response to terrorism.

For Democrats, the HIG became a symbol of a better way forward, after the notorious episodes of prisoner abuse at Abu Ghraib, Bagram Air Base, and elsewhere. They saw the HIG as a smarter, more efficient, more effective way of interrogating terrorist suspects. For Republicans, the HIG was a sign of how far the country had fallen and proof that the U.S. had gone soft on terrorism. What were we doing sending FBI people in front of terrorists and reading them their rights? Terrorists don't have rights. They deserve whatever they get.

When I went to the Hill to brief members of Congress and testify before committees, that was the conversation I became a part of. A conversation with no middle ground. I went to the Hill to brief or testify about the HIG more than fifteen times during my first year on the job. These were my initial experiences testifying before Congress, and the first few times I went, members of Congress wanted to hear about Abdulmutallab.

Republicans would ask, Isn't it true you didn't even get in front of him for weeks before he lawyered up, and he didn't want to talk to you? And you lost all that time, and you didn't get much of anything out of him? I would answer, Yes, true, he wasn't questioned the night he was arrested, but we did convince him to cooperate, and we collected significant intelligence. They did not want to hear that. They were not willing to acknowledge what we learned. They could only see the case as an example of a single effect of Obama's new policy, an effect they viewed like this: Now a terrorist could get arrested and be treated like a criminal defendant—be allowed to tell the federal government, Screw you, I don't want to talk.

Democratic congressman Adam Schiff, a former U.S. attorney from California—and now the chairman of the House Permanent Select Committee on Intelligence—was one of the few members of Congress who asked to have a real conversation with me, one on one, about interrogation. He said, I'm really interested in this concept of the HIG, tell me about it. He wanted to know what works, what doesn't, how he could help. Was he doing that because he had been told to support the president's agenda? Or was he legitimately interested in finding a mode of interrogation that was guided by the Constitution and the rule of law? I got the sense that he was legitimately interested in national security. I was looking for friends. I took them where I found them.

The pitch of rhetoric around the interrogation of terrorist suspects—and about the HIG—rose higher through 2010 and into 2011, as the House flipped and the Tea Party moved Republicans even further to the right. I was constantly appearing on the Hill and elsewhere around town, arguing that a constitutionally consistent approach to interrogation works. Sometimes you'll get a guy who decides not to talk, and in this country we have to respect that. Most suspects who decide not to talk on the day they're arrested do talk eventually. And rapport building—the relationship-building process of getting to know suspects, breaking down their defenses positively, building trust—gets you higher-quality, better intelligence than scaring the hell out of them or beating them into telling you anything you want to hear to make the beating stop. That's my position. Always has been and always will be. I'm not throwing a rock at anybody who's done interrogations differently. But my experience has been that law-enforcement interview techniques produce great volumes of valuable intelligence.

More than half of Congress disagreed, because law-enforcement techniques were not in their political playbook. Mike Rogers, a Republican from Michigan, became chair of the House Permanent Select Committee on Intelligence in January of 2011. He said one of his first priorities as chair was to get rid of the HIG. Rogers was hard to deal with in part because he had once been an FBI agent. He spent about five years in the Chicago field office, where he worked on organized crime—enough time to give him some dog-with-bone opinions.

What I learned, in my appearances on the Hill, was that the goal of every trip up there was survival. There was no convincing anyone of anything. Everyone walks into the room with predrafted talking points and questions. Success is coming out with a sound bite that will advance an agenda. A congressional hearing is not fact-finding. It's theater. As the witness, you have one goal: Get out alive.

'Fine! Done!'

When I wasn't battling my way through the Capitol building, I was in LX-1 building teams. Teams were organized by target. The HIG charter designated two kinds of targets for our deployments, predesignated and pop-up.

Predesignated targets were the highest of the high-value people. If Osama bin Laden or Anwar al-Awlaki ended up in detention, the HIG would deploy predesignated teams on those people. To create that list of targets, we sent out a survey to the agencies and had knowledgeable people rate each terrorist on a few different scales, such as operational value or intelligence value. We then submitted the list of the top twenty-four to the National Security Council for approval.

Pop-up targets were more common. Anyone anywhere in the intelligence community could nominate a target for a pop-up HIG deployment. Abdulmutallab was a pop-up. Nobody knew who he was before he got on that plane, but then he became the most important person for anyone to talk to. Any person captured who knew a lot about Awlaki, Asiri, or al-Qaeda in the Arabian Peninsula would be a prime pop-up candidate.

Each team had interrogators, analysts, and reports officers. The FBI and the Defense Department provided a lot of these resources. The CIA always provided the fewest. The CIA is the smallest of the intelligence services and is very careful, to the point of reticence, about assigning people and spending money.

We were constantly poring over intelligence traffic to pick up information about high-value targets who had been detained. The Agency held back on this kind of information, too. One notable early failure for the HIG was missing the chance to interrogate a high-level terrorist leader who had been captured and held by Pakistani forces in early 2010. The CIA was allowed to question him, but (as *Newsweek* reported at the time) the HIG was not. On the Hill, members of Congress grilled me about this lapse: If the HIG is so good, why did you miss this guy? To expose all the details of interagency tension would have been a mistake. Frustrated as I was with my reluctant CIA partners, calling them to account in front of Congress would only have made things worse.

Art Cummings and Director Mueller wanted frequent updates from me about relations with the Agency. I tried and tried to make it work, and finally had to tell them I couldn't. Mueller said, Okay, I'm coming in. He set up a meeting at Langley with the CIA director, Leon Panetta, and a few of us went and joined them. The seventh-floor conference room was gorgeous: hardwood paneling, a forty-acre table, bottles of water and little mats in front of every chair. And in the middle of the table sat a bowl of fresh raspberries. I had never seen a fresh raspberry in a government office before. Had not known such things could exist in such places. We had no fresh raspberries in the Hoover building. I really wanted to eat one, but I did not eat one. I opened the bottle of water next to my place mat—heard the little whoosh, felt the rush of air on the edges of my fingers. It was *fizzy* water. These guys knew how to live.

The Agency team came in, including Panetta, whom I'd never met before. He whipped off his suit coat, threw it on a chair, looked sideways at Mueller, and said, Get the hell over here, you son of a bitch! The backslapping, the questions: How's that golf game? Do you still suck? How's Ann? How's Sylvia? Mueller took his own jacket off, put it on the back of his chair. We all sat down.

Then Mueller leaned back—easy, heavy lidded—and said, All right, what the hell are we gonna do with this thing? What are we gonna do? Panetta said, We're gonna do it. What do you need? Mueller looked at me: What do you need? I said, Well, sir, I need three analysts and a logistics officer. Panetta said, Fine! Done! Next week.

They moved on to other topics. The whole meeting seemed unnecessary. And in that way it was a lesson. This is how government works. There's no need to get histrionic and polarized and scream and yell. We all want the same thing. Sometimes we don't all agree on how to get where we're going, but if we just sit down and talk, we can figure it out.

A year later, in September, Anwar al-Awlaki was killed by a drone strike in Yemen. The following month, Umar Farouk Abdulmutallab pleaded guilty to all eight charges on which he was indicted, including conspiracy to commit an act of terrorism transcending national boundaries, attempted murder within the special aircraft jurisdiction of the United States, and attempted use of a weapon of mass destruction. At some point, after all the cooperation he provided in all the interrogation sessions, he just shut down. He went back into his shell, and off to Colorado—to ADX

Florence, the federal Supermax prison. Five years after that, in 2017, in response to a Freedom of Information Act request from *The New York Times*, the U.S. government released almost two hundred pages of the 302s of Abdulmutallab's interrogation. The same ones I'd read in the FBI computer system back when they'd first been filed. The *Times* story about the documents, by Scott Shane, noted that Abdulmutallab, in his interrogation, had "tried to reconstruct the layout of a training camp, Mr. Awlaki's house and many other Qaeda buildings. His descriptions were so precise that it is likely they have helped shape targeting decisions in the American drone campaign in Yemen."

Déjà Vu

Now, to bring the story forward: During the 2016 campaign, candidate Donald Trump was clear about his views on some traditional hot-button national-security issues, such as the use of torture (he was for it), the prosecution of foreign terrorists in regular criminal courts rather than by military tribunals (he was against it), and the future of the detention facility at Guantánamo (he wanted to keep it open and put more people in it).

For many of us in national-security positions, this was like being dragged back into a part of your past that you did not wish to revisit. We had been through these issues before, fought these battles many times, and over the years found what we believed were the best ways to do the job of keeping America safe. After eight years of finding ways to hold, interrogate, and prosecute terrorists that did not involve sending them to Cuba—eight years of doing these things successfully, with a track record that "enhanced" methods have not matched—we found ourselves having these conversations all over again. And needing to justify our success all over again. And arguing once again that torture, in addition to being wrong, was not necessary—and not even helpful—to the project of collecting the best, most reliable intelligence from subjects. And trying to persuade policy makers once again that confinement for life in maximum-security federal prisons—from which no one has ever escaped—without the possibility of parole was a pretty reliable way to keep terrorists from harming anyone. All the facts were on our side, but I got the distinct feeling that we might lose the arguments this time.

Attorney General Sessions had strong preconceived beliefs about all of these issues. Early in the new administration, George Toscas, the deputy attorney general in the National Security Division, expertly used the ongoing trial of a hard-core al-Qaeda fighter known as Spin Ghul as an example to show why trying a foreign terrorist here in the United States was sometimes the only reasonable course. Ghul was responsible for the deaths of two American servicemen in Afghanistan in 2003. After spending years in a Libyan prison, he was arrested for attacking a police officer on a boat while en route to Italy. The Italians couldn't prosecute him for anything other than simple assault, and Ghul was likely to be released into the wilds of Western Europe—only a plane ride from the United States. The Italians would never give him to us if they knew he would be sent to Guantánamo—most Western nations did not approve of our use of that facility, or of the jerry-built and controversial legal regime that had grown up around it, and the European Union's Court of Human Rights would not permit such a transfer. But they would give him to us for federal criminal prosecution. Ghul was tried and convicted in New York and will spend the rest of his days in prison. The attorney general was not impressed.

The issue came to a head a few months later with the case of a detainee in custody overseas—a detainee whose situation, suffice it to say, was parallel to the case of Spin Ghul. The attorney general flat-out refused to allow this detainee into the United States for trial. He seemed not to appreciate that the likely alternative was the detainee's imminent release from custody.

And he did not just oppose bringing the detainee here—he was volcanically offended that we had even proposed it. This sent Sessions into a mode that I witnessed a number of times: He would grab the arms on his chair and prop himself up a bit higher in his seat. His face would redden. His voice would rise. Then he would stare, not at anyone in particular, but at the table, his eyes darting back and forth, as he berated us for treating terrorists like criminals. For giving constitutional rights to enemy combatants. He was not able to see the work as we saw it: as taking one more terrorist out of circulation.

At a Principals Committee meeting in early 2018, I remember Sessions erupting at Defense Secretary James Mattis over another aspect of the same issue. He tore into Mattis for the Defense Department's role in detaining terrorists on foreign battlefields and then proposing that those detainees be tried in U.S. courts. Defense was creating problems that Justice had to solve, Sessions declared. Mattis politely answered that he would work on establishing a facility for detaining military combatants in the United States.

Nobody even bothered to point out to the attorney general that the so-called problems he believed Defense created for Justice were in fact an example of how the system was supposed to work: a prime example of two very different departments, with different powers and different techniques, collaborating on their shared mission. No one said this, I think, because everyone understood that such collaboration was no longer valued by the federal government's most powerful decision makers. Not anymore. This was the new team. Things were going to be different.

President's Daily Brief

Finished Intelligence

Information is the lifeblood of effective government. You can't manage the administration of anything unless the people involved draw on the same knowledge and understanding, and the same sense of what needs to happen and in what order. Interrogations produced raw intelligence—reports eventually written up as 302s. Then these 302s were analyzed, interpreted, and discussed by the investigators in counterterrorism. Working with prosecutors, agents used information from those 302s—about the detainee's associates, his habits, the places he visited—to build cases, using techniques described by the enterprise theory. Analysts also took the raw intelligence in select 302s from all the FBI's operational divisions—primarily the criminal, counterterrorism, and counterintelligence divisions—and turned it into the finished intelligence of briefings. An "operational" division is one that is responsible for some piece of the FBI's investigative work. "Finished" intelligence means that it has been contextualized, rewritten, and presented in a way that can be understood by informed readers whose government positions—in departments such as State, Treasury, Homeland Security, and Justice; and, most critically, in the White House—require them to make decisions about how the government should act on the briefing's information.

Traditionally, the briefing structure that maintains the flow of information between Justice and the Bureau has been regular and reliable. (I am describing that structure as it was during my time in FBI leadership; I do not know the present structure of briefings.) Every Monday, Wednesday, and Friday morning, the Bureau's director and members of his senior team briefed the attorney general, the deputy attorney general, the National Security Division folks, and some other Department of Justice staff members. As I rose in the ranks at the FBI, I dealt with Justice officials of corresponding rank. In my first years at headquarters, I was occasionally called in to brief the attorney general. During the administration of President George W. Bush, I gave one briefing each to Alberto Gonzales and Michael Mukasey. One of them seemed very bored and the other one actually fell asleep. I didn't take it personally. I started briefing the attorney general on a regular basis when Eric Holder held the job and I had become assistant director of counterterrorism at the FBI. Holder was President Obama's first appointee to lead the Justice Department.

What mainly drove these thrice-weekly meetings was a presentation of intelligence called the President's Daily Brief. If intelligence is information for decision makers, the President's Daily Brief is the information that the intelligence community believes the ultimate decision maker must have. It covers a wide—literally, global—range of subject matter, from migration patterns to weapons sales to economic intelligence. The briefing is assembled in the Office of the Director of National Intelligence, and to the extent that the FBI is involved in preparation of the PDB, the work chiefly concerns terrorist threats and counterterrorism work—highly classified stuff. You need a whole suite of security clearances and read-ins to different compartmented programs to even read the document.

For a small number of people in offices that are not Oval—including about half a dozen each from the FBI and from Justice—it is also helpful to know what the president knows. In an elemental way, the President's Daily Brief gets all the relevant people focused on the same targets at the same time, especially when crises are breaking. The PDB also organizes the fire-hose blast of information these people require so that they can do their jobs more broadly. For Bureau officials who read it, the PDB shows how our cases fit into the wider world of national-security threats and the government's other priority issues and concerns.

A Rough, Rough Gig

At the PDB meeting with the attorney general, everybody from the FBI would sit on one side of the table and everybody from Justice would sit on the other side, like in a strategic-arms-negotiating meeting or a summit with a foreign leader. The briefer, an FBI analyst exclusively assigned to the PDB, sat at the head. Every day, except Friday and Saturday, that person arrived at work in the early evening and worked through the night reviewing the book, looking hard at every piece of new intelligence and trying to anticipate all possible questions about every issue that anyone might ask. The main qualification for becoming the briefer: having brains to burn. The job is a one-year assignment. By the end of that year, the person in the job is smoked. It's a rough, rough gig. But smoke gives flavor. Briefers know this country's most sensitive intelligence as well as or better than anyone else. When people left that role, I always tried to steer them into jobs in counterterrorism or counterintelligence.

The briefer generally began the PDB meeting like this: In the book today, I'd like to draw your attention to . . . And then he or she orally presented the most important pieces of intelligence. That has been, for a long time, the baseline of the established process for the PDB meetings. Beyond that, every attorney general has adapted the process to his or her liking. Attorney General Holder asked many questions, and there was a lot of discussion back and forth.

When it came to FBI operations, I discerned no defining political or philosophical slant in Eric Holder. Never did I sit there and think he was speaking from a set of firm biases or preconceived opinions. He was focused on the work in the way you'd expect a good attorney to be. I also never thought of Holder as someone I needed to educate or for whom I needed to provide background information. He had been acting attorney general under George W. Bush, deputy attorney general under Bill Clinton, and U.S. attorney for the District of Columbia before any of that. Also, he was firmly in charge as attorney general when I started briefing him, which would not be the case years later when I briefed President Trump's first attorney general, Jeff Sessions.

I only saw Holder get angry once in the many dozens of times I briefed him, and that was because we pushed. It was on a complicated, difficult issue. The FBI wanted to do something and Justice was holding the Bureau back. We pushed the disagreement all the way to paper: wrote him an actual letter to try to put him in a corner. At the FBI, even something as seemingly straightforward as a letter on stationery has an acronym—LHM, for "letterhead memorandum." You know you're in a bureaucratic war when "going to paper" is the equivalent of DEFCON 5—it means there's now a record, something to judge future decisions and behavior against. And Holder did not appreciate that. Looking at the matter from his point of view, I can understand his reaction and might well have had the same one if I had been sitting in his chair. He read the memorandum right there at the table, then stood up and said, This is bullshit. He threw the paper down. Walked out. Slammed the door. With

Mueller sitting right there. Even Mueller reacted to that one. It got a Hmmm out of him.

At the next briefing, Holder walked in, and the first thing he said was, Listen, I just wanted to say I got a little heated the last time we were in here, and I apologize for that. I should not have reacted that way. I was not happy about what I was reading. But I don't want you to take that the wrong way. I respect the work you are doing and the work you are putting into this. We just need to work through it.

Holder made lots of decisions I disagreed with. Fine. The ball bounces. But I admired his generosity, his sense of responsibility, his magnanimity, and his intelligence. Others at Justice followed that example. His deputy attorney general, James Cole, was another official I disagreed with a lot. One day we got in each other's faces. I made an argument, he shut me down, I kept arguing, he kept shutting me down. Eventually he said, Enough—meaning, Don't say another word. And I shut up. And felt that second-guessing afterburn: Did I overstep my bounds? At the end of the meeting—papers shuffling, briefcases clasping, Florsheims clopping—Cole caught me for a second and said, You know, I did not agree with you today, but I respect the way you advocate for your position, and I thank you for that.

When Holder left and Loretta Lynch took over, the atmosphere around the table changed. There was less talking, more reading. I don't know if Lynch hadn't read the book before she came to the meeting, or if she didn't like to listen to the briefer as much. Whatever the reason, there were a lot of us sitting there while the attorney general and deputy attorney general would read in silence.

Loretta Lynch is gracious and considerate. She comports herself in a way that is controlled at all times. She speaks in the measured tones of an NPR broadcast: positive but not peppy, concerned but not angry. I never went into a meeting with her afraid of what I was going to hear. Edges, though, are useful for a leader. It's okay for a leader to have limits that others do not want to test. That can be motivating. Lynch seemed to loathe conflict. Oftentimes she and her people would have little to say in the President's Daily Brief. We had a run of very intense counterterrorism events in 2016 and 2017 when Lynch was attorney general, and I don't remember her asking many specific questions. Sometimes I wondered if she spent so much time reading and so little talking in those briefings because she wanted to avoid the possibility of any friction or dispute.

'Where's He From?'

After Trump's inauguration, when Jeff Sessions came in, we were ready to help orient him to this process. Or to adjust the process, to reshape it to suit his preferences—to make the briefings more effective for him. Sessions changed the venue for the Bureau's meetings. He asked that instead of holding them in the Hoover building, we come over to the Justice Department's operations center in the Robert F. Kennedy building, where his own office was.

Sessions had been a senator for twenty years. He had been attorney general of Alabama for two years and U.S. attorney for Alabama's southern district from 1981 to 1993. In public statements he frequently indexed back to his experience as a prosecutor, even though the Justice Department in those days was very different from the department he inherited. The National Security Division was not even a twinkle in anyone's eye when he was a U.S. attorney. (The National Security Division of the Justice Department was created by the USA Patriot Act, in 2005.) And Sessions had never received the PDB. He had never been a part of the intelligence community. As soon as he became attorney general, he began to encounter all kinds of information that he hadn't seen before. To understand the documents he was receiving now, to see what those documents could show, he needed to be able to register at a glance the author, source, and subject. It's not hard to learn to read those documents. But it is a skill. And it was all the more important to learn the shape of this information because the substance was largely unfamiliar to him, too.

In the first few briefings with Sessions, conversations necessarily covered a lot of basic material. Jim Comey was the FBI director, and he began at the beginning. Described the differences between the Sunni and Shia practices of Islam. Explained which terrorist groups lined up with which religious philosophies. During the PDB, Comey and Sessions would have religious discussions: wide ranging, even free flowing. As a double major in chemistry and religion, Comey was well positioned to engage the AG on the groups we tracked and the religions they followed. Sessions believed that Islam—inherently—advocated extremism. The director tried to explain that the reality was more complicated. Talking about religion was Comey's way of trying to connect with Sessions on terrain familiar to them both.

Leading the Justice Department is one of the biggest responsibilities a person can have in this country. Getting up to speed on intelligence, and categorizing it properly in memory, is a basic part of the job. Sessions did not compartmentalize the new knowledge he acquired. He would say, I saw in the paper the other day . . . and then would repeat an item that we had briefed him on a few days earlier, intelligence from the PDB. Sessions was confusing classified intelligence with news clips. It was an early sign that this transition would be more challenging than we expected.

As time went on, I observed many things about Attorney General Sessions that gave me pause. I observed him to have trouble focusing, particularly when topics of conversation strayed from a small number of issues, none of which directly concerned national security. He seemed to lack basic knowledge about the jurisdictions of various arms of federal law enforcement. He also seemed to have little interest in the expertise and arguments that others brought to the meetings, or in some long-standing commitments by Justice and the Bureau. I observed his staff to be somewhat afraid of him—reluctant to voice opinions because they did not want to make him angry.

His major interest in any given topic tended to be the immigration angle, even when there was no immigration angle. Before disruptions of U.S.-based counterterrorism cases, we would brief him. Almost invariably, he asked the same question about the suspect: Where's he from? The vast majority of the suspects are U.S. citizens or legal permanent residents. If we would answer his question, Sir, he's a U.S. citizen, he was born here, Sessions would respond, Where are his parents from? The subject's parents had nothing to do with the points under discussion. We were trying to get him to understand the terrorist threat overall. Trying to explore the question, Why are Americans becoming so inspired by radical Islam and terrorist groups such as ISIS that they're going out and planning acts of terrorism against other Americans right here in this country? That question cannot be exhaustively explored by reference solely to immigration policy.

In February 2017, less than a month after he was sworn in as attorney general, Sessions began sending requests for the FBI to analyze our counterterrorism cases through the immigration lens. This was the period when the Trump administration was revising the president's first executive order on immigration, "Protecting the Nation from Terrorist Attacks by Foreign Nationals," which had provoked many legal actions and had resulted in a hold on the action by a federal judge. Sessions wanted answers to questions like these: How many counterterrorism cases did we have against immigrants? How many people from outside the country had we arrested?

The FBI does not keep those statistics in that form. In the course of an investigation, we may uncover someone's immigration history. That immigration history may or may not prove to be significant. We do not keep aggregate figures on how many Syrians were arrested this month. And there are so many ways of construing the how-many-immigrants question that we would not know how to answer it. Do you mean how many people arrested? How many people convicted of terrorism offenses? Do you mean people who came here from Syria as immigrants? If yes, at what age? What if they came at age five with their parents? Because those people are not Syrians, they're Americans—they've become citizens by now and spent their whole conscious lives here, but yes, technically they did come here as Syrians, thirty years ago.

Any one of those numbers presented without context can be wildly misleading. But then what would be the point of gathering those numbers anyway? The attorney general's questions about immigration and terrorism were troubling to us. We knew what thin ice they would put us on, in terms of accuracy. It's very hard to provide a true count in answer to a question like that. It is also incredibly labor-intensive to come up with an answer, even one that is inadequate or even wrong. It would require taking analysts who are working substantive issues and telling them, instead, to start counting the angels on the head of a pin.

'How Much Longer?'

The briefers set a goal. They wanted to engage the attorney general's attention. They took note of things that interested him, aside from immigration. He was very interested in narcotics trafficking—an important issue for the country, but not usually central to the kinds of national-security issues that are the focus of the President's Daily Brief. Still, to try to get his attention, the briefers started putting updates about narcotics shipments from Colombia in the book.

Someone had told Sessions that even if we knew in advance about every drug shipment destined to leave Colombia by boat or ship, the U.S. wouldn't allocate enough vessels to intercept them. This made Sessions apoplectic. Drugs were flooding into the U.S., he believed, simply because we weren't making the necessary interdictions. Many times, when he was briefed on narcotics trafficking, he would burst out with questions: Why don't we have more boats down there? Why don't we put more boats in the water? Is that all we need—more boats? This is ridiculous! I'll go talk to the White House chief of staff. I'll get us more boats. Sometimes he went on like this for fifteen minutes. He seemed to think that the FBI had some kind of navy at its disposal, and that this navy was off doing other things. We had to tell him, We don't have the boats in Colombia. We are not able to do that. That's not us.

Trying to interest Sessions in matters that he was not predisposed to care about was a lost cause. One of those matters was the disappearance of Robert Levinson. A former agent for the Drug Enforcement Agency and the FBI, Levinson worked as a private investigator after he retired from government service. In 2007 he went to Kish Island, off the coast of Iran, where he disappeared. The circumstances have never been fully explained. Aside from some pictures of him that came to light in 2011—wearing an orange jumpsuit, as a prisoner would—there has been no sign of Levinson since then. Many people believe he is being held by the Iranian government.

When Levinson disappeared, the FBI started trying to find him and bring him home. This is an important issue to FBI agents. It was important to Attorneys General Holder and Lynch, and to Directors Mueller and Comey. I was present on several occasions when Director Mueller told Levinson's wife, Christine, that the FBI would never stop looking for Bob. I was present when Jim Comey told her the same thing. In each of my many meetings with her, with her children, and with her sister, I conveyed the same message: The FBI is committed to this search.

Sessions did not seem to see the importance. He asked, How much longer are we going to do this? How much money are we going to spend on this? Sessions questioned not only the search for Levinson; he questioned why the federal government bothered to search for other Americans detained or taken hostage overseas. The implication was that some of these people had it coming: If you traveled to Iran and then found yourself locked up, it was your own damn fault.

I see a glimmer of brutal logic there, up to a point. In recent history, though, when Americans have gone missing overseas, the federal government's response has been guided by a broader set of values than cold expediency. We do not abandon people. We work to find them and bring them home, even if they have been irresponsible and stupid. We do everything possible to bring them home. We are in this together.

Many of Sessions's questions were awkward. He would ask a question that was implicitly critical of the Department of Justice and look at those of us from the FBI expectantly, as if we could or should answer the question with our Justice colleagues sitting right there in the room. We would simply say, That's not our area of responsibility.

An example: He expressed frustration that many U.S. attorneys, in cases where the death penalty was an option, were not recommending or pursuing the death penalty. It's nonsense, he would say. We have this law, and if we have the law then we've got to start using it. Sessions spent a lot of time yelling at us about the death penalty, despite the fact that the FBI plays no role of any kind in whether to seek the death penalty—that's a job for Justice. All the people on Sessions's side of the table would look at their laps. No one would chime in and try to answer his questions, calm things down, redirect the conversation. We were always hanging out on a limb.

Maybe they were so quiet over there because they, too, brought limited experience to the table. That was fine. It could have given us the opportunity to engage. But no one ever gave us an opening. I would look at the line of them and think, Pitch in here, be the translator, help me out. Show me how to get through to him or help him understand. To be fair, they may have had their own difficulties charting the byways of his mind.

You never knew when you'd bump into some distorted perception. On one occasion Sessions launched into a diatribe about whom we were hiring at the FBI. Back in the old days, he said, you all only hired Irishmen. They were drunks, but they could be trusted. Not like all those new people with nose rings and tattoos—who knows what they're doing?

The difficulty of dealing with Sessions personally was compounded, I believe, by the political nature of the Department of Justice. Political, meaning staffed with officials who are appointed and are therefore cautious—not political as in partisan. When a new attorney general comes in, survival instincts are triggered. People try to figure out where they stand. No one wants to say anything controversial.

Another reason they were so quiet may have been that they weren't reading the briefing material. Most people who received the PDB still got a hard copy, but by this time the attorney general and the deputy attorney general were receiving theirs on secure tablet computers. One day one of the briefers came to me, concerned, and said, I don't know what to do about this—we keep getting the tablets back, and they haven't been opened. The tablets were sent out with a passcode that had to be entered to get access to the briefing information. The machines kept logs of when they had been opened. The logs were empty.

It is possible that the attorney general and the deputy attorney general had been reading the hard-copy version. It was my impression, however, that Sessions arrived at the briefings unfamiliar with the book. The lack of interest was confounding. More than that, it was demoralizing. The work of these briefings is important. The President's Daily Brief is how the intelligence community joins in a communal understanding of what is most important to the national security of this country. To blow that off sends the wrong message.

We tried to interpret that choice as revealing no more than the intense degree of focus that Attorney General Sessions devoted to criminal matters, such as immigration and narcotics: very important things. But in time it became impossible to avoid the overwhelming evidence that the attorney general had little use for serious discussions of national security. And an attorney general can't ignore that conversation. Engaging on counterterrorism is not optional.

The PDB, or Putin?

These days, another person who derives little benefit from the PDB is the president. Like former attorney general Sessions, President Trump appears not to be paying attention, or not to care, or not to trust the intelligence community. Although it may be that both these men don't understand the importance of this information or don't understand how it is different from other information, it may also be that they do not appreciate the pains that are taken to acquire and process it.

Whatever the reason, this profound disengagement sends a very clear signal back when briefers go in and try to talk to the president about the topic they've been told to talk to him about, and the briefing goes off the rails—when the principal, as he's called, slams you with questions about totally unrelated things and makes all kinds of bizarre statements and pronouncements, and you come back to the Bureau thinking, My God, where do I even begin? The Bureau gets feedback like, He wants more video. But you can't tell every story in a video. Sometimes you need a written narrative. Sometimes you need empirical data and statistics. These interactions have a debilitating impact on our capacity to process and present the intelligence that's essential for the most crucial decisions concerning national security. It affects the way our analysts think about what they need to produce and present.

In July 2017, the White House requested a briefing for the president on the Russian dachas—two Russian diplomatic facilities in the United States, one on the Maryland shore and the other in New York. Both of them were closed in December 2016 at the direction of the Obama administration, as part of the sanctions placed on Russia for Moscow's sustained interference in the 2016 U.S. presidential campaign. By the following July, the sanctions were about to expire, and the Trump administration had to decide whether to allow the Russians back into these properties or not. This was an important issue to the FBI, because we believed the Russians had used the dachas for intelligence purposes, not just as sites for diplomatic recreation.

On a briefing of such importance, it would be customary for the FBI director to attend, and at this time I was the acting director. There had been a lot of back-channel signs during the spring that the president and the administration saw me as a kind of enemy. Just a couple of days before the dacha briefing, an administration official told a member of my staff that I should not attend. For good measure, the official added that "they"—unnamed powers in the White House—had decided to get rid of me as soon as a new director was in place. That was the phrase that was reported to me about their plans: "get rid of."

Based on these signals, and on my knowledge that senior staff from other agencies would be in the briefing, I decided that I would delegate the job. The briefers returned to the Hoover building when the meeting was over, and one of them came to my office to tell me how it went. This is standard practice. Briefings to any president are assiduously prepared, with oversight from the director as needed, and if the director is not present, the senior official in attendance comes back to the director to report. This is because, in normal circumstances, the president would provide direction—assign us a task, request more information, or ask questions that the director should be aware of.

But when this official came into my office, where a number of us had gathered, he was dumbfounded. I remember asking, How did it go? and watching him shake his head in response, then explain that the briefer on the dachas spoke for no more than a few minutes. For practically the whole rest of the meeting, the president talked nonstop. That day, North Korea was on the president's mind. North Korea had recently conducted a test of an intercontinental ballistic missile, potentially capable of striking the U.S.—Kim Jong-un had called the test a Fourth of July "gift" to "the arrogant Americans." But the president did not believe it had happened. The president thought it was a hoax. He thought that North Korea did not have the capability to launch such missiles. He said he knew this because Vladimir Putin had told him so.

The PDB briefer told the president that this point of view was not consistent with any of the intelligence that the United States possessed. The president said that he believed Putin.

Then the president talked about Venezuela. That's the country we should be going to war with, he said. They have all that oil and they're right on our back door. He continued on, rambling and spitballing about whatever came to mind.

As my colleague told this story, he was sitting at the conference table, his hands out in front of him, palms open to the sky. When the meeting was all over, he said, he got into the car with the analyst who had prepared to brief the president on the dachas. He said the analyst was distressed. Overwhelmed by the experience. Thought she had somehow screwed up, that it was in some way her fault that the president had failed to learn anything about a matter of critical importance. My colleague tried to reassure her: I'm sorry. I'm sorry you had to see that. That didn't have anything to do with you. It's not your fault.

Every time something like this happens, the concern becomes more real, the question becomes more urgent: What is going on here? The fields of law enforcement and intelligence, when stripped to their essentials, are both driven by human conversation. Law enforcement is a conversation about how to order and safeguard society. Intelligence is a conversation that aims to describe the true state of the world. The president of the United States has, traditionally, been an indispensable participant in these conversations. But when a president is incapable of listening, or at least unwilling to listen, to any voice but his own, how can the other participants in that conversation go on doing their jobs?

A lot has been said about the president's demands for loyalty pledges—loyalty pledges to him personally, which were demanded from Jim Comey and from me. We did not make such pledges. One of the things that has been most startling is the starkness of the difference, just night and day, between how the former administration and the current administration expected to deal with the FBI. The current administration comes to everything—not just the FBI, but everything—with a mentality of, You're with us or you're against us. That's incredibly corrosive to an organization responsible for protecting people's liberty. The FBI has to be independent and guided only by the truth and the Constitution.

A functional relationship between the FBI and the White House is paradoxical, as Jim Comey told his senior leaders at the Bureau many times. Comey also tried to explain this to President Trump. He explained that some presidents tried to bring the attorney general and the FBI director close to the White House, believing this would protect them from the sort of problems that usually come from Justice. This tactic expresses an instinctive feeling: I need this guy protecting me, I need this person on my team and in my corner. What presidents should do is the opposite, Comey believed. A president needs the attorney general and the FBI director to be independent. He needs them to have the credibility that comes from that known independence. The FBI and Justice need to have the political independence to be honest brokers in all situations. Obama probably came closest to that ideal. The current administration is the furthest away—it's like nothing we've ever seen before.

5

Benghazi to Boston

RELIVING THE HORROR, AGAIN AND AGAIN

No Red Lines

Try to hit the alligator closest to the boat. In 2011, when I returned to headquarters from the HIG, that was the counterterrorism division's guiding strategy. And the water was teeming with alligators. As in the case of Zazi and the New York City subway plot, sometimes we got lucky. In May 2010, a Pakistani named Faisal Shahzad left a Nissan Pathfinder packed with propane, gasoline, fireworks, and timing triggers parked in Times Square. Vendors called the police when the car began smoking after a failed detonation. Three days later, Shahzad slipped past FBI surveillance teams outside his house and was pulled off a flight by Customs and Border Protection officers minutes before the airplane was to leave for Pakistan. In October of the same year, we were spared the loss of possibly two airliners when security officers found bombs packed in toner cartridges on aircraft at East Midlands Airport, in the United Kingdom, and Dubai International Airport, in the United Arab Emirates. Both packages were the creative and deadly work of AQAP bomb maker Ibrahim al-Asiri. In January 2011, observant workers discovered a backpack containing a radio-controlled pipe bomb on the route of the Martin Luther King Jr. Day parade in Spokane, Washington. Investigators determined that the perpetrator, a white supremacist named Kevin Harpham, had laced the bomb's shrapnel with rat poison to aggravate the injuries.

In September 2016, a man named Ahmad Khan Rahimi gave us three near misses in a single day. One Saturday morning, a bomb made by Rahimi detonated in a garbage can just before the start of a fun run in Seaside Park, New Jersey. No one was injured. That night, a pressure-cooker bomb made by Rahimi detonated on a street in Chelsea, in Manhattan, injuring a number of people but producing no fatalities. A second pressure-cooker bomb made by Rahimi, also left on the street in Manhattan, miraculously failed to detonate despite being handled and moved by several passersby. The next day multiple bombs—all the work of Rahimi—were discovered at the train station in Elizabeth, New Jersey. Rahimi was taken into custody after a shootout with police in Linden, New Jersey.

Unfortunately, near misses were not our only experiences during those years. In Fort Hood, Texas, in Oak Creek, Wisconsin, in Overland Park, Kansas, in Chattanooga, Tennessee, in San Bernardino, California, in Orlando, Florida, terrorists killed or wounded many people. With each tragedy we improved our ability to respond and, we hoped, to prevent the next one. The inevitable next one. I had returned to CT during a milestone month of what I still nostalgically refer to as the "War on Terror." On May 2, 2011, U.S. forces killed Osama bin Laden. Though still a danger, al-Qaeda was no longer the monolithic, overriding threat it had once been. Counterterrorism now required thinking about a larger variety of extremist groups, including state-sponsored groups. Did Lebanon's Hezbollah, or the Quds Force of Iran's Revolutionary Guard Corps, have a presence in the U.S.? How could they act against us here?

The case of Mansour J. Arbabsiar shifted our perspective on those questions. Before Arbabsiar, we thought there were still some things that state-sponsored terrorists would not do. The Arbabsiar case, which ended with his arrest in October 2011, showed us that nothing was beyond the realm of possibility. With financial support and direction from known members of the Quds Force, Arbabsiar—a used-car salesman in Corpus Christi, Texas—sought to hire Mexicans from the Los Zetas drug cartel to assassinate the Saudi Arabian ambassador to the United States at a restaurant in Washington. That was such a clownfish-crammed saltwater aquarium of a situation that I will gut it for you: The Iranian government ordered a hit on American soil. We had always thought that was a red line they would never cross. They crossed it.

Proliferating terrorist groups and techniques made coordination of U.S. intelligence work even more important. Cooperation among the relevant agencies—staffed by individuals whose defining characteristics include reticence and skepticism and, on our worst days, paranoia—did not come naturally. Adapting to meet new threats, agencies had to cross red lines of their own. People stopped concentrating so much on protecting their lanes and started thinking about how to share resources and information. The Arbabsiar case was a milestone in the relationship between the FBI and the intelligence community. Soon after we started developing the case, we brought our colleagues over and said, This is what we've got. We have a great source, great access. We'll tell you everything. We want your help. They said, Yes, we want in.

The information architecture of threats, and of investigations, was changing fast. The Arab Spring had just passed, and new threat actors emerged. Some were purely local, such as the Libyan militias, and some were regional, such as the Nusra Front, a Syrian rebel group that splintered off al-Qaeda in Iraq. Terrorists were improving their public relations skills, packaging their messages for increasingly mainstream consumption. For al-Qaeda in the Arabian Peninsula, Anwar al-Awlaki produced a glossy propaganda magazine called *Inspire,* with article headlines such as HOW TO MAKE A BOMB IN THE KITCHEN OF YOUR MOM.

The U.S. government's Middle East foreign policy discussions focused on what role this country should play in the civil war in Libya. Many of us in counterterrorism were much more concerned about Syria. That country was going south, hard. The population had become so fractured, the country was a completely lawless place. After a war broke out between the old-timers in al-Qaeda in Iraq and the new, better-packaged generation in the Nusra Front, the younger generation relocated to Syria. Then that group split and gave birth to what eventually became ISIS. It was a volatile, violent situation, and few people in the U.S. government were paying attention.

In the counterterrorism division we were all very concerned. Maybe we should have done more to raise the alarm with Congress, but I don't think we ever seriously considered that option. In those days, the FBI interacted with the Hill as little as possible. When Congress wanted a briefing, we went up, fulfilled our responsibility, and got back to work. Bob Mueller's approach to the Hill was: only go when it is unavoidable. He, like all directors after Hoover, fiercely guarded the FBI's nonpartisan integrity. Mueller protected the FBI from congressional partisanship by following the standard rules for dealing with radiation: minimize your exposure time, don't get too close to the fissile material, keep something in between you and the danger. Time, distance, and shielding.

On the night of September 11, 2012, in Benghazi, Libya, a mob attacked a U.S. diplomatic compound and a nearby CIA base. Four Americans were killed: J. Christopher Stevens, the U.S. ambassador to Libya; Sean Smith, an employee of the State Department; and CIA security contractors Tyrone S. Woods and Glen Doherty. The FBI immediately opened an investigation, as it does whenever any U.S. facility is attacked. The FBI counterterrorism division—which by this time I led, as assistant director—oversees those investigations, because initial suspicion for such attacks always falls on terrorist actors. But the FBI was denied diplomatic access to the Benghazi crime scene by the Libyan government, such as it was, and the risk of violence was in any case too great for us to go in immediately.

The FBI pursued this investigation according to procedural guidelines, within diplomatic limits. Still, the problems of access drew criticism right away. When I went to brief Congress, one member said, I saw a CNN reporter in Benghazi walking through the crime scene—if CNN can be over there already, why can't the FBI? I answered, If you don't own the environment, you can't access the environment. Benghazi was not like a bank robbery in Kansas, where FBI agents could go charging in to dust for fingerprints and interview the tellers. This was a foreign country. To send in U.S. law enforcement after the host country had denied access could be considered an act of war. It would take a lot of time and effort before we could get the right conditions on the ground to be able to send people in to do anything.

Outside the FBI, the Bureau's work was viewed through a partisan lens. During the week following the attack, Obama administration officials offered two different explanations for the violence. Susan Rice, most prominently, said it was part of a spontaneous demonstration against an anti-Muslim video that had been produced by an American. Others said that it appeared to be a planned terrorist attack. Some Republicans considered these ambiguous or inconsistent statements as indications of a cover-up. With a presidential election less than two months away, Republicans seized on the idea that Benghazi was an al-Qaeda attack as a way to discredit President Obama on the issue of national security. On the other side, Democrats were eager to suggest that, no, the attack had nothing to do with terrorism.

Everyone on both sides of the aisle wanted explanations as to why this attack had happened—Was it the movie? Was it a terrorist plot?—before the FBI had a clear sense of who had been involved. That picture would begin to emerge only through a grinding, tedious investigation that began in late September, when a small team of FBI investigators arrived in Tripoli. Our embassy there was spartan. Only the security was elaborate. The investigators were not allowed to leave the building except in caravans of fully armored vehicles manned by U.S. soldiers. Even a trip to a local police department to develop liaison contacts who could corral witnesses involved a massive military movement. We had immense numbers of questions and requests, and in any given week, if the Libyan police did even one of the twenty things we asked them for, that was a pretty good rate of return.

On the Hill, there was no understanding of realities on the ground. Congress found a hundred ways of asking the one question that hijacked their minds: Was this al-Qaeda or just the movie? My colleagues and I always provided the only clear and honest answer we could credibly provide, on the basis of the information we had: We do not know yet. It may have been both. We have unsubstantiated indicators that people with connections to al-Qaeda may have been involved, and we also know that the video provoked violent protests in Cairo and other places around the world.

The honest answer was not acceptable. It was dismissed as equivocating. The exchanges we had on the Hill when we went to give briefings did not concern the process of investigation. The only thing I saw members of Congress learning, during these early Benghazi briefings, was that the way to gain the upper hand in a confusing situation was to keep on repeating yourself, louder and louder, and never to listen, never to rest.

Patriots' Day

Skepticism was general and trust was low where national security was concerned. As 2013 arrived, politicians, journalists, academics, and, it seemed, almost everyone with an internet connection had harsh words for the intelligence community's work—especially interrogation, drone strikes, and electronic surveillance. The government's use of technology was a frequent target. But that spring, when a new crisis exploded, technology proved itself an asset.

On the afternoon of Monday, April 15, 2013—Patriots' Day, as it's celebrated in Massachusetts—I went to a meeting at the office of the National Security Council, next door to the White House in the Old Executive Office Building. The building is a time capsule. Chandeliers, black-and-white tile floors, grand staircases: You could round a corner and not be surprised to bump into Dwight D. Eisenhower. I had arrived a few minutes early. I was unpacking my lock bag when someone said, Have you heard what just happened at the Boston Marathon? By the time this person said the word "explosion," and then the word "bomb," I was making for the door, back to the Hoover building, and into crisis mode—where I stayed until we found the people responsible for detonating two bombs near the finish line of the world's oldest marathon, killing three people and maiming and wounding more than 250.

In the aftermath of the bombing, my first job was to manage the competing demands for information and resources that had been instantaneously activated by the attack. I spoke immediately with all four of my deputy assistant directors—in charge of administration, domestic terrorism, international terrorism, and intelligence—and we gathered every shred of available information about what had happened. I organized it in my mind to brief the deputy director, who would convey the information to the homeland-security adviser at the White House, who would convey it to the chief of staff, who would convey it to the president. Other agencies are our partners in counterterrorist operations, but the FBI has foremost responsibility for responding to acts of terrorism in the United States.

Then I went down to SIOC—the Strategic Information and Operations Center—for a conference call involving agents in the Boston field office along with representatives from every FBI division and office that could possibly have anything to offer. SIOC is the one part of the Hoover building that looks and functions like something you'd see on the TV show *24*. SIOC operates in a constant state of readiness. This is where the FBI coordinates federal responses to major incidents like the 9/11 attacks. Connected to the top secret computer network linking the White House with Defense and other agencies, SIOC also allows FBI officials to watch faraway events in real time, events such as the initial search of the Benghazi compound—via aerial surveillance assets over Libya. The facility covers forty thousand square feet: almost an acre, almost as big as a football field. One big room, the Watch Command Center, is divided into an A side and a B side by a removable video wall, like a massive TV screen that can be divided up into many individual screens. Lining the room are some six hundred computer stations on long rows of tables and more than a thousand phone lines. The tables are dotted with little signs like place cards, saying ITOS-1 or U.S. ATTORNEY, giving everyone a clearly defined place. The cards do not bear people's proper names. In SIOC, individual identity matters less than job description: You are your office before you are yourself.

For the conference call, in addition to practically everyone in counterterrorism, we pulled in assistant directors of other divisions and SACs from surrounding field offices. They had personnel or assets that could help. People from the Victim and Witness Assistance Program were on the call, too—they would send counselors and people who could provide all kinds of practical help with logistics for the victims and their families: transportation, foreign-language translation, assistance communicating with local government officials, repatriating bodily remains. Human Resources was on the call, because we were moving so many people around and needed help getting them to the right places. The FBI Lab was on the call, to initiate the plan to collect evidence, exploit evidence, handle electronic evidence. Special Flight Ops was on the call, because airplanes would be heading up to Boston full of people, gear, and equipment, and we would have airplanes coming back with evidence, including hazardous evidence—you can't fly bomb-making material in cargo on Delta or United Airlines. The Hostage Rescue Team—which has an air service of its own—was also on the call, because we could well need high-speed tactical assets supporting the field office in the event of high-risk arrest and search-warrant situations. The Evidence Response Team Unit was on the call, to figure out what kind of help Boston's own evidence-recovery group might need. The crime scene at the finish line was several blocks long, so we were going to need a boatload of teams to process the whole thing. Which field offices could we draw from, and how quickly could they be on-site? But first we had to find enough bomb teams—FBI agents specially trained to clear an area of explosives—because the entire crime scene, the zone encompassing the scene of the attack on Boylston Street and the area around it, had been filled with spectators, most of whom got away unscathed. Practically all of those people, when the bombs went off, dropped whatever they were carrying—backpacks, purses, briefcases, bags of groceries—and ran. So at a scene where bombs had likely gone off inside some sort of bag, the ground was covered with thousands of bags and backpacks, every one of which had to be cleared by a bomb team before we could even begin the process of evidence recovery. And how would we keep track of everything? Hundreds of agents were about to converge on the Boston field office. How would anyone know who was there, when they arrived, when they left? We had to know where our people were—not just to keep the whole operation moving smoothly, but also because everything would have to be paid for—so logistics officers were on the conference call, too, and on their way to Boston. Finance was on the call, to make sure the field office had enough credit cards and to locate hotel space.

All of this was scaffolding for one monumental question: Who was responsible? Was it one person or more than one? What might happen next? We had no good leads. More than a hundred victims were in the hospital. Some of the victims were in a condition where they could talk to us. A few of them thought they'd seen someone acting suspicious. We had to get sketch artists to them.

Coordinating a crisis response on this scale, involving all these resources, requires prior experience of similar events. The job is teachable in only one way—by going through it. Crisis learning can't be taught by a book. No link chart or algorithm could account for all its variables. Crisis learning happens only in relationship: by being part of the group whose job is to manage such urgent, gigantically intricate, high-stakes responses. On the day of this attack—the anniversary of the first battles of the American Revolution, the Battles of Lexington and Concord, commemorated as Patriots' Day—I found myself in the middle of all these competing demands for attention and resources, in the role of go-between, pulled in many directions. The main reason I was ready was that I had been part of managing the response to such attacks for years.

This array of actions had been launched, executed, or in process as we rolled into day two of the investigation, April 16. Now we had to focus on converting everything we knew into actionable leads. And we had to move faster. Phone records were not being pulled, video-surveillance footage was not being acquired quickly enough. I provided Boston with extra resources and support. When this did not fix the problems, I did something I have done only a handful of times in my career. I flipped out.

In a call with Boston, we were talking about video coverage from a bank along a route we assumed the attackers had likely taken as they left the scene. I asked the assistant special agent in charge if we had gotten the video from the bank. She said, No, we haven't. And then silence. Until I asked, Well, why? She said, We've got a lot to do, it's 6 P.M., the bank is closed, we'll talk to them tomorrow. That was the breaking point for me. This kind of stuff had to stop—I lit into her. I said, You do not get it. You are not handling this thing the way it needs to be handled. This is a terrorist incident. This is the counterterrorism division. You are working the biggest terrorism case we've seen in the last decade, and that means you are on it twenty-four hours a day, seven days a week. There is no break. Nothing gets done tomorrow. Everything gets done today. When you develop a lead it gets handled immediately. If you need more people to get that done, I will send you five hundred more people by tomorrow morning. If you need video coverage from that bank, I expect you to be at that bank five minutes after the thought occurred to you. If the thought occurs to you in the middle of the night, you should be at the manager's front door, banging on the door, waking him up. That is how we respond to a terrorism incident. And if you don't know who the manager of the bank is, and you don't know where his house is, just tell me you don't know and I will find that out for you and push that information to you. She said, Okay, okay, I get it. I understand. There was no pushback. Every minute clicking away was making it harder and harder to find the attackers.

I ended the call and immediately felt bad about it—regretted administering that kind of public discipline, which I don't believe in. Praise in public, discipline in private—that's the best course most of the time. But in the moment, I could not hold this back. As I stewed about my outburst, I received a message: The director and deputy director wanted to see me. The deputy had been on the call. It felt like getting called to the principal's office.

I went upstairs. Hello, Wanda. She made go-on-in gestures—slight tilt of the head, sideways-pointed thumb. Mueller sat in the conference room, wearing his Mueller face. Hand on chin, chin tilted down, peering up at me through thickets of eyebrows. I tried to head him off—I'm sorry you had to hear that, I didn't know what else to say. He put his hand up, the stop-talking gesture. In a low, calm voice, he said, You had to do that. It was the right thing to do. The voice of authority.

Authority was an important part of my experience as a special agent of the FBI. An orientation to authority is unfashionable. Many people see authority as inherently suspect, even alien to their experience. I take a different view. I value authority, and I believe we all need it. It is a necessary element of meaningful civic life. I am not talking about egocentric authority, authority for its own sake—the punitive force of compulsion, exerted to gratify the individual who exercises it. I am talking about legitimate, contemplative authority, which serves as a pillar of any institution or community—authority exercised within a system built on respect and accountability. This kind of authority can deliver a warning. It can discriminate between right and wrong. It can discern. It can punish. It can praise. Authority is activated by a crisis. And it must be earned, as Mueller had earned his. It keeps us solid when things are falling apart.

White Hat, Black Hat

By day three of the investigation, April 17, we had two suspects. Beginning on the first day, as after any attack, we had gone back to look at every current subject of investigation in the area. We scrubbed every counterterrorism case, not just in the Boston field office but also in the whole surrounding area, including the New Haven and New York City field offices. We looked for any bit of information that perhaps we hadn't seen or correctly interpreted—any clue that someone knew about or was involved in plotting this attack. We also looked to see if any subject of those cases seemed like the kind of person who might have been involved in this attack or was located in a place that made involvement plausible. In addition to evaluating these known potential subjects, we worked with informants and witnesses, and analyzed images and videos, to identify persons of interest. We began surveillance operations on some of those people, and we received reports on their activities. By day three, the surveillance reports were not much more promising than this: He went to the mini-mart, he bought a slushy, he went back to his apartment.

After all the potential bomb packages on Boylston Street had been cleared as safe, evidence-collection teams brought the bags to Black Falcon Pier, on the Boston waterfront. By now we knew something about the bombs themselves—they were homemade devices that consisted of pressure cookers packed with ball bearings, nails, and explosives rendered from firecrackers. They had been detonated by means of a remote-control unit designed to be used for a motorized toy car. A marking on the lid of one of the pressure cookers gave us the name of the foreign manufacturer. We identified the importers who sold that brand and model in the U.S., identified every store in the Northeast region that stocked it, and then tried to figure out everyone who had purchased one in the recent past. We went to Amazon and other online retailers. We did the same kind of source analysis on every element of the bombs and on the backpacks that carried them. The backpacks came from Target. We purchased similar ones. We built models of the bombs to get a better understanding of how they worked.

The FBI also asked the public for help: We asked that people send us their video and still photographs of Boylston Street. When you ask the public for help, you get it—and much of the help you get is not much help at all. We had such a flood of information, including video footage from businesses in the blast area, that it became a challenge to review and analyze it all. We needed every set of eyeballs we could muster. At headquarters we pulled together a video- and photograph-exploitation team to assist the work being done in Boston, sorting through evidence in twenty-four-hour shifts.

On day three, an analyst in Boston identified the video that became the investigation's turning point. From forensic evidence, we knew that the second bomb had detonated on the ground, next to a mailbox in front of the Forum restaurant. The analyst reviewed commercial video from across the street, looking at the Forum. The footage showed a man, wearing a white baseball cap, walk up to the spot with what appeared to be a backpack on his shoulder. We then looked at the Forum's footage, which pointed in the opposite direction, showing the back of the crowd on the sidewalk, in front of the restaurant, watching the finish.

The Forum was a restaurant with a small bar that abutted an outdoor seating area. The restaurant was located on Boylston Street, on the final stretch of the race, a few blocks from the finish line. The camera on the restaurant showed a festive crowd of people drinking, eating, and watching the runners, and a line of spectators standing on the sidewalk. The man in the white baseball cap—he wears it backward—walks into the frame. He has a backpack slung on one shoulder. He looks around. He pushes up into the crowd on the sidewalk, not far from a woman with a stroller. There is a child in the stroller. The man in the white hat takes the backpack off his shoulder. The bomb is in that backpack. He places the backpack on the ground. He waits a moment, looks around, and then meanders off.

Suddenly, there is a loud noise to the left of the Forum crowd. It is the sound of the first bomb detonating, at the finish line. In the video you see the faces of the spectators as they shudder and gasp. They all turn their heads to look in the direction of the sound—everyone turns except for one man, the man in the white hat. He is the only person who is not taken by surprise. He just steps away from his backpack and walks out of the frame to the right. Seconds later, this second device detonates.

With that video, we were confident we had a solid picture of one of the bombers. Analysts then went back through all the commercial surveillance video previously obtained from the stores that lined Boylston Street to see if we had additional footage of the man with the white hat. We did—and it revealed a second man. The footage, spliced together in sequence, showed the two men walking together along Gloucester Street, turning left onto Boylston, and proceeding toward the Forum and the finish line. Both men wore backpacks, and both wore baseball hats. One hat was black, one hat was white. We knew we had our bombers: White Hat and Black Hat. Their backpacks contained the bombs.

I remember being in my office later that day when someone from the team walked in with a CD. He handed it to me, and I pushed it into my computer. On the monitor I saw the entire Forum video. I was struck by the carefree nature of the crowd, the lightness of the scene. The horror of the video was compounded because I knew what was about to happen. But I wasn't prepared for what I saw. The video continued after the explosion. A man, a young boy, and a younger girl had been standing outside the restaurant. After the detonation, people were running everywhere. The boy was lying in the street. The girl was screaming. The man scooped her up. He talked to the boy. Bent down to pick him up. The boy was his son. The boy's name, we would later learn, was Martin Richard. He was eight years old. That is where the video cuts off. Martin Richard was one of the three people killed by these bombs.

I watched this at my desk. Later that night I went back to the office and watched it again and again. I must have been trying to push through it in some way, to get past the emotional reaction. I never have.

We did not yet know who these two men were, but we knew they were responsible. We had to figure out their identities. So the next day, Thursday, day four, the question became, What do we do with the footage we have? We would not of course release the more graphic video, the one that I had watched the night before. That was never in question. But what would we do with the video that showed White Hat and Black Hat? Should we continue to work our leads quietly, in the usual way, or should we ask for the internet's help—in effect, crowdsource the manhunt? We had never done that before.

I felt strongly that we should make the videos public. I went upstairs to discuss this with Mueller, Deputy Director Sean Joyce, Stephanie

Douglas, who was the executive assistant director of national security, and Michael Kortan, the head of public affairs. We all knew that asking the public for help in this way would bring an avalanche of bad leads. We would have to run through every one of them. We risked wasting resources when we had none to spare. But the press, thanks to a leak, already knew we had footage of a suspect and were ready to tell the world. The general public had been crowdsourcing the manhunt all week without our supervision or encouragement. Online and in newspapers, innocent people were being falsely identified as suspects. We all made our arguments. I came down strong in saying that such insanity would continue and could turn violent. We had no reason to wait. Joyce, Douglas, and Kortan agreed. Mueller said, Let's do it.

Kortan had mocked up a poster of what it would look like if we decided to make the images public. The Boston special agent in charge, Richard DesLauriers, used a version of this poster during a scheduled press conference at 5 P.M. that day, and we pushed the video to TV stations at the same time. The FBI.gov website crashed from all the incoming connections. But with expanded capacity, we were back up and running later that night. At Quantico, a hundred analysts worked on incoming tips and pored over video. I reviewed some of the video myself, then went home. I had been asleep only a couple of hours when the phone rang.

Guardian

Jane Rhodes, a section chief in counterterrorism who was night watch command, called me to say that a police officer had been shot in Cambridge, and there had been a carjacking in Boston. She did not know of any connection between these events and the bombing. Since the events were anomalous, and since they occurred within the general region of our investigation, she felt I should know about them. I showered, dressed, and then Jane called again. There had been a shootout in Watertown. One suspect escaped, the other was shot and run over, and was being taken to a hospital. I headed for headquarters with lights and sirens on, ran every red on Constitution, and then the briefings started.

We soon had more details. The carjacking victim revealed that the two carjackers had told him they were the bombers. More important, for the work of identification, was that we had someone rush to the hospital with a Quick Capture Platform, a piece of electronic gear that can take fingerprints under almost any conditions, sync with the FBI database, run the print, and confirm identification in the field. The suspect, who was pronounced dead from his injuries at 1:35 A.M., was identified as Tamerlan Tsarnaev. In the video, Tamerlan was Black Hat. We still had no idea who White Hat was.

Off the Watch Command Center in SIOC are breakout rooms with SVTC capacity. By about 3 A.M., Mueller, Joyce, and I had gathered in one of these rooms. Analysts here and at LX-1 were gathering information about Tamerlan Tsarnaev, running his name and his identifiers through every database and database aggregator. The first thing they did was to answer the most basic, top-level questions the Bureau asks about any person of interest: What do we know, from our own information, about this individual? Does he exist in our files anywhere? Do we have a case on him already? Did we ever investigate him in the past? From the answers to those questions, all further questions will proceed. Where does he live, whom does he know, what does he drive, whom is he related to, has his name ever surfaced in any FBI documents? Every name that has been mentioned in any 302 in the system is indexed, so we can type "Tamerlan Tsarnaev" into a computer and see a list of any other subjects who have ever mentioned him in an interview.

Mueller's chief of staff, Aaron Zebley, who had been gathering information about Tamerlan Tsarnaev, walked in with a piece of paper in his hand. His mouth started moving. He was saying words that no one in counterterrorism at the FBI wants to hear. He was saying, We had a Guardian on him.

Guardian is the name of the FBI system that organizes complaints and baseline evaluations of every person who comes to our attention in the context of criminal activity, including terrorism and cybercrime. Having a Guardian means that you have been a subject of an investigative inquiry of some kind. A name comes in, it gets entered into Guardian, the person or the lead gets assigned to an investigator, and the process begins. The results of any investigative effort then get loaded back into Guardian, and if there's not much there to go on—if it's not enough to predicate the opening of a full investigation—it eventually gets closed. That's what had happened with Tamerlan Tsarnaev.

In an agent's life, few things are more excruciating than finding out you had run an investigation on someone who later perpetrated an attack. A nightmare come true: We knew this person posed a potential threat, and then he turned around and blew up the Boston Marathon. The strafing, regretful sense of responsibility: Could we have stopped it? Could I have stopped it?

As Zebley handed each of us a copy, there was half a second before I started reading where I thought, Please, let us have done a good job on the Guardian. I've seen outstanding Guardian work, and I've seen bad Guardian work. We all three read as hard and as fast as we could. This was good work. After a few minutes, we all started to offer comments. They did their homework . . . Interviewed him, his parents, his employer . . . Interviewed a college friend . . . Says he has a brother, that could be the other guy . . .

The brother was the other guy, the second suspect—White Hat. By 6 A.M., the hunt for Tamerlan's brother, Dzhokhar Tsarnaev, had shut down Boston. The manhunt lasted all day. We had a more or less open line with the White House Situation Room and an SVTC with Boston. I went back and forth from one to the other. The head of hostage rescue said he needed a team up there, with helicopters—asked if it was okay to move those air assets and team forward. I told him yes, send the Black Hawks. I worked with Justice Department attorneys on aggressive telephone analysis of Tamerlan's number, which required a 215 warrant, to figure out whom Tamerlan called, and whom those people called, and whether any of those numbers hit the numbers of known terrorist suspects overseas. Strings of possible analysis pinwheeled out from every phone number or email address. We traced each string, just in case there might be someone else out there, connected to this, planning another attack.

Zebley and a group of other lawyers, after studying the Guardian, discussed what to do with the knowledge that the FBI had, at one point, interviewed Tamerlan. We decided we needed to make an announcement. We needed to put out a statement acknowledging that the FBI had a preexisting inquiry. It is significant and undeniable. And we have learned, through many crises, the truth of yet another old cliché: Bad news does not get better with age. It took us the entire day to arrive at wording we were satisfied with, and in the early evening we released a statement to the media.

By that point, the manhunt in Watertown involved thousands of cops searching house-to-house for Dzhokhar Tsarnaev. Around 6 P.M., Massachusetts governor Deval Patrick lifted the "shelter-in-place" order on Boston-area residents. A man in Watertown walked out into his backyard to smoke a cigarette. He saw that the cover on his boat was disturbed, and the side of the vessel was stained with blood. He called the police. Within minutes, cops converged on the property and trained their guns on the boat. At the first sign of movement, dozens began shooting at the boat. In SIOC, we watched live video of the fusillade and wondered—if Dzhokhar was in fact in there—whether there would be anything left to take into custody. The ground team hit the craft with explosives and even probed it with a robot, and finally Dzhokhar emerged.

Much later, people sometimes asked me how I felt in that moment, when the manhunt was over. I understand why a person would ask that question, but the main thing my honest answer reveals is the distance between the mind-set required to do my job and the mind-set of a person following the news. Psychologically, to manage a crisis like the Boston Marathon bombing response is an extreme exercise in compartmentalization. Whatever bolt of relief I felt at finding Dzhokhar, my life was actually no less complicated the minute he climbed out of that boat. The cloud of questions to be answered just got thicker. Where's he going to go? Who's going to talk to him? *How* are we going to talk to him? Can we ask questions before we give him his *Miranda* warning? When does he get presented to the judge? Do we do a bedside arraignment? Dzhokhar had been shot multiple times, including in the neck: So could he still even talk? The limit of the relief I allowed myself was, We're not going to be doing this manhunt again tomorrow. But it was not as if this freed me up to lie on the sofa for a couple of days. I probably did get a good night's sleep that night, for a change.

I was not the only one with limited energy for celebration. It was not long before the FBI was pilloried for waiting to issue its statement about having the Guardian on Tamerlan. We would be pilloried much more for having closed the Guardian to begin with—even though closing the Guardian was the only thing that made sense to do, under the legal system as it is—and probably under any legal system we would want to have. This was the backstory: In March 2011, the FSB, the Russian Federal Security Service, had told the FBI that Tamerlan and his mother, Zubeidat Tsarnaeva, ethnic Chechen immigrants to the U.S., held radical Islamic beliefs.

We asked the FSB for more specifics, since we don't investigate beliefs. We never got any more specifics. Russian disseminations were like that. You never knew exactly what you were getting. Could be a legitimate warning, or could just be the Russians trying to get us to track down someone for political reasons. The agents here did the best they could with what they had. They interviewed both mother and son, interviewed people who knew them, and conducted thorough background checks. None of that work raised questions of terrorism, much less the "articulable factual basis" necessary to open a full investigation. What else should the FBI have done? Every time a person of interest comes to our attention, should we be obligated to keep investigating that person forever? To do so would overstep the bounds of our legitimate authority. It would violate subjects' privacy. It would waste FBI resources. The Boston Joint Terrorism Task Force opened more than a thousand Guardians in 2011 alone. It is not humanly possible to investigate everyone forever.

Investigating everyone forever, though, seemed to be the only thing the FBI might have done that would have satisfied the congressional leadership, judging from the conversations that took place after the crisis had passed. Reviews of the investigation were initiated soon after the event and continued for at least three years. Many people to this day will say the Boston bombing was a failure on the FBI's part. Whether you believe that reveals where you stand on the spectrum of a defining issue in counterterrorism: acceptance of risk. Counterterrorism involves risk. It involves trade-offs. Go too far in one direction—toward the all-seeing eye of a national-security state on a permanent war footing—and you undermine the rights and liberties we cherish as a nation. I wish the trade-off did not exist, but it does.

After Boston, much misinformation circulated about our investigation. Congress devoted a great deal of energy to questioning how and when the FBI shared information with state and local partners—in the process displaying unrealistic expectations of how seamlessly information can ever be shared, and how equally all information can ever be weighed. To help manage these expectations, Mueller, Joyce, and I decided on a new communications strategy with Congress. We would make more effort to inform congressional leadership of the details on the front end of a crisis, in hopes that we could spend less energy correcting mistaken impressions on the back end. We began making personal telephone calls to the congressional leadership during the earliest hours after major incidents and following up with regular updates.

We also decided that whenever we found ourselves in an analogous situation to the one we had with this Guardian, we would announce it right away. And we have been in similar situations a number of times. The best-known one occurred in 2016, when Omar Mateen, the shooter who killed forty-nine people at the Pulse nightclub in Orlando, turned out to have been the subject of a prior FBI investigation. Until or unless terrorism disappears from the world, or the U.S. becomes a surveillance state, the FBI will continue to open and close cases on a very small number of people who go on to do terrible things. But now, when the FBI finds out that this has happened, it takes us an hour to acknowledge the situation. There is no debate anymore.

6

Examination

COLLECTIVE INSANITY AND
THE CLINTON INVESTIGATION

Always Sunny in the Caliphate

About two weeks after the FBI's first-ever crowdsourced manhunt, in Boston, the FBI launched a second crowdsourced manhunt. We released photos of three men from the Benghazi attack site, and we asked for the public's help in identifying them. Also that spring, in Syria, a new name began emerging into prominence from the shuffle of schisms among extremist groups: ISIS, which is an acronym for "the Islamic State of Iraq and Syria." Keeping track of ISIS would be part of my new job, as executive assistant director of the National Security Branch, overseeing all FBI work on counterterrorism, counterintelligence, weapons of mass destruction, and the HIG. The month I accepted that position, Edward Snowden, a onetime contractor for the National Security Agency—the agency primarily responsible for collecting and monitoring electronic communications—began to leak the vast trove of information he had stolen. For the better part of a year, as Snowden fled the country and sought safe haven elsewhere, the biggest part of my work would be managing the fallout from those leaks.

The FBI's Snowden problem had two dimensions: exposure and spoilage. His leaked documents brought counterintelligence under intense public scrutiny—not a situation in which counterintelligence thrives. Before Snowden, counterintelligence had always existed in a netherworld, right where it belongs. As a field of endeavor, it favors sheltered, quiet conditions and was rarely much discussed even internally. In presentations of the President's Daily Brief and the director's briefings, where the counterterrorism division was always under the gun, the counterintelligence division was almost never under the gun. Now, all of a sudden, because of Snowden, Mueller could not get enough counterintelligence. He brought out a twelve-gauge full of questions: Where is Snowden now? What is he telling the Chinese? What is he telling the Russians? What are we doing to get him charged? Have we figured out the full extent of what he took? How deep are we into the damage assessment? The assistant director of counterintelligence had never before looked down the barrel of Mueller's questioning. He is the only person I ever saw come near to telling Mueller where to go.

External exposure of those leaks caused more damage. For a year afterward, our division fought to defend capabilities we had relied on. The NSA made a desperate effort to save its bulk-data collection program under section 215 of the Patriot Act. Its ability to create a pool of metadata—not communications content—that could be queried with an individual search term upon a finding of reasonable suspicion was an important tool; we had just used it to analyze Tamerlan Tsarnaev's phone records. The post-Snowden environment killed that capability and cast suspicion on all of the government's lawful surveillance efforts. The White House ordered a full review of the intelligence community's surveillance and national-security activities, and because the FBI is the most public and most outward-facing of those agencies—the broadest target in the intelligence community—we took more than our share of the criticism. It seemed as if our ability to pursue the mission of protecting national security, which requires us to be able to investigate terrorists and spies, was under assault not just by our most vocal critics but also by our most dependable supporters.

The FBI's biggest Snowden problem, though, had less to do with the information he took than with the way his actions reframed the relationships we had with technology companies and the work those relationships made possible. Overnight, the business model changed. Suddenly, everybody using the internet was newly focused on the security of their communications. Tech companies competed to position themselves as market leaders in terms of privacy. Marketing campaigns projected new images of these companies as defenders of liberty who would no longer freely support government intelligence or law-enforcement work. Tech companies framed their choice as moral or ethical. I saw the choice, frankly, as a bottom-line business decision. The cooperative relationships we had with these companies in the pre-Snowden world were suddenly a thing of the past.

This was in the background during the year when ISIS entered the vanguard of violent extremism. ISIS produced the most seductively packaged, ostentatiously violent, technologically savvy terrorist propaganda I had ever seen. Their work made the al-Qaeda magazine *Inspire* look as if it had been run off a ditto machine. They created videos with Hollywood production values, appealing to the range of audience demographics about as well as any mainstream media company. For believing strivers, there were jihadi-lifestyle-oriented infomercials, as enticing as the Home Shopping Network—It's Always Sunny in the Caliphate. For isolated, unstable loners, there were splatter and snuff films—as gory as the most explicit scenes of violence in a big-studio action movie, but real. ISIS even had its own version of a breakout star: "Jihadi John," an actual executioner, who gained a following in some quarters for his beheading videos. On the distribution side, ISIS was even more adept. The first group to make full use of social media, ISIS pushed propaganda to countless phones on the platforms of mainstream apps. Eventually the group learned how to monitor users' interaction with content, assess an individual's vulnerability to their message, and then contact them directly with IMs that dinged like any others: Hey, brother, reach out to me at this WhatsApp handle . . . From there, conversations would continue under end-to-end encryption that law enforcement has no power to surveil.

In this period, the percentage of communications that law enforcement could not see began to grow. It has kept on growing. Widespread use of encrypted connections has been unambiguously good for online banking and consumer purchases on the web, but it has also created a danger, by staking out large swaths of the digital world that exist beyond the reach of any lawful court order. In the United States, that situation is unprecedented. In the U.S., there is no physical space that is beyond the reach of law enforcement. Americans have always acknowledged that if a judge determines there is probable cause, law enforcement can access any person or place in this country with the proper legal authorities: warrants issued under court oversight and executed with Fourth Amendment rights observed and respected.

Now we cannot always do that with cyberspace. The makers of the encryption technology have brought about a state of affairs that they themselves cannot control. Or will not control. In 2016, after the San Bernardino shooting—when an American couple, inspired by ISIS, killed fourteen people and injured twenty-two at a public-health training event and Christmas party in California—I hoped that the FBI and Silicon Valley would negotiate a truce. I hoped that we would all be able to agree that, yes, it was important that law enforcement be able to have access to a phone that was carried by the man who helped to kill all these people. This was someone who had sufficient connections overseas that we couldn't be sure he was not directed by a terrorist organization, and we wouldn't be sure until we took a look at his communications devices. Apple, the maker of his phone, did not agree. Tim Cook, the CEO of Apple, made provocative statements: "The government is asking Apple to hack our own users and undermine decades of security advancements that protect our customers." As if Apple were the only reliable guarantor of public safety. Really? But that's the position the company took, and still takes.

Law enforcement should never be allowed to unilaterally decide what sort of access we should have. But democratically elected representatives need to engage in a thorough and meaningful debate over questions like these: How are we going to balance privacy and security? Under what conditions should the government have access to private communications? What kinds of laws should we apply to data in motion (as it traverses our networks and lands on our devices) and what kinds should we apply to data at rest (in the server farms and data centers of the world)? We need to start having this conversation in some organized fashion. After San Bernardino, nobody on the Hill wanted to take the lead, though, because any choice might alienate some constituency.

And also because people on the Hill were consumed by other distractions, such as Benghazi. Yes, still. Benghazi. Over a period of four years there were eight separate full-scale congressional investigations of the attack. The last one was conducted by the House Select Committee on Benghazi, chaired by Representative Trey Gowdy, of South Carolina. That committee's appointment and hearings made big news for a long time; the next month, when the FBI collaborated with Defense on the capture of Ahmed Abu Khatallah, a ringleader of the Benghazi attack, the news seemed to come and go in a week. (In 2018, Khatallah was sentenced to twenty-two years in prison for his role in the attack.) The first Benghazi investigation, by the House Intelligence Committee, was just ending its second year of work when Jim Comey was sworn in as the new FBI director. That first committee's report found no evidence of a cover-up, no evidence of wrongdoing by the president or the secretary of state, and no evidence that the Obama administration's conflicting statements about the cause of the attack had been intentional. The findings of the next seven investigations of Benghazi revealed little more. I continued to be called to testify and brief Congress on Benghazi throughout those four long years. There were weeks when ISIS was posting videos to YouTube of Americans being beheaded, and I was being called to the Hill to testify about Benghazi yet again.

Americans have freer access to more information than at any other time in the history of our country. What happened when we were let loose on that landscape of possibility? People raised their voices, louder all the time, and the boundaries of the landscape we had known wore down as volumes rose. The country started seeming like a village in a folktale under a spell, where the more the people see, the less they know.

In Walked Jim

September 2013: Entering his first morning staff meeting as FBI director, Jim Comey loped to the head of the table, put down his briefing books, and lowered his six-foot-eight-inch, shirtsleeved self into a huge leather chair. He leaned the chair so far back on its hind legs that he lay practically flat, testing gravity. Then he sat up, stretched like a big cat, pushed the briefing books to the side, and said, as if he were talking to a friend, I don't want to talk about these today. I'd rather talk about some other things first. He talked about how effective leaders immediately make their expectations clear and proceeded to do just that for us. Said he would expect us to love our jobs, expect us to take care of ourselves . . . I remember less of what he said than the easygoing way he spoke and the absolute clarity of his day-one priority: building relationships with each member of his senior team.

Comey continually reminded the FBI leadership that strong relationships with one another were critical to the institution's functioning. One day, after we reviewed the briefing books, he said, Okay, now I want to go around the room, and I want you all to say one thing about yourselves that no one else here knows about you. One hard-ass from the criminal division stunned the room to silence when he said, My wife and I, we really love Disney characters, and all our vacation time we spend in the Magic Kingdom. Another guy, formerly a member of the hostage-rescue team, who carefully tended his persona as a dead-eyed meathead—I thought his aesthetic tastes ran the gamut from YouTube videos of snipers in Afghanistan to YouTube videos of Bigfoot sightings—turned out to be an art lover. I really like the old masters, he said, but my favorite is abstract expressionism.

This hokey parlor game had the effect Comey intended. It gave people an opportunity to be interesting and funny with colleagues in a way that most had rarely been before. Years later, I remember it like yesterday.

That was Jim's effect on almost everyone he worked with. I observed how he treated people. Tell me your story, he would say, then listen as if there were only the two of you in the whole world. You were, of course, being carefully assessed at the same time that you were being appreciated and accepted. He once told me that people's responses to that opening helped him gauge their ability to communicate. Over the next few years I would sit in on hundreds of meetings with him. All kinds of individuals and organizations would come to Comey with their issues. No matter how hostile they were when they walked in the door, they would always walk out on a cloud of Comey goodness. Sometimes, after the door had closed, he would look at me and say, That was a mess. Jim has the same judgmental impulse that everyone has. He is complicated, with many different sides, and he is so good at showing his best side—which is better than most people's—that his bad side, which is not as bad as most people's, can seem more shocking on the rare moments when it flashes to the surface.

That does not mean he is two-faced. No one's words or actions are perfectly consistent over time. No one moves through life in a state of complete "transparency." Anyone who believes that unfaltering transparency goes with the job of director of the FBI knows nothing about how power is exercised, much less how institutions of government function. Comey does have charm, and it is sincere. Upon arriving at the FBI, he used that quality to build a deeply affectionate sense of camaraderie, which was especially pronounced in his relationship with the deputy director, Sean Joyce. The relationship between the director and his deputy—the appointed head of the institution and the most senior special agent in the Bureau's ranks—is complementary, and in the case of Comey and Joyce it was also very close. The director is like a CEO, managing external relationships and internal strategy, laying out the FBI's ten-year plan, and inspiring the entire workforce to think about what happens to the Bureau over the long term. The deputy director is the action arm of the partnership, the executor, managing the FBI's day-to-day operations and intelligence collection. From the time Comey arrived, there was no apparent barrier between him and Joyce. The director was always seeking authentic, almost raw, feedback. The deputy responded with what seemed like total candor. Comey thrived on that—with Joyce most of all, but with many others, too. Tell me what you really think, Comey would say in meetings, trying to tease out opinions and insights from everyone in the room, not just the same three people over and over again.

Though his manners were more informal than Mueller's, Comey shared the previous director's larger-than-life sense of rectitude. In their own times and their own ways, each had shown true courage in protecting the rule of law against the encroachment of politics. We all knew the story from 2004, during Comey's time as deputy attorney general, when the

White House tried to force Justice to sign off on a surveillance program despite the department's concerns about legality and oversight. It was Comey who refused and held the line. He did so during a dramatic showdown in the hospital room where John Ashcroft, then the attorney general, was recovering from surgery.

In September 2013, when Comey took the helm at the Hoover building, many of us believed his uprightness and open mind could serve as antidotes to the poisonous atmosphere that had engulfed Capitol Hill in particular. We needed antidotes urgently. The town, and maybe soon the country, seemed to have gone halfway berserk. In Congress, almost no one seemed capable of hearing any story, or accepting any shred of information, that in any way departed from preexisting notions of what the truth was or of how things ought to be.

For law enforcement, a sufficiently fractured public conversation can pose a mortal threat. When a population loses any sense of a shared story—when each segment of a population believes that only its own perceptions are valid—then that population can become ungovernable.

"Part of the Solution"

I was the head of the Washington field office now, responsible for FBI operations not only in D.C. and northern Virginia but also in Central Asia, the Middle East, Afghanistan, and Pakistan. Through that spring and summer, ISIS occupied a lot of my energy. And we had a big spike in counterterrorism arrests: more in 2015 than in any year since 9/11.

In the beginning, the Clinton email case had nothing to do with my job. The case started for me the way it did for everyone else. I was just a guy reading the news. *The New York Times,* Tuesday, March 3, 2015: CLINTON USED PERSONAL EMAIL AT STATE DEPT., POSSIBLY BREAKING RULES. Next day, same newspaper: USING PRIVATE EMAIL, CLINTON THWARTED RECORDS REQUESTS.

Day by day, the story emerged in pieces. Hillary Clinton, during her four years as secretary of state, had never used a government email account, relying exclusively on her own private email account. This became public knowledge when the House Benghazi Committee contacted the State Department to ask for some of Clinton's emails, and State found that it had no Clinton emails at all. That was a head-scratcher. The idea that Clinton would use a personal email account to do government business for any reason—she herself cited convenience—didn't seem plausible.

But I did not spend much time thinking about Hillary Clinton that week. I spent a lot of time thinking about my wife and our future. I did not anticipate that anyone would ever think the first topic was related to the second.

On March 5, a giant snowstorm walloped Washington, unseasonably late, as Jill and I celebrated our twentieth wedding anniversary. We were in a hotel in Washington, watching the snow fly and talking about what we imagined our life might look like in another twenty years. Out of the blue, about ten days earlier, Jill had been asked if she would consider entering the race for one of Virginia's forty state senate seats. At a stage of life when circumstances can seem very settled, the call was a reminder that life is full of possibilities.

The year before, in February 2014, Virginia's governor, Terry McAuliffe, had paid a very public visit to the hospital where Jill worked. The next day, *The Washington Post* published a story about the visit. IN VA, FIGHT OVER MEDICAID EXPANSION CONTINUES, was the headline. The piece described McAuliffe's push to expand access to medical care in our state. The Affordable Care Act had expanded Medicaid, the partnership between state and federal governments that provides health insurance to poor people, the elderly, and the disabled—and then the Supreme Court ruled that each state had to choose whether to participate in that Medicaid expansion. In Virginia, Medicaid expansion would have extended health-insurance coverage to four hundred thousand people who had none, but the Virginia General Assembly's Republican majority blocked it. McAuliffe fought back. His visit to the hospital where Jill worked was part of a road trip of press events intended to persuade the public. As head of the hospital's pediatric emergency room—where the impact of Medicaid expansion would be especially dramatic—Jill helped to show the governor around. A *Post* reporter covering the event asked for Jill's professional opinion about Medicaid expansion, and her answer was so good—clear, precise, nonpartisan, persuasive—that it showed up as the story's closer in the paper the next day. Jill's main point was that regardless of the complicated politics of health-care reform—these are her words—"I think expanding care for the folks who need it has to be part of the solution. . . . I'm faced with patients every day who are struggling because they don't have that access." If Medicaid were expanded, she added, more patients could seek primary care, the emergency room would not be so crowded, and children would be healthier. "They'd be on medication to manage their asthma. They would have good preventative care. They would get their immunizations. . . . They would address their obesity. All of the epidemics that are coming along, primary care wants to try to address that. . . . But if they don't have access, how are they going to get that taken care of?"

In the kitchen the next day, we read the story out loud as a family. It was the first time Jill had been quoted in a big-city newspaper. She blushed. The kids cheered: So cool! And that was that—or so we thought.

Twelve months later, in early February 2015, Governor McAuliffe, Lieutenant Governor Ralph Northam, and the Virginia Democratic Party were still working to expand Medicaid in our state. This was their number-one legislative goal, and to realize it they were developing a strategy to flip the state senate—focusing their efforts on a handful of districts, in-

cluding the one where we lived. In the thirteenth district, our state senator was Dick Black. A staunch McAuliffe enemy, Black led the Republican
effort to block Medicaid expansion in our state. Black is also known for
his stances on many other issues, including abortion, which he has described as "a greater evil than segregation or slavery." When Virginia's
General Assembly voted on bills relating to abortion, Dick Black handed
out plastic fetuses to his colleagues. McAuliffe and the Democrats decided that their dream candidate for this district in the 2015 election would
be the diametric opposite of Dick Black: a woman, preferably a medical
professional. Their brainstorming process led them back to Jill's quote in
the 2014 *Post* story about the governor's hospital visit.

When the lieutenant governor's chief of staff asked Jill to consider
running for the state senate in order to help expand Medicaid in Virginia,
she was intrigued. I was in a work meeting when she emailed to say that
she'd been invited to run. I thought she was joking, but I played along.
Then came the next message: I said Yes.

She had not yet said yes, but she was interested, so she investigated the
prospect. The first week of March, Jill met with a couple of state senators. She learned that, if elected, she would not have to give up her medical practice, since Virginia's General Assembly is in session for no more
than a month and a half per year. The next step, as Jill weighed her
options—and the Democrats weighed whether they wanted her to run—
would be for her to meet the governor. She wanted me to go with her.

If Jill wanted to run for office, my support for her would be as solid as
hers had always been for me, since the day that I told her I wanted to join
the FBI. If Jill wanted to run for office, I would also respect absolutely all
legal and ethical limits that her service might place on my own. I called
Adam Lee, special agent in charge of the FBI's Richmond field office, to
tell him that Jill was considering running for office and to let him know
that I would accompany Jill on her trip to Richmond to meet McAuliffe
on Saturday, March 7.

Concerning any politician with the history and connections that McAuliffe has, I am always cautious. I certainly knew about his long and sometimes controversial career. But I had absolute faith in Jill. She would never compromise herself or do anything inappropriate. When we met with him at the governor's mansion, McAuliffe told Jill he saw her as the best person to run against Dick Black and a potential leader of the fight to expand Medicaid. She acknowledged their agreement on that issue, and she asked how he might handle disagreements that might come up on other issues. McAuliffe said he would always expect her to vote her conscience. Jill's interest was rising.

I was excited for her, but I could not help worrying about her, too. On the way home from Richmond, I remember saying, This is politics—you have to be prepared for people saying horrible things about you. How are you going to feel, to wake up in the morning and see despicable things in the newspapers or online? She said, I'm not going to be afraid of name-calling.

From the beginning, Jill had been clear that she would run only if the FBI leadership was satisfied that her campaign would create no problem for the Bureau or for my work there. Now that she was seriously interested in running, I made every effort to learn about the full range of implications her campaign might have. Over the next few days, I spoke with many people who provided guidance and encouragement, and who advised me on the requirements of laws and regulations that would allow me to avoid conflicts of interest. I spoke with, among others, Patrick Kelley, the assistant director of the FBI's Office of Integrity and Compliance—the chief ethics officer; with my direct supervisor Mark Giuliano, deputy director of the FBI; with James Baker, general counsel of the FBI; and with Director Comey's chief of staff, Chuck Rosenberg, who spoke with Comey on my behalf and reported back to say the director had no concerns. No one said the campaign would be a bad idea. The day I talked to Rosenberg, I told Jill the FBI had no objections. Jill decided to run.

Delete, Delete, Delete

I removed myself from any involvement in cases that had anything to do with Virginia politicians. Jill's campaign went into high gear when the summer began. To avoid any potential issues, I decided not to be involved in the campaign in any way. Instead, I spent practically all of my spare time working toward a big personal goal of my own: I trained for an Ironman triathlon. "Patience," I wrote with a Sharpie on one of my forearms. "Discipline," I wrote on the other. Leaning forward on my bike, in the aero position, with my forearms together, I looked down and saw those words, day after day.

During the summer and fall of 2015, in Washington, patience and discipline were countercultural values. The Benghazi investigations were spinning their wheels. The Clinton email story was gaining traction. Congress was riled. The intelligence community inspector general became concerned—had classified material spilled into Clinton's private email server?—and referred the matter to the FBI for investigation. In July, the FBI opened a case to see if such a spill had occurred, and, if so, whether it occurred accidentally or on purpose.

Then, in September, I took a new job and headed back to headquarters as associate deputy director—the Bureau's version of chief operating officer and chief financial officer combined—overseeing beans, bullets, buildings, computers, and people. The next month I finished the triathlon in a respectable time, and the month after that Jill lost the election for state senate. With both our races run, life at home started returning to normal—until three months later, when I switched jobs again, to the

Bureau's number-two position—deputy director. Among the many duties that were a part of my new job, I assumed oversight of the Clinton email investigation. Only then—three full months after Jill lost her election—did I gain substantive knowledge about that case. It was a head-quarters "special"—I had learned that fact before it hit the news. Some-times, for a particularly sensitive case, for reasons of discretion, the FBI runs its investigation out of headquarters instead of the relevant field of-fice, to limit the numbers of eyes and ears and mouths involved. A case like that is called a special. The Bureau has run specials since the 1930s. Calling a case a special does not give the subject special treatment. It just means the case is handled in the one distinctive way I have described: from headquarters, not from a field office.

"Midyear Exam" was the code name of the case. I don't know how the name was chosen, and it was an occasional source of confusion because the regular assessments of the fifty-six field offices were marked on my calendar as "Midyear Reviews." The only worse code name would have been "Lunch." The Midyear team took over a small room down in the center of SIOC. We called that room the Bubble, and the team worked there seven days a week for months and months. Midyear was a classic FBI muscling effort. The team muscled through mountains of data, in-cluding even mountains that had crumbled into the void.

The setup for Midyear was simple. As noted, the Benghazi committee had asked the State Department for Clinton's emails. State quickly dis-covered that Clinton's emails were kept on a private server. In order to comply with the committee's request, Clinton's staff downloaded her emails—some sixty thousand of them—onto a couple of laptops. Then the staff members performed the Sisyphean task that, in due course, drove America bonkers. The Midyear team called this task "the sort."

The sort divided Clinton's emails into two batches: personal emails here, work emails there. The two batches were roughly equal in size, about thirty thousand each. Personal emails were kept back. Work emails were sent to State to send on to the committee. Then the thirty thousand emails Clinton's staff deemed personal were deleted—destroyed.

Those thirty thousand emails, by their absence, became an inescapable presence in American life. A mystery of mysteries, a terra incognita. The missing emails were a blank space on which many people projected dark fantasies about government secrets and illegal activity. From the week the missing emails became publicly known, those fantasies dominated all other news about Hillary Clinton. They still do.

Leaving fantasies aside, there were two basic aspects to the Midyear investigation: technological and human. On the technology side, the Midyear team had to review every work email that was saved and to recover or reconstruct as many of the deleted personal emails as possible, in order to find out which emails contained classified information. In the course of that search, the team had to reconstruct Clinton's private computer network. The team did both of these things, in spectacularly meticulous feats of computer forensics and data recovery.

On the human side, the team had to assess the motives of scores of Clinton's associates and correspondents—to evaluate the intentions behind their actions and determine whether these people meant to do anything illegal. The legal standard for a criminal charge involving the compromise of highly sensitive classified information is intent. If there is no criminal intent, there is no crime.

The tech side of the case revolved around Clinton's private email server. That makes it sound like a little plastic box. But to call Clinton's computer network a private server is an oversimplification. The network started as an old Apple computer in the basement of the Clintons' house in Chappaqua, New York. The family's computing needs quickly outstripped what that machine could provide. They replaced it, but before long found themselves again needing more capacity. The Clintons eventually outsourced responsibility for their computing situation to a server farm in Secaucus, New Jersey.

None of this was known at the beginning of the Midyear investigation. Painstakingly, the Midyear team pieced together the whole timeline of what constituted Clinton's "private email server" at every moment from 2008 through March 2015. It seemed as if every time the investigators turned over another rock, they found yet another laptop that was used to fix or process or transfer Hillary Clinton's data and yet another place where some of Clinton's emails, which could have contained classified information, might have been.

And because there were persistent questions about the missing thirty thousand emails, the team had to shed light on every dark corner of that network—had to find every machine and thumb drive and phone, and do whatever it took to reconstruct every piece of gear that had ever been a part of that network.

That was hard. But it was easy compared to other things the Midyear team did. When you press Send, the email that goes out no longer belongs only to you. It also belongs to the person you've sent it to. So if I come to you and say, I want to see all the emails in your account, and you say, I already deleted half of them, I can still retrieve those emails if I know which other accounts you were corresponding with. Clinton's surviving emails provided a target list of her correspondents. So the team pulled email records from the time in question for every person on that list, searching for additional emails that had been thrown out—emails from the missing thirty thousand—and trying to slowly chip away at that number of the missing and amass a collection that would come close to the total number.

The most extreme feats of data recovery were barely distinguishable from magic. Clinton used one machine that was subsequently taken out of service and reformatted. But wiping emails from a machine does not make them go away. It just sweeps them into the so-called slack space of the server. The content of the emails is not lost. What is lost is the structure that organizes the emails into content that you can read. Imagine

pulling the frame and the foundation out of a house, and everything inside that house falling into the pit where the basement used to be. Computer servers have a pit like that—the slack space. The team spent weeks
and months analyzing the slack space of one particular server in an effort
to piece together, word by word and letter by letter, emails that had been
jumbled into this cyber pit full of other, unrelated code. I half wondered
if we'd find an email from the California Brothers in there somewhere.

Every email we recovered from all these different processes was reviewed to make an initial determination as to whether we thought it
contained material that could be classified. Once that was done, the material we thought might be classified was sorted out by owner. Some of it
belonged to the FBI, some to the CIA, some to the NSA, some to State,
some to others. We then farmed all that material out to its origins—called
its classification authority—and said, Please review and let us know if any
of this stuff is classified.

That, in and of itself, became a massive endeavor: sending information out, following up, constantly asking, requesting, demanding. Responding to our requests required a significant amount of effort on the
part of these other entities. They had to go back and review the old emails
to try to figure out if the information was, in fact, theirs, and if it was,
what was its classification status. As it turned out, none of the emails bore
clear classification markings—headers, footers, or paragraph markings
indicating confidential, secret, or top secret content. According to the
inspector general's report on Midyear, only a handful of emails bore paragraph markings indicating confidential content.

The human side of the case revolved around the question, What were
they thinking? We had to find out each person's intentions. Did people
know they were discussing classified matters in their unclassified email
exchanges with Secretary Clinton? What was the tech guy thinking when
he took the data off one device, put it on another one, and then went back
to the original device and reformatted it? What was some senior staffer

thinking when she told the junior aide to hit Delete, Delete, Delete? What was Hillary Clinton thinking by not using her government email like every other cabinet secretary? Were people simply careless or stupid about how they handled information? Or were they trying to cover things up so Congress or anyone else couldn't get to it—or processing and storing information in a way that was specifically designed to evade federal records-retention laws? The only way to answer such questions was by conducting interviews with people, to try to determine intent—which, again, was the key to any possible criminal charges.

Assessing intent, I would argue, is a feat just as indistinguishable from magic as drawing ones and zeroes out of the digital void and reassembling them into whole emails. And assessing intent is an FBI specialty. For more than a century, agents have been performing this feat. Sitting in rooms with witnesses, talking with them about things they've done and not done. Tuning out the noise. Tuning into lines of truth in people's stories. Tracking the tells of behavior that was bad or careless, devious or dumb. Probing for statements that reveal what someone is thinking. Searching for evidence that corroborates or disproves those statements.

A Fatal Choice

At least once a week, the Midyear team had a standing meeting with the FBI's senior leadership—Comey, his chief of staff, the Bureau's chief counsel, and me. Midyear's lead analyst would start by walking us through the numbers. Here's what we've viewed so far. Here's the new stuff we found in the slack space. Here's how the agencies have responded. Here's how many thousand emails are still out with the agencies. Here's how many classified emails we have found on this server, here's how many classified email strings. Here's how many of those strings were not classified when they were written but now have been up-classified—classified in retrospect. Of those classified emails, here's how many are confidential, how many secret, how many top secret. The level of detail was extreme.

Then Peter Strzok, the lead agent, briefed us on the interviews. Here's who we talked to, what we expected to find, what we actually found. Here's who's next. But here's the roadblock coming into view on that one. Here's the problem we're having with prosecutors as we try to schedule these next two witnesses.

From the time I joined the meetings on this investigation, in February 2016, the Midyear team was bridling at what they perceived to be a lack of aggression on the case among their partners at Justice. Bridling was in this team's nature. It was a group of aggressive, determined people—typical FBI investigators. They knocked heads with Justice on many points of procedure.

Point of conflict number one: gathering evidence. In a different sort of investigation—in what some might call a normal investigation—if investigators wanted access to a device or if they wanted to seize evidence, they might serve a subpoena: You have to produce this evidence by Tuesday. In this investigation—of a candidate for president, lawyered up to here, in the middle of a campaign—Justice was mindful of the risks and wary of the tensions that might be activated by ordinary investigative techniques. The department didn't want to risk subpoenas getting tied up in long litigation battles. It also wanted to have friendly conversations: Hey, we need to look at your client's laptop—can we work this out? In the department's view, negotiation would be better than compulsion in this case.

Point of conflict number two: interview techniques. In an ideal FBI world, as has been the case since long before my first partner and I went out for our very first interviews in Brighton Beach, an interview means two agents, one subject. For a big, important interview, a case under the spotlight, or in the homestretch of nailing down a prosecution strategy, it would not be unreasonable to have the assistant U.S. attorney sit in.

But three's a crowd. Midyear case interviews, in contrast, had become extravaganzas, with Barnum, Bailey, and every Ringling brother invited: two FBI agents, five attorneys, the witness, the witness's attorney. My people would come to see me and complain—all these lawyers chill the witnesses—and then we would push back on Justice, and they would say, It's been negotiated: They're bringing six attorneys so we're bringing six attorneys.

Lots of people, lots of feelings. In May, the issue came to a head over the interview with Clinton's chief of staff, Cheryl Mills. Mills was the one who had supervised the sort on two computers that, at one point, each contained all sixty thousand emails. The interview with her was a big deal. We thought she was uniquely positioned to shed light on how the sort was done, where it was done, under what guidance and direction it was done, and steered by what intent. Was the intention simply to weed out Clinton's private emails from the cache being turned over to Congress, or was a more nefarious purpose involved?

We had many questions for Mills. Our team was concerned about how to communicate that fact to her. From the get-go, they wanted Mills to know this was just the first of what might be several interviews. If the team had follow-up questions, it was going to require her to come back and sit down again. At the start of the interview, the team wanted to read a statement explaining that.

A day or two before the interview, the team showed me the statement. They said they were afraid to tell Justice they wanted to read it. They thought Justice would go off the deep end and force them to spend the next two weeks changing periods to commas and "happys" to "glads." I saw their point, and I took their side. FBI agents know how to do interviews—know how to build rapport and have a conversation. FBI agents do not need to confer with lawyers to clear the language they intend to use when they introduce themselves to a witness. But that's how pedantic Justice had gotten. Overwrought review, constant comment, six more meetings convened to converse about conversing. At the same time, the Midyear team was starting to overread Justice's overreading, spinning it up into suspicion: Why are they doing this to us? Are they trying to slow us down?

Just do it, I told the agents—just read the statement. Get it done. If you feel you need to tell the witness you might have to talk to her again, it's your interview, you're conducting it, tell the witness what you need her to know.

So they did, and brought the interview to a screeching halt before it even started. Mills and her attorney had to leave the room and take a break. Consultation. Attorney came back, yelled at Justice: What is this? They all survived. Got through the interview. But the Justice team was so angry that the FBI team had done this, the next week we all had to have a follow-up meeting so everyone could air their grievances and apologize. That's how fraught this thing was now. That's how much pressure had built up on this case. At every step, everyone was aware that everything that happened could have potentially huge implications for God knew what.

The Midyear conflict between Justice and the Bureau went deeper than tactics. It was grounded in a difference between their natures. This conflict has existed for a long time. Though the Bureau represents the instrumental aspects of law enforcement, while Justice represents the ideal, both institutions are more complex than that. Each contains elements of the other's defining characteristics. This raises the tension between them. Agents often unfairly read a Justice prosecutor's caution as political. Similarly, prosecutors often view an agent's intentions as overly aggressive or even reckless. And the tolerance among agents for any whiff of politics in prosecutions runs from low to zero. Politically appointed officials are not a big part of the internal FBI world. The Bureau's only political appointee is the director, and few agents interact with that person day to day. A lot of the leadership at Justice, on the other hand, is politically appointed. Early on in Midyear, the politically appointed leadership—Attorney General Lynch and Deputy Attorney General Sally Yates—had decided not to recuse themselves. Somehow, they saw the investigation of Hillary Clinton—former First Lady and former secretary of state, current candidate for the presidency, likely nominee of the Democratic Party, who was being supported by the president of the United States, to whom they owed their jobs—as a case they could handle without prejudice. Recusal would have been a reasonable and, I would argue, better decision for those political appointees to have made. A special prosecutor could have been appointed to oversee the case, to work with the career professionals at Justice or other attorneys. It would have been an extreme choice but also a safe one. I don't know why they didn't do that.

Instead, they made a feckless compromise. They designated career professionals in the National Security Division as decision makers in this case but didn't unambiguously commit to abide by those people's decisions. The leadership at Justice chose not to be involved but also not to be recused—the worst possible choice afforded by the situation. They were not far enough removed to eliminate suspicion of partisan motivation, and not closely enough involved to exercise the active discernment that such a sensitive case demanded.

It was a fatal choice. Had there been a competent, credible special counsel running Midyear Exam independently—the way Bob Mueller's Russia investigation has been run—I think circumstances might have been very different, and we would not have been where we ended up in July.

"Extremely Careless"

Investigation involves constant evaluation. What do I have? How does this case look? Is it getting stronger? Is it languishing? What sort of evidence do I need to build this charge or that one? The investigator steadily asks

these kinds of questions. As does the prosecutor. Individually and together. On Midyear, we were having these conversations all along. With
every update on the emails and the interviews. What were we seeing,
what were we hearing? Were we learning anything that indicated to us a
guilty state of mind—a level of intent that we could prove?

Consistently, time and time again, what the team was finding was, No,
we're not finding much of anything here. No smoking gun. No sign of
any vast conspiracy to trick the House committee, the State Department,
or the American people. By March or April, we all knew in what direction the investigation was heading. It was clear to the whole team.

Comey and I started having general conversations about how to proceed. The investigation had two possible outcomes. Option A would be
the easy path. At the last minute, we would find evidence that, the FBI
and DOJ would agree, should be put in front of a grand jury, and a charge
would be pursued. An indictment would speak for itself. Option B would
be the thorny path. What if we found no more evidence? After we'd looked
under every rock and found nothing, what would we do? Typically, the
case would be closed. Everyone would walk away quietly. Typically, out
of fairness, we don't make a public statement about not charging people.
We try not to draw attention to that outcome. We keep silent, to avoid
further damage to the reputations of people we've been investigating.

This case was different. It was public before we got it. The inspector
general's referral had been public. The world knew we had this investigation. There was nothing private about it. The attorney general and the
director had publicly acknowledged it. A front-page refrain had repeated
itself all through the spring: What's the FBI finding? When will the FBI
be done? So if we concluded there was no criminal case to bring, we could
not just put the genie back in the bottle. We would have to somehow publicly acknowledge our decision.

How would we do that? Would we push a two-sentence press release
out into the world, give no answers to the questions people would ask, let

them screech and howl? Or would we do something more? Should we issue a long statement, reviewing details and spelling out a rationale for the choice not to go forward? Should it be a written memo? Should it be a speech? Who would make a speech like that? The attorney general? The FBI director? Would they do it as a duet?

A leader on the Justice team, John Carlin, pushed for Comey to be out front on this. Nobody has Director Comey's credibility, Carlin said. Nobody can deliver a speech like Comey can. In a general way, I agreed with that logic. But I didn't want to sign the Bureau up for all the dirty work. The signal was clear, though. Justice wanted the director to be prominently involved in the announcement, whatever form it took. Comey and I had been talking about the same thing. With his chief of staff, Jim Rybicki, and the general counsel, Jim Baker, we'd been having these same sorts of theoretical conversations about the forms that Option B could take.

Then one day, when the four of us were talking, Comey said, I've been thinking, I had this kind of crazy idea: What if I just went out there and did it? What if I just spelled out our conclusion for people? What if I just told them? What if I did it solo? When Comey said this, I was sitting to his right, Rybicki to his left. Our normal seating arrangement. I looked over at Rybicki and could tell without a word his reaction, which was the same as mine. Oh, my God, I thought. We don't do that. That is not what we do. I remember looking at Comey and just kind of shaking my head, and saying, Ooofff, I don't know, that seems like really putting us out there. That's really abandoning tradition and practice, and could set a bad precedent. I don't know that there's a specific policy about that, but that's not who we are most of the time.

Comey reacted: I know, I know, I feel the same way about it, it seems crazy—but just think about it. . . . He argued that we were in a situation and a fact pattern that, with even a small amount of luck, would never, ever happen to this agency again: investigating a candidate for president in the middle of the campaign for using a private email server. Umpteen investigative efforts had rendered zero prosecutable results. Comey acknowledged that announcing the null result would break with precedent. But he believed that his announcement could be a singular event.

He also doubted the Department of Justice's credibility to make this sort of an announcement because of its half-in, half-out posture of involvement in the case. And because the attorney general had said odd things about it from the start. In September 2015, the first time Lynch and Comey discussed how they would publicly acknowledge the case, she told him not to call it an investigation. She told him to refer to it as a "matter." This became a running joke whenever anyone at the FBI felt like Justice was dragging its feet. If someone on our side of the street felt slowed down by someone on their side of the street, someone would ask, What have we become, the Federal Bureau of Matters? The matter of the "matter" did have a serious effect on the director. It planted the question, Was the attorney general trying to minimize what we were doing? The question festered. He'd heard that the Clinton campaign was trying to avoid the word "investigation," too.

I want to be clear. Neither Attorney General Lynch nor Deputy Attorney General Yates at any time during the course of this investigation ever said or did anything that caused me to believe that they were sandbagging, obstructing, slowing down, or influencing the investigation in any way. Much less in any way based on politics. Those two officials didn't talk about it with us. We didn't talk about it with them. We never briefed them. Maybe they were getting information on the case from the Justice team—I don't know. As far as we knew, they were totally hands-off.

As tends to happen, thought became action. One weekend, Comey wrote a draft statement to work up an idea of what he might say if he were to make the close-out announcement solo. On Monday, May 2, he sent it to Rybicki, Baker, and me. I read it and talked to him about it. The more I thought about the situation, the more I also believed, as Comey did, that Justice couldn't make a statement like this—but somebody needed to. I thought it would be important that the country knew three things. What we had done, what we had found, and what we thought about it.

What we had done—people needed to know the scope and the significance of the investigative effort. What we had found—people needed to know the result of all that effort, literally the numbers of emails, numbers of classified emails. What we thought about it—people needed to know not just our conclusion, but how much study and consideration went into drawing that conclusion. We had asked Justice to go back through more than half a century of records and produce for us the results of every single prosecution for mishandling classified information. We made a comprehensive review of who had been charged, be it misdemeanor or felony; whether prosecution resulted; whether cases were dropped; whether pleas were guilty or not guilty; and what the sentences were. We knew with great specificity what it took to go forward with a case. Comey asked for all this. Justice sent a huge spreadsheet, thirty or forty pages long, with all the details on those sorts of cases over a long period of time. It showed how weak this case was compared to cases that had actually been prosecuted.

Comey's draft went to a few more people. Some readers noticed that the draft called Clinton "grossly negligent." That was statutory language— the language you'd use to indict someone for mishandling classified information—and the statutory meaning did not match Comey's intended meaning, which was simply to use the words the way ordinary people would to characterize an action in a nonlegal way. In a meeting involving five people, a lawyer on the Midyear team said "extremely careless" would more accurately describe the behavior Comey's first draft had called "grossly negligent." The lawyer's argument was, If we're saying we shouldn't charge her, then you shouldn't describe her using those charged words.

That change, like the rest of the group's edits to the draft at that meeting, was entered on Peter Strzok's computer. More than a year later, I would learn—and six months after that, it would be widely reported—that during and after the investigation, Strzok had had an affair with another member of the Midyear team, Lisa Page, who, as the deputy director's chief counsel, was my lawyer. The two conducted their relationship in secret, sending thousands of text messages to each other on their work phones. Some of their text messages expressed dread, shock, fear, and disgust concerning Donald Trump's behavior during the presidential campaign. Although their personal views did not affect the investigation—I know that, because I was their boss—and this assessment has been corroborated by the inspector general's Midyear investigation—the mere fact that the change from "grossly negligent" to "extremely careless" was typed on Strzok's machine was used to eviscerate Strzok, Midyear, the Department of Justice, and the FBI. The suggestion was that Strzok tampered with Jim's statement, that Strzok wanted to save Hillary Clinton from a felony charge and therefore took out the language consistent with a felony charge. As if this proved the fix was in.

The truth is, it was Comey's statement. The statement he delivered personally on July 5 at that podium in the William H. Webster Conference Room of the Hoover building was one he pored over a million times. There's not a letter, not a comma, not a change of any kind to that document that Comey did not read, reread, ponder, weigh, and approve. Comey agreed with and approved the suggestion to change "grossly negligent" to "extremely careless." He accepted the suggestion because it clarified his statement. Comey had drafted the statement to explain that no prosecutor would seek a charge based on the evidence we had. We knew that because we had looked at every single case that had ever been charged. Clinton's conduct did not demand that a charge be sought.

That was not an empty statement or a dramatic statement. It was a statement of fact. Meanwhile, the Midyear team still had one more interview to do, with Hillary Clinton herself.

A month passed. Five days before the final interview, at the end of June, on a hundred-degree afternoon, two small planes were parked on the tarmac in Phoenix, Arizona. A man got off one of those planes, walked over to the other, and climbed the steps into the cabin. He met for half an hour with the woman inside. The man was Bill Clinton, the woman Loretta Lynch. The two had never met before. The conversation may have been completely innocent. Lynch and Clinton would both recall that they mostly talked about their grandchildren. Even granting that, the tarmac meeting was a horrible lapse in judgment by Loretta Lynch. She should have recused herself from Midyear at that point. She did not—she made things worse. Three days into the furor over the meeting, which had quickly become public, Lynch announced that she would accept the FBI's recommendations in the Midyear case. On the same day, Lynch's spokeswoman reasserted the attorney general's authority over the final decision. Half-in, half-out, and all confused. That was the last straw for Comey.

In the end, the Hillary Clinton interview revealed nothing new. It did not change the way we saw the strengths and weaknesses of the case. The Midyear team concluded formally that no charges should be pursued. Justice could not credibly announce that conclusion because its credibility had been compromised. On the morning of July 5, we invited the media to come in at eleven. We placed some courtesy calls to Justice and said we were making an announcement about the case but did not reveal the conclusion. Justice watched the statement on TV like everybody else. We did it that way for this reason: Comey wanted to stand up there and say, I have not coordinated this with the Department of Justice in any way. What I am giving you is the raw, pure FBI perspective—what we did, what we found, what we thought about this case.

The Department of Justice was not happy. No one said thank you until the next day, when they came to appreciate what the FBI had done. We took all the risk and all the criticism for delivering the result we thought was fair and just. To do this, we leveraged the Bureau's credibility, because by this point Justice had none. If we had it to do over again, would I want it done the same way? We do not have it to do over again. In the moment, we made the best decision we could with the facts and analysis and circumstances we had.

We gambled heavily on Comey's status as a great communicator. We had, and he had, considerable confidence in his ability to lay out the situation in a way that was convincing. We hoped people would listen with an open mind and that the general reaction would be one of understanding. Of course, that makes total sense: We believed in our own good intentions. We believed that the American people believed in us. The FBI is not political. The FBI did not pursue this investigation with any sort of political intention in mind. Our confidence in Comey's ability to convince people that we had done the right thing turned out to be excessive. No question about that.

Leading up to the speech, Comey and I had also talked about people in the Bureau who were not going to be happy about the approach he was taking—and how to communicate internally about the decision and help people understand. Afterward, there were a few people who talked to reporters. Or talked to other people who then talked to reporters. Or passed information to third parties such as Rudy Giuliani, if he can be believed; people who then spun rumors into full-blown conspiracy theories.

I look back now and see how far the FBI was stretching, how completely we were leveraging our own credibility. Had I imagined how polarized and vicious the reaction to Comey's statement would be—had I foreseen how his statement would erode the credibility of the FBI, and specifically that of the FBI director, in a way that could do long-term damage to the institution—I want to believe I would have assessed our chances for success very differently. Made different arguments. Listened differently.

Had I thought this whole thing through more skeptically, had I been more resistant to Comey's idea that he could make this statement in a way that connected with people both inside and outside the organization, had I made a more realistic appraisal of how many of those people would not have accepted anything short of seeing Hillary Clinton in handcuffs being dragged off to the Metropolitan Detention Center, then perhaps I would have said to Comey, Don't do it. Let's be the normal Bob Mueller, say-nothing FBI of old. Let's stand there on the dais with them and say nothing, and let DOJ step into the spotlight and take the hit. I think that was an option—but I'm aware that I think this only in retrospect.

After working the Benghazi cases, I of all people should have seen this coming. The Benghazi investigation—the seed that gave rise to the Clinton investigation in the first place—revealed the surreal extremes to which craven political posturing had gone. I should have thought more about that. Should not have seen it as an anomaly. Should have realized it was a microcosm of the new reality. Should have understood that whatever we concluded about Midyear was not going to be thoughtfully considered but rather ground to powder for political warfare.

Or should I have known that? When is the right time to give up on people's general ability to understand any slightly complicated statement that they don't agree with? When do you declare that the political process, or the press, no longer has the power to facilitate comprehension? When is the right time to act from skepticism and cynicism, rather than from faith in a society you have always believed in?

The Other Shoe Drops

Midyear ended. Midyear's afterlife began. For the rest of our lifetimes, everyone involved will be asked questions about Midyear, the zombie

apocalypse of counterintelligence cases. After Comey's July 5 announcement, the Bureau was pounded by FOIAs and requests from Congress
for more information—everyone wanted to know everything. Satisfying
those requests, in addition to completing normal end-of-case housekeeping
tasks, such as preparing a comprehensive letterhead memo describing
everything we did on the case, took up the rest of the summer. At the
same time, unfolding events called for our attention, too.

In July, three days after the Republican Party nominated Donald
Trump as its candidate and three days before the Democratic Party nominated Clinton as its candidate, WikiLeaks released more than nineteen
thousand emails that had been stolen from the Democratic National
Committee, in a hack for which twelve intelligence officers of the Russian
government would later be indicted. On the last day of that month, the
FBI began investigating a variety of links between the Russian government (or people close to it) and Trump's campaign. Also during this period, the FBI's New York field office was pursuing an ongoing investigation
of the Clinton Foundation, which in August provoked a confrontation with
the Justice Department. In a phone call, the principal associate deputy
attorney general expressed concern about FBI agents working on this investigation during the presidential election. The tone sounded a lot like pressure. I asked straight out, Are you telling me I need to shut down a validly
predicated investigation? The answer was no. We all went back to work.

September threw a wrench. The New York field office and the U.S. attorney's office for the Southern District of New York opened a criminal
investigation of a disgraced former congressman, Anthony Weiner, for
transmitting obscene material to a minor, sexual exploitation of children,
and activities related to child pornography. When the case agent obtained
Weiner's iPhone, iPad, and laptop computer and began searching for evidence on the devices, he realized that Weiner's wife, Huma Abedin, a
longtime senior aide to Hillary Clinton, had also used the laptop, and

that the laptop contained emails that might be relevant to the Clinton email investigation. New York's assistant director in charge told me about the emails in late September. I spoke with counterintelligence about it the same day, and I understood that someone would go up to New York right away to put eyes on the situation—to figure out what we had, and what, if anything, we should do about it.

The laptop was a find, but finding the laptop was not self-evidently a six-alarm situation. During Midyear, each of the many, many times we got a new tranche of emails, a first order of business was having them "de-duplicated"—that is, compared with the ones we already had to see what might be new. This time, we would do the same thing. I tasked the job of looking into this to the counterintelligence division, and I expected to receive reports as things developed. I mentioned it to Comey—maybe in person, maybe by phone, I don't remember which—and I mentioned it to Justice; and the world turned. I hit the road for a couple of weeks of work trips. When I came back to the Hoover building, much was afoot. I'd been home for two days when the Bureau applied for and received a FISA warrant to surveil a subject in connection with the Russia investigation. This investigation into possible collusion between Russia and people associated with the Trump campaign had begun during the summer and was continually expanding. On the same day, FBI public affairs mentioned that *The Wall Street Journal* planned to run an article about Jill's state senate campaign a year earlier and my involvement with Midyear. In an email, I mentioned it to Comey. The story was published on the *Journal*'s website on October 23 and in the print edition the next morning. It focused on large donations, totaling approximately six hundred seventy-five thousand dollars, that Jill received from the state Democratic Party and a political action committee controlled by Virginia's governor, Terry McAuliffe—donations that, the story insinuated, created a conflict of interest for me in Midyear because McAuliffe was a longtime friend and ally of, and fund-raiser for, the Clintons. The headline innuendo was not subtle: CLINTON ALLY AIDED CAMPAIGN OF FBI OFFICIAL'S WIFE.

As noted, I had nothing to do with Jill's campaign. And Jill's campaign had nothing to do with the Clinton email investigation. The Hatch Act of 1939 prohibits certain kinds of political activity by federal employees. When Jill ran for state senate, as I've explained, I sought ethics advice and followed it, observed all of these prohibitions and more, avoiding even activities that might have been permitted. I was not aware of the donation reported by the *Journal* until I read about it in the newspaper. The donations were entirely lawful, reported as required, and consistent with similar donations to other candidates. And even if McAuliffe had wanted to curry favor with me on Hillary Clinton's behalf, he would have had to be clairvoyant. Jill's campaign was over—and she lost—in November 2015, months before I had any knowledge of, or involvement in, the Clinton case.

Donald Trump immediately picked up on the story. First he tweeted it. Then, in a Florida campaign rally that same day, he built the innuendo into a full-blown conspiracy theory. Yelling and waving his arms, he touted "shocking new revelations which you've seen—front page of *The Wall Street Journal*—about how the Clinton campaign has corrupted our government." He said that Hillary Clinton knew about the money—which the article did not assert, and which no evidence suggests. Trump's speech was not a misinterpretation of the article. It was a fabrication. His hatred was palpable. The crowd's angry response was chilling.

But a lot was happening that day. George Toscas, in the National Security Division, told me that the Weiner laptop had still not been searched, because the legal authority to read the emails had not been arranged. The search warrant in the Weiner case allowed searches for images of child pornography, but opinion was divided as to whether that warrant also gave us the right to look at the Clinton emails. The New York field office and prosecutors briefed most of the Midyear team on what limited information concerning those messages they could legally view—the number of messages and the range of dates that might potentially be covered. The day after that, October 26, when the team briefed me on this, it seemed clear that we had to get a warrant. Obtaining a warrant would change the status of the Midyear case. It would mean that Midyear wasn't closed—it was still open. It would mean the FBI was still investigating Hillary Clinton. Before sunrise the next day, as I got ready to leave town to visit family, I emailed Comey to say the Midyear team had to brief him on an important issue.

When they did, Comey decided to seek the warrant and ultimately to notify Congress. I was not present for that meeting. When Comey and I spoke by phone after the meeting was finished, he said, I don't need you to weigh in on this decision. I already know what I'm going to do. It's going to be easier to keep you out of it, because it avoids putting you in the position of having to answer any questions about it. I later learned that Comey was uncomfortable with the insinuations of impropriety that had been stirred up by the *Journal* article.

He was about to steer the FBI into the boiling rapids of one of the most acrimonious presidential campaigns in American history. The next day, in his October 28 letter to FBI employees explaining his decision, Comey wrote, "Of course, we don't ordinarily tell Congress about ongoing investigations, but here I feel an obligation to do so given that I testified repeatedly in recent months that our investigation was completed. I also think it would be misleading to the American people were we not to supplement the record."

Responsibility and Risk

I think it was a mistake to send that letter. I did not believe we knew enough about what we had to make any kind of statement to anyone about

it. I believed that we should get the warrant and review the material to
see whether there was anything new in there. Or at least figure out how
long it would take to review, or even just de-duplicate, these hundreds
of thousands of emails. Taking that level of action, in my view, would
not have violated the assurance the FBI had given the Hill that the investigation was finished and that we would let them know if anything
changed.

I know Jim saw it differently. Later, he publicly stated that it would
have been more dangerous to keep silent, but I disagree. My way would
have taken on a fair degree of risk to the organization. Taking the aerial
view: Sometimes the riskier choice is the more responsible one.

Had I been in his shoes, I think I would have taken that chance. People
have criticized him by saying that he was more concerned with his own
reputation than the reputation of the organization. I do not know that to
be the case. But I do believe it weighed heavily on him that he thought
he might be perceived as taking action that was inconsistent with what
he told the Hill and the American people—that the investigation was concluded. He has said he felt he had a choice between going through a door
marked "Terrible" and a door marked "Even Worse" to explain why he
chose Terrible. That makes sense to me. I understand how he viewed the
situation at the time and how he made his decision.

That weekend *The Wall Street Journal* prepared to publish another article about the FBI. This one alleged an intersection between the Clinton
Foundation case and Midyear. As with the previous story, I kept Comey
and his chief of staff in the loop as this story developed. Published under
the headline FBI IN INTERNAL FEUD OVER HILLARY CLINTON PROBE, this
article, like the previous week's, strongly implied that the FBI gave Hillary
Clinton preferential treatment and also implied that I was responsible for
this. No facts supported that hypothesis. And my attempts, with help
from colleagues in my office, to provide the *Journal* reporter with facts
for the story had not succeeded in changing its tone. We had even told

the *Journal* about my telephone confrontation with the official at Justice the previous August, but the reporter supplemented that, perhaps for reasons of "balance," with false information—about an episode in which I supposedly told agents on the Clinton Foundation case to stand down. That incident never occurred.

Some people began to question whether I should recuse myself from matters involving the Clintons. The standard for recusal is whether a person with knowledge of the facts would assume there to be a conflict. No one with knowledge of the facts would conclude that there was a conflict. If I recused, many would see the decision as an admission that the insinuations were true—and more important, would cast retrospective doubt on Midyear. None of that was true.

On October 31, Comey and I had a quick chat about the second *Wall Street Journal* story, which clearly bugged him. He was concerned about falsehoods in the article that seemed to be coming from within the Bureau—the same ones that had compelled us to push back on the article. We were both frustrated with how the story had turned out. I also wanted to talk to Comey about the recusal issue. He advised me to discuss it with Baker and let him know what we thought. I later learned that he was more concerned about the donations to Jill's campaign than he had let on. A couple of days later, I went to Comey's office to make the case against recusal. Comey said that my legal argument was sound, but in light of the controversy he asked me to recuse. I did not think it was the right decision, but I did as he asked.

On November 6, Comey sent Congress a second letter, saying that the FBI did not find anything new on Weiner's laptop. November 8 was Election Day. As a matter of policy, the FBI does everything possible not to influence elections. In 2016, it seems we did.

Beautiful Black Sky

Everyone was surprised by the results of the election, starting with the president-elect. It would be months before we understood how utterly different the new team was going to be, if "team" is even the word. Many of the officials in the new administration had little or no familiarity with national government and were deeply distrustful of everything about Washington. They were wary of the FBI, though I believed that once they experienced firsthand our capabilities and professionalism, they would come to rely on us in the same way that the last team had, and the team before that. What I remember most vividly from the days immediately after the election is how quickly we in the Bureau just got on with it. We all suspected that what lay ahead was going to be more like a roller-coaster ride than a walk in the park, but I don't think any of us anticipated that the cars would go off the rails. Looking back, I don't know whether the best word to describe my attitude is hopeful or naïve.

In any case, there was work to do. After the election, President Obama tasked the intelligence community—specifically, the CIA, FBI, and NSA—with synthesizing everything we knew about the possibility of Russian involvement in the 2016 election and putting it all together into one product. We referred to this internally as the ICA, the Intelligence Community Assessment.

By this point, we already knew a lot. The Russia investigation had been initiated in the summer of 2016 and was conducted scrupulously, according to long-established procedures. Unlike the Clinton email investigation, which was inevitably public from the very start, and in that sense out of the ordinary for the FBI, the Russia investigation was pursued quietly, as virtually all Bureau cases are, for principled reasons. There would have been little the Bureau could say even if saying little were not Bureau policy: Much of what we knew was based on intelligence that could not be revealed without damaging sources or alerting unfriendly actors to their existence. Going public would have impeded the investigation itself. There was also a political issue, which President Obama and his advisers had to wrestle with. Sounding the alert in the middle of a national election, when the full picture was not yet known, could be perceived as an attempt to sway the electorate. At the very least, it would cause widespread confusion and dismay—doing the Russians' work for them. The administration eventually did release an official statement, in October, explicitly fingering Russia for computer hacks and other forms of interference. The president spoke to Vladimir Putin. A few journalists received confidential briefings. Some in the White House, after the election, lamented that they had not done more, and done more sooner. But even in hindsight, it is hard to conclude with confidence that doing more would have been wise or effective. President Obama faced his own version of the choice between Terrible and Even Worse.

But now the election was over. The unclassified version of the Intelligence Community Assessment was eventually published as "Assessing Russian Activities and Intentions in Recent U.S. Elections." We spent a lot of time on this during November and December. Near the end of December, the administration and the National Security Council prepared sanctions on Russia as punishment for their involvement in the election, and for some extremely aggressive surveillance and intimidation that Russia's intelligence services had directed at American diplomats in that country. The sanctions were announced on December 29.

The next day, Russia's president, Vladimir Putin, issued an unusual and uncharacteristic statement, saying that he would take no action against the United States in retaliation for those sanctions. The PDB staff decided to write an intelligence assessment as to why Putin made the choice he did. They issued a request to the intelligence community: Anyone who had information on the topic was invited to offer it for consideration. In response to that request, the FBI queried our own holdings. We came across information indicating that General Mike Flynn, the president-elect's nominee for the post of national security adviser, had held several conversations with the Russian ambassador to the U.S., Sergey Kislyak, in which the sanctions were discussed. This information was something we had from December 29. I had not been aware of it. My impression was that higher-level officials within the FBI's counterintelligence division had not been aware of it. The PDB request brought it to our attention.

An analyst shared it with me; I shared it with Comey; Comey shared it with the director of national intelligence, James Clapper; and Clapper verbally briefed it to President Obama. Many people were trying to figure out what to make of this. After high-level discussion at the relevant agencies and at Justice, the question arose: Was this a violation of the Logan Act? The Logan Act, passed by Congress in 1799, prohibits private citizens from negotiating with foreign governments that have disputes with the U.S. The FBI's position was that we should consider this possible violation in addition to our continuing inquiries into General Flynn. We felt we needed time to do more work to understand the context of what had been found—we don't just run out and charge someone based on a single piece of intelligence. We use intelligence as the basis for investigation.

Justice was more concerned about doing something immediately. The department began pressing us to brief the president-elect's team about Flynn. We were concerned that this might make it back to Flynn and destroy our ability to continue vetting the information quietly. I also had some concern about how open the president-elect would be to hearing what we had learned. In early January, when the unclassified version of the ICA was released, Trump called it "fake news" and suggested that the work of the U.S. government's intelligence community was comparable to the way things were done in Nazi Germany. He made that comparison to Nazis more than once. On January 12, news of Flynn's contact with Kislyak leaked out. In TV interviews, Vice President Elect Mike Pence vouched for Flynn. Pence said Flynn had told him that the contact was "not in any way related to the new U.S. sanctions."

At that point, Acting Attorney General Sally Yates felt very strongly that we should inform the new administration about what we had. She and I discussed it at length before the inauguration. She felt, based on the information in our possession, that there was good reason to believe General Flynn had lied to the vice president, which created a national-security vulnerability. The mere fact of a lie, Yates believed, made Flynn vulnerable to blackmail by Russians. This vulnerability seemed plausible, but it did not seem imminent enough to warrant disrupting the ongoing investigative work. We did respond to Justice's sense of urgency by hastening the FBI's own work. Four days after Trump's inauguration, and after conferring with Comey, I called Flynn on the telephone. I remarked on how many people were curious about his contact with Kislyak, and I asked if he would mind sitting down with two agents that day to answer a few questions. He said, No problem at all—happy to. I said, Okay, let me know if you feel compelled to have attorneys there, whether White House counsel or your own attorney, that's perfectly fine with us, but if you do, then I will have to ask someone from Justice to come down with the agents. He said, No, no, no, I don't need to do that, it's fine, just send your guys down here. I'm happy to talk to your guys. Okay, great, I said. We agreed on a time. The tone was as friendly, and as detached, as if we were planning a playdate for our kids.

One thing he said stands out in my memory. When I told him that people were curious about his conversations with Kislyak, Flynn replied, You know what I said, because you guys were probably listening. To Flynn's specific point, I had and have no comment. But I had to wonder, as events played out: If you thought we were listening, why would you lie?

The two people we sent to see Flynn were accomplished, seasoned agents. After the interview, they came back to my office and described it to a small group of us. They said that Flynn had a very good recollection of events, which he related chronologically and lucidly. They did not feel he showed any outward behavioral signs of deception. He did not appear to be nervous or sweating. Not looking side to side. Displayed none of the mannerisms commonly associated with dissembling or lying. They said he related his comments in what appeared to be a very credible fashion.

However, what he said was in absolute, direct conflict with the information that we had.

It was a very odd conversation. The agents kept saying, It seemed like he was telling the truth. The rest of us kept saying, Yes, and it completely contradicts the information that we have. And their response was, Yeah, we know, it's weird. They weren't saying they believed him, and they weren't saying they didn't believe him. They struck me as being mainly surprised by the encounter. Surprised at the difficulty of resolving their observations. As if they had just met a man who seemed completely normal, even when he glanced out the window and remarked, at noon, and then again an hour later, and a third time shortly after that, What a beautiful black sky.

After Sally Yates was briefed on this interview, she decided the time had come for the White House to know everything we knew about Flynn's contacts with Kislyak. She went to see Don McGahn, and then McGahn asked her to come back to see him a second time. On Monday, January 30, she and Mary McCord, the acting assistant attorney general for national security, pulled Comey and me aside after the morning meeting on the President's Daily Brief. McCord told us how they had walked through the Flynn details with McGahn and other White House staff members. Yates explained to McGahn how the Russians' awareness of Flynn's deception could make Flynn vulnerable. I was shocked to learn that McGahn hadn't known Flynn had been interviewed by the FBI until Yates told him—apparently Flynn did not mention it to the White House counsel.

Later that same day, Yates was fired, ostensibly because she found the president's executive order banning entry to travelers from seven countries with predominantly Muslim populations to be unlawful. Yates disagreed with the legality of the order. The disagreement could have been aired, and in some fashion resolved, if the order had gone through a customary interagency process before it was issued. Her dismissal stood out for another reason. She had spoken her mind, done her job, and stood by her principles—a fatal trifecta in the eyes of this White House.

Tiny Shakes of No

When a new president and vice president take office, everyone who works for them becomes a potential surveillance target for foreign intelligence services. To help those people protect themselves, the FBI provides defensive briefings. On February 10, I helped give a defensive briefing to a fairly large group of the vice president's staff—between twenty and thirty people. As I was leaving, a call came in from the White House counsel's office. McGahn wanted to see me. I found my way to his office, and his secretary said, They want to see you now in the vice president's office. Someone walked me down there. The vice president's office is not an oval—more of a square. The walls are blue. I was shown to a seat. Vice President Pence sat in a chair to my left. McGahn, Reince Priebus, and some other staffers sat on two large sofas. News played on a TV. Pence was courteous but reserved. After saying hello, he barely spoke. He has a very controlled presence. I sat down, and Priebus asked me about our information concerning General Flynn. We want to see it, he said in a very demanding tone, and then they all got distracted by something that was on a television news program. Everyone turned toward the screen, and they all began to talk about the story, which they said had been leaked. I don't remember what the story was, only how much it upset them. They had a heated conversation. I waited for that to finish. When it was done, attention returned to the topic of General Flynn. Priebus said, again, that they wanted to see the information. I said, That's fine, I can arrange that for you whenever you want. Priebus said, We want it now—we want to see it right now. I said, I don't carry it around with me, so I don't have it at the moment, but I can get it for you. Priebus said, How soon can you get it? I said, It's in my office, so just as long as it takes to get to my office and back. Priebus said, Where's your office? I said, the Hoover building. He said, Where's that? I thought, Are you kidding me? I said, It's five blocks away.

I stepped out of the office and called Jim Baker to get clearance for the briefing. He said, As long as you observe classification restrictions, and everybody has clearances, you're fine. A colleague retrieved the material for me, and we met in the West Wing and walked down to the Situation Room, next to the White House mess. We waited for the vice president and the others to arrive. I took out the information, and I explained it to the vice president, the details around it, and he started reading. The opening passages were not very interesting or germane, and Pence was saying things like, Oh, this is fine. No problem with this. Fine, fine, fine. I said, Keep reading. He reached the part that we had been focused on, and immediately his face changed. His expression turned very cold. It hardened. His reading became very focused. His head shook, but barely—tiny shakes of no. He spoke very little. He said a few things along the lines of I can't believe this, and This is totally opposite, and It's not what he said to me.

Moments later, Pence and the others returned what I had brought them, they stood, and then Mike Pence composed himself, ever the gentleman, and shook my hand and thanked me. Three days later, Flynn resigned.

The day after Flynn's resignation, President Trump asked Comey to drop the Flynn investigation. Since Election Day, Trump and his associates had, on an almost daily basis, made decisions and statements that raised serious questions about his desire to faithfully execute the duties of president of the United States. Each interaction between the FBI and the president seemed stranger and more inappropriate than the last. Now that he had asked the FBI to drop the case against Flynn, his friend and associate, he was demonstrating an intention to apply a standard in unqualified contradiction to what the Bureau stood for. After Comey's conversation with the president, he called me on the phone to tell me what Trump said. This was the moment when I realized that the president and his administration were not just inexperienced, not just unfamiliar with the established norms of democratic government. They wished to manipulate the functions of government mainly for their own interests.

Through the winter into spring there proceeded a series of odd interactions with the White House. I was invited to brief Jared Kushner one day, and then was suddenly uninvited; the official who had invited me explained the change of plans by saying that Kushner is "a private person." The day after I briefed Vice President Pence about General Flynn, I heard—thirdhand—that Ezra Cohen-Watnick, at the time an official at the National Security Council, had questioned my "commitment to the Trump administration," as well he might—the commitment of an FBI agent is to the Constitution and the American people, not to one administration. (Cohen-Watnick later became the national security adviser to Attorney General Sessions.) The week after my commitment was questioned, Reince Priebus asked me to speak with reporters to refute a story in *The New York Times*. When I told him I could not, because doing so would violate the FBI's policy of not confirming or denying FISA coverage, he told me that I, personally, and the FBI as a whole, were "not being good partners."

In March, during testimony before the House Permanent Select Committee on Intelligence, Comey made the first public acknowledgment that the FBI had been investigating the Russian government's sustained efforts to interfere with the 2016 U.S. presidential election. In the White House, in the FBI, and elsewhere, the problem of leaks had been growing, and so the issues of surveillance and information security seemed to be on everyone's minds. Trump's accusation that "Obama had my 'wires tapped' in Trump Tower just before the victory" had jacked up the drama.

On March 17, the FBI press office got a call from a reporter at Circa News, which is owned by the right-wing media powerhouse Sinclair Broadcast Group. The reporter said that sources had told her that I had announced in staff meetings that I hated the president. Said I was out to get Michael Flynn. Said that when Flynn got fired, I slapped high fives with everyone in the room. The reporter made my staff meeting sound like the towel-snapping scene in *Top Gun*.

There was no truth to any of this and we flatly denied it. In any normal, reasonable world, that would be the end of it. But we're not in that world. We lost that world at some point. Instead, our denial touched off a new standard cycle of story development. The FBI press office would receive inquiries about fictional scenarios from right-wing news outlets; we would shoot them down; the news outlets were unable to go forward. Then the story would appear on some fringe, alt-right website, without a byline. Once it was picked up by the blogosphere and on social media, an outlet such as Sinclair would have cover to repeat it, which would enable Fox News to get on board, and then Sean Hannity and Laura Ingraham would talk about it for weeks. This is a practiced, intentional strategy of news circulation. The stories may be fictional and the information false, but the consequences of this strategy are real.

The afternoon of May 9, FBI's inspection division—the INSD—dropped by to talk with me about the Circa News leak, which I had asked them to investigate. They also had a few questions about the

October 30 *Wall Street Journal* article. The conversation was short, and my memory of it would be all but obliterated by the blindsiding turn of events that began later that day, when I was summoned to meet with Jeff Sessions and told that Jim Comey had been fired.

The Attorney General Guidelines

Tools of the Trade

I am not aware of another president who has weighed in against ongoing criminal prosecutions in the overt, hostile, and unrelenting way that President Trump has. This is a breach of propriety and of historical norms. Presidents don't weigh in on those things. They don't try to tip the scales of justice for or against a particular defendant. In our system, intervention from the outside is not only considered inappropriate—it *is* inappropriate. It undermines the operation of a fair system of justice. It sows seeds of mistrust. President Obama was rightly castigated for a single offhand remark, when he said of the Clinton investigation that he thought there was nothing there. The political world exploded: Was he trying to telegraph something to investigators? Was he sending a coded message to the attorney general? It was not a smart thing to say, as Obama surely realized. And yet it was not even in the same universe as what President Trump does on a daily basis—casting doubt on the legitimacy of the prosecution of Paul Manafort, as he has done since June 2018, and calling the Mueller investigation a "witch hunt," as he does all the time.

For an FBI agent, watching the president seek to interfere with the ordinary process of justice is especially galling—an affront to our constitutional system. The work of every agent at every waking moment is governed by intricate procedures whose aim is to ensure that every step taken is by the book. The process has to be fair and rigorous from start to finish—for the sake of subjects and for the sake of justice. It is a high-minded regime. The Bureau suffers lapses, of course, as any institution does, but the standards are taken very seriously.

Let me walk through how this plays out in real life. The FBI receives an enormous amount of information every day. People bring the Bureau tips through phone calls, emails, and texts, or by simply coming into one of our field offices, sub-offices, or legat offices around the world. More than seventeen thousand police departments and agencies in America, and hundreds more beyond our borders, routinely pass on leads to the FBI. Our partners in the U.S. intelligence community and friendly foreign services share information about potential national-security threats. The FBI is constantly recruiting and developing informants to augment its effectiveness. Meanwhile, the tens of thousands of ongoing FBI investigations are generating new information about previously unknown threats and crimes. Paradoxically, as the Bureau improves its ability to collect information, it becomes harder to sort through what we have and decide whether to open a new case. The FBI's ability to make those decisions in an impartial and independent way is the foundation of public confidence. It doesn't take shortcuts, it doesn't skirt the law, and it regards the web of rules and guidelines that govern all official activity as formal structures worthy of our dedication and of public faith, not as impediments to an all-against-all battle of wills.

Historically, determining which cases to open has been a source of controversy. For most of the FBI's history, until the mid-1970s, the Bureau was accused—with cause—of investigating people and groups based on their political beliefs or social activism rather than on any actual threat. Exercising a hold over powerful individuals, in the form of subtle or not-so-subtle blackmail, was another motivation: Thick dossiers were compiled on figures such as Martin Luther King, Jr. and John F. Kennedy. Intelligence cases on some political figures sometimes went on for years, pointlessly and unjustifiably. Congressional investigations such as the Church Committee hearings in 1975 led to calls for a charter to establish clear restrictions on the FBI's activities. In 1976, Attorney General Edward Levi issued the first set of official guidelines to govern the FBI's domestic operations. For the first time, the agency had a clear set of ground rules that, if followed, would ensure that the FBI executed its mission fairly, independently, and according to the law.

In 2008, Attorney General Michael Mukasey issued a revised set of guidelines. The FBI has been operating under them ever since. To ensure that agents understand how to operate in compliance with the AG guidelines, the FBI created the Domestic Investigations and Operations Guide—usually referred to by the acronym DIOG (pronounced "DYE-ogg"). The DIOG is a public document. Anyone can read it.

What follows is based on the unredacted portions available on the FBI's website. The guide lays out the framework for how the FBI conducts different levels of investigations. It identifies the tools, or investigative techniques, available to investigators at each level. It defines the threshold, or "predication," that is necessary to initiate an investigation, and it specifies the oversight regime that monitors compliance. Finally, it sets the requirements for FBI involvement in sensitive investigative matters, enterprise investigations, undercover operations, foreign-intelligence investigations, and undisclosed participation in criminal organizations and other illegal activity. The guide specifically prohibits the initiation of any type of FBI investigation based solely on race, ethnicity, national origin, or religion, or on what people say when exercising their First Amendment rights.

The DIOG identifies three types of investigations that agents can initiate. The most basic level is called an assessment. To begin an assessment, an agent need only have an authorized purpose and a clearly defined objective. Most assessments are initiated when the FBI receives unsolicited, unvetted information that someone has done something suspicious. Assessments are documented in the Guardian system. Although there are different types of assessments, the most common authorized purpose is to seek information about possible violations of federal criminal law or threats to national security. The agent's supervisor has to approve an assessment and, like every Bureau investigation, it must be documented on specific forms in FBI systems. For an assessment, the permissible tools include reviewing FBI information, receiving information from other government entities or the public, querying online resources, interviewing people, conducting physical surveillance, and using confidential informants. Agents can also use grand jury subpoenas to compel the production of information or testimony, but they cannot use search warrants. The justification for the continuation of an assessment must be reviewed by a supervisor every thirty days.

The next level up is the preliminary investigation, or "PI." To initiate a PI, an agent must have "information or an allegation" that activity constituting a federal crime or threat to national security has taken or will take place. This could be as simple as an informant telling you a person is a member of a known terrorist organization or finding an online threat to a specific person. The PI uses all the same tools as an assessment but adds some others. For a PI, an agent can use closed-circuit TV to monitor a location without needing on-site physical surveillance. Agents can surreptitiously listen to and record a subject's conversation as long as they do it with the consent of another participant to the conversation. Undercover operations are permitted in a PI. Agents can use national-security letters to secure information from communications providers—such as account information and toll records—but not the content of those communications. Agents can ask the post office to tell them whom a subject receives mail from but cannot read that mail. The opening of a PI must be approved by a supervisor, and its term is limited to six months, with the possibility of a single six-month extension. An agent's work on a PI must be reviewed by the supervisor at least once every ninety days. During the PI, it is likely that an agent might also ask for the involvement of a prosecutor to provide legal support to the investigation.

The full investigation, or "FI," is the most robust. The purpose of the investigation is to collect information about, or to prevent, a federal crime or threat, and an agent must have an "articulable factual basis" for believing there is such a crime or threat. With an open FI, an agent is free to use any of the FBI's most sophisticated and sensitive investigative techniques, many of which require elevated levels of approval and oversight. An agent must have an open FI to request a search warrant, conduct a polygraph examination, or seek court authorization to conduct electronic surveillance. Opening an FI requires at least a supervisor's approval and may require additional approval from FBI lawyers and senior managers from the FBI and the Department of Justice. A full investigation has no time limit, but the work must be reviewed every ninety days by the agent's supervisor. The case agent on an FI usually has an assistant U.S. attorney to provide legal support.

Day to day, agents and analysts sort through the relentless tide of incoming information. They don't open cases or conduct investigations for political reasons—that is out of bounds—or because they happen to find the circumstances interesting. Rather, agents review the facts they have against the framework of authorities provided by the attorney general's guidelines and the DIOG. They discuss the result of that review with their supervisors and together make a decision. If they fail to initiate an investigation when the facts and the guide call for one, they are not doing their job.

That mandate, that directive, is burned into the conscience and the soul of every agent. No matter who the subject is.

Sensitive Investigative Matter

Let's imagine, for example, that the Justice Department receives a complaint from someone who says that a well-known political consultant has published an article in an online trade magazine arguing for more favorable U.S. trade policies toward China. The complainant alleges that the consultant is advocating on behalf of the Chinese government. Justice reads the article and checks to see if the consultant has registered with the department as a foreign agent, which is required by law. When they discover that she has not, Justice refers the matter to the FBI to determine if the matter should be investigated

The FBI reviews the referral. The content of the statement by itself is not an issue—it's a free country, and protected speech by itself can't form the basis of an investigation. However, the fact that the consultant could be on the payroll of a foreign government and has not registered as a foreign agent raises the possibility of a violation of the Foreign Agents Registration Act of 1938. On that basis, and because the political consultant lives and works in D.C., the FBI passes the referral to the Washington field office for follow-up. After reviewing the information, the political-corruption squad opens an assessment. The assessment doesn't yet have a lot of information, but the agent does have an authorized purpose and a defined objective: to collect information about a possible violation of the Foreign Agents Registration Act.

With the assessment open, the agent checks FBI databases, other government information, and publicly available information online. From that work, he fully identifies the consultant and collects information about her business, her residence, and her employees, clients, and associates. He conducts physical surveillance to confirm this information, and in the process of doing so he observes a car registered to a Chinese corporation pull up to the consultant's office. His review of public information and other government intelligence tells him that the Chinese corporation is a state-owned and -controlled enterprise. Realizing that one of his squad mates has an informant who works in the same building as the consultant, the agent meets with the informant and asks him to try to interact with the consultant.

Several days later, the agent gets a call from the informant, who has just had lunch with the consultant. The informant reports seeing a group of "Asian businessmen" leaving the consultant's office before they met for lunch. At lunch, the consultant revealed that she has just agreed to work for a prominent governor who has decided to run for the U.S. Senate.

As good agents do, this agent reviews what he has. The vehicle registered to the Chinese corporation, the meeting with the Asian businessmen, and the public statements advocating for China, combined with the lack of a foreign-agent registration on file with DOJ, all add up to an "allegation or information indicative of criminal activity or a national security threat"—the official standard for a preliminary investigation. The agent proposes to his boss that they convert the assessment to the next level. The supervisor thinks about the additional fact that the consultant is working for a governor who is also a candidate for high national office. The supervisor knows that according to FBI guidelines, any case involving a domestic political official or a domestic political candidate must be considered a "sensitive investigative matter," which means that the field office's chief division counsel and the special agent in charge will have to approve the opening of a PI. Also, he will need to report the investigation to the local U.S. attorney and FBI headquarters within fifteen days. And headquarters must report the matter to the Department of Justice. This investigation now has extensive, high-level oversight.

The PI also gives the agent new investigative authorities. He can install closed-circuit television to identify other vehicles and people at the consultant's office. He can use national-security letters to request information from the phone company and the internet service providers that serve the consultant and her office. This will not get him the content of her communications, but he can get important historical account information, toll records, and information that can reveal the identities of people who are in contact with the consultant. He can also get authorization from the court to collect information about the consultant's incoming and outgoing calls as they occur—though he can't listen in. Further, he can ask the prosecutor for a grand jury subpoena that will compel a bank to provide the agent with financial records for the consultant and her business. Finally, he can now have the informant consensually monitor conversations with the consultant. The informant will do this by wearing a wire to their meetings.

Imagine now that from all this work, the agent confirms that the consultant is indeed deeply engaged with a Chinese corporation, one that is owned and controlled by the Chinese government. The consultant's bank records show regular payments from the corporation to the consultant. The telephone records show numerous calls to the corporation. Email records indicate correspondence between the consultant and the president of the corporation, who also holds a position in the Chinese government and has close ties to the Chinese leadership. Additionally, the informant has produced a recording of a conversation with the consultant in which she tells him about a trip she took with the president of the corporation to Mexico City, where she was introduced to a high-level Chinese government minister.

The agent knows that these facts all add up to an "articulable factual basis." He reviews his findings with his supervisor in the field and officials at headquarters. Both tell him to convert his PI to a full investigation. Both remind him that the matter remains a "sensitive investigative matter." He documents the conversion, obtains the necessary approvals, and makes all required notifications. In addition to the potential violation of the Foreign Agents Registration Act, the agent knows he has uncovered activity that may be of interest to the foreign-counterintelligence squad, and they agree to join forces. With the authority of a full investigation, they are now free to pursue a federal court order to conduct electronic surveillance of the consultant's communications. If it were a purely criminal matter, their assistant U.S. attorney would suggest obtaining that order in a local federal court under Title III authority. However, with the possibility of national-security implications, the agents and the prosecutor would likely request authorization from the court established by the Foreign Intelligence Surveillance Act (FISA), in Washington. FISA court proceedings are classified and designed to enable investigators to investigate national-security threats without exposing the investigation to sophisticated state actors. The secrecy of FISA proceedings is also an important protection for the person under investigation—if no violation is found, a classified investigation is closed quietly without damaging the reputation of the subject.

So here's the bottom line: The FBI derives its authority from federal law and executive orders. The guidelines on how to operate within the law are promulgated by the attorney general. Supervisors and division attorneys apply the same standards to every case they oversee. Intelligence and evidence are collected and documented in the same deliberate manner in every case. All of these procedures are drilled into agents starting on their first day at Quantico. In this way, the FBI tries to ensure that its approach to each assessment is consistent, lawful, and free from bias. It operates in this manner in order, first, to protect the dignity and privacy of the people it is looking into—the vast majority of whom will never be subject to a preliminary or full investigation, much less charged with a crime. Second, it operates this way to ensure that cases going forward are built on a solid foundation of evidence, lawfully collected and fairly evaluated.

Army of Trolls

It's in this context that, on June 15, 2018, I read what the president wrote about the Paul Manafort case on Twitter—not understanding what has happened in the courtroom, evidently not even knowing what sentencing is, but saying that the judge had been unfair. Manafort, the former manager of the Trump campaign, had been indicted on a variety of charges and had just had his bail revoked after new charges of obstruction of justice and witness tampering. The president tweeted, "Wow, what a tough sentence for Paul Manafort, who has represented Ronald Reagan, Bob Dole, and many other top political people and campaigns. Didn't know Manafort was the head of the Mob. What about Comey and Crooked Hillary and all of the others? Very unfair!" Earlier that day, the president had walked out onto the White House lawn and taken impromptu questions. He said, about Manafort, "He worked for me, what, for forty-nine days, or something? A very short period of time." You *think* it was forty-nine? It was 144.

Imagine what the judge must have been thinking when she heard the president's comments. Judges abhor witness tampering. They regard it as a crime committed against themselves and their court. Under normal circumstances, anyone accused of witness tampering who was out on bail would lose that bail and go to jail. That is what happened to Paul Manafort. But what was it like for that judge on her way into work that morning? I had to wonder if she asked herself, What is the president going to say about me if I do the right thing today? Is he going to tweet about this? Send his army of trolls after me? This judge, Amy Berman Jackson, if she thought about it, didn't care—she went ahead and did what she had to do. But my fear is that someday a judge *will* care. Someone *will* be cowed. The fact is, plenty of people in Washington are cowed already: such as the Republicans on Capitol Hill, many of whom believe that the president is unfit for office but are afraid to stand up to him.

If the principle of noninterference with the wheels of justice holds for a president as a broad, general matter, it is a hundred times more important that he not weigh in on anything that affects him personally. Today we have a president who is willing not only to comment prejudicially on a criminal prosecution but to comment on one that potentially affects himself. He does both of these things almost daily—and directly and repeatedly—to millions of followers on Twitter and viewers on television. He is not just sounding a dog whistle, weighing in with a glancing suggestion that can be interpreted. He is lobbying for a result. He is telling the judge, the defendant, and the world his preferred outcome.

People don't appreciate how far we have fallen from normal standards of presidential accountability. I was offended by Bill Clinton, who plainly lied in his deposition in the Paula Jones case when he denied having sexual relations with Monica Lewinsky. Many people minimized the significance of those lies, saying, So what if he was dishonest about his personal sexual activity—everyone lies about that, it's okay. It was not okay. But now, with President Trump, we are being battered every day. Every day brings a new low. A new ridiculous assertion. There are literally hundreds of examples. During a fund-raising speech in Missouri, he revealed that he got into an argument with Justin Trudeau and started citing statistics to the Canadian prime minister he acknowledged he had just made up. In a press conference with British prime minister Theresa May, he directly denied saying what anyone can hear him saying in an interview recorded the day before. The president exposes himself as a deliberate liar, someone who will say whatever he pleases to get whatever he wishes. If he were on the box at Quantico, he would break the machine.

What more could a person do to erode the credibility of the presidency? But news reports of such episodes come and go in a blink of an eye. A common reaction is, Of course he did that—it's Trump. That's what he does. How is the whole nation not offended?

The president, by calling the Russia investigation a witch hunt, is basically telling the judge, the system, and the investigators: This is what I want to happen. In the end, whatever Trump does, he will not get his way. Even if he were to fire Bob Mueller, the various investigations and prosecutions now reside in too many hands and too many locales to be contained. But that's beside the point. The president is doing exactly the thing a president is not supposed to do. There are no shades of gray here. The president is trying to destroy what Americans have long assumed about who we are and how the justice system works. He is doing two kinds of damage. There's the head-on-collision damage: the "phony Witch Hunt," "FBI corruption," in-your-face insult damage. And there's the much more insidious damage that results from remarks like the ones he made before Manafort's hearing. They continually lower the bar on presidential conduct, now and for the future.

7

Mess and Crisis

ABOVE ALL, PROTECTING THE RUSSIA CASE

'Can You Come Over?'

On Wednesday, May 10, 2017, my first day on the job as acting director, I arrived at the office early, went through the morning meetings, did my briefs, and by 10 A.M. I was sitting down with senior staff involved in the Russia investigation, many of whom had also been involved in Midyear Exam.

As the meeting began, my secretary relayed a message that the White House was calling. The president himself was on the line. This was highly unusual. Presidents do not, typically, call FBI directors. Federal policy, written by the Department of Justice, strictly restricts such contact. There should be no direct contact between the president and the FBI director, according to the White House contacts policy, except for national-security purposes. The FBI does have frequent, routine, and direct contact with the White House by way of the National Security Council and other facets of the national-security structure, but when it comes to topics that do not concern national security, the FBI is supposed to go through Justice, which then makes contact with the White House counsel's office. And vice versa: If the president or any other senior White House official needs to get a message to the Justice Department or the FBI, that message is supposed to go through the White House counsel to the deputy attorney general before it gets to us. The reason for all this is simple. Investigations and prosecutions are delicate and complicated, and can affect the lives of many people; they need to be pursued according to fixed rules, without a hint of suspicion that someone with power wants to put a thumb on the scale. That means those on the front lines must have insulation from politics—or even the perception that political considerations may be at play. So the president calling the acting director of the FBI is, and was that day, remarkable.

The president was waiting on the line. The Russia team was in my office. I walked over to my desk and took the call on my unclassified line. Another strange thing about this call—the president was calling on a phone line that was not secure. He did not call on the yellow TS phone—yellow being the color for Top Secret. (Red is the color for Secret and green is the color for Unclassified. When agents talk among themselves about sending emails or texts, they'll say things like, I'll send on the red side, or, I'll send on the green side.)

It was the president's voice on the other end of the line, not the voice of an assistant waiting to connect him. The voice said, It's Don Trump calling. I said, Hello, Mr. President, how are you? Apart from my surprise that he was calling me at all, I was surprised that he referred to himself as "Don."

The president said, I'm good. You know—boy, it's incredible, it's such a great thing, people are really happy about the fact that the director's gone, and it's just remarkable what people are saying. Have you seen that? Are you seeing that, too? What're you doing over there?

I was taken off guard, now understanding that this topic—how the Bureau judged what the president had done—was not going away.

He said, I received hundreds of messages from FBI people, how happy they are that I fired him. There are people saying things on the media, have you seen that? What's it like there in the building?

This is what it was like in the building: You could walk out of my office on the seventh floor and go to any floor of the Hoover building, and you would see small groups of people gathering in hallways, standing together, some people even crying. Tears streaming from their eyes, from the distress that you would expect if there had been a death in the family. The death of a patriarch, a protector.

I can't speak for every agent and employee of the FBI. But the overwhelming majority of people in the Bureau liked and admired Director Comey. They liked his personal style, the integrity of his conduct, the changes that he instituted. For many of us, myself included, it was a point of pride that the FBI had such a leader, who honorably represented us in the world. Many other agencies struggled because they lacked capable people at the top. We felt lucky. We had someone who would stand up for us and always try to do the right thing. Even among people who disagreed with Comey—and there will always be disagreements, even serious ones, in a complicated place like the FBI—few ever doubted that he habitually acted in good faith. Now he was gone, and we felt as if we'd been cast onto the dustheap. We were laboring under the same dank, gray shadow of uncertainty and bleak anxiety that had been creeping over so much of Washington during the few months Donald Trump had been in office.

I didn't feel like I could say any of that to the president on the phone. I'm not sure I would have wanted to say it to him in person, either, or that he would have cared. I told him, Most people here were very surprised, but we are trying to get back to work. We've had our whole series of morning meetings, and my leadership team is just keeping everybody focused on the job we have to do.

The president said he thought most people in the FBI voted for him—

he thought 80 percent. He asked me again if I knew that Comey had told him three times that he was not under investigation.

Then he got to the reason for his call. He said, I really want to come over there. I want to come to the FBI. I want to show all my FBI people how much I love them, so I think maybe it would be good for me to come over and speak to everybody, like tomorrow or the next day.

That sounded to me like one of the worst possible things that could happen. He was the boss, and had every right to come, but I hoped the idea would dissipate on its own. I said, You are welcome to visit FBI head-quarters anytime you want to.

He said, Why don't you come down here and talk to me about that later? Can you come over, and maybe we can talk about how I could come out to the FBI and show the FBI people how much I care about them? When can you come down?

I was tempted to make a joke of this—When can I come down? No other appointments on my calendar today with presidents of the United States. Nothing that would conflict with this one. But I didn't make a joke. I told him I'd be there whenever he wanted.

After we agreed on a time to meet, the conversation turned in another direction. The president began to talk about how upset he was that Jim Comey had flown home on his government plane from Los Angeles. He wanted to know how that had happened.

I told him that I had talked to Bureau lawyers about the matter here last night. They assured me that there was no legal issue with Comey coming home on the plane, and I decided that he should do so. Even though he was no longer the director, the existing threat assessment indicated he was still at risk, so he needed a protection detail on his trip home. Since the members of the protection detail would all be coming home, it made sense just to bring them back on the same government plane, the one they had used to fly out there. The plane had to come back anyway.

At this, the president flew off the handle: That's not right! I don't approve of that! That's wrong! He reiterated his point five or seven times.

I said, I'm sorry that you disagree, sir. But it was my decision, and that's how I decided.

He said, I want you to look into that! I thought to myself: What am I going to look into? I just told you I made that decision. There's nothing left to look into.

The president asked, Will Comey be allowed into the building? Will he come back in, to get his personal stuff out of his office?

I said I didn't think he planned to come in. His staff was going through his office and packing his personal effects, which would be taken to his residence.

The ranting spiraled: I don't want him in the building. I'm banning him from the building. He should not be allowed, I don't want him in FBI buildings.

I waited until he had talked himself out.

Finally, toward the very end of the conversation, he said, How is your wife?

I said, She's fine.

He said, When she lost her election, that must have been very tough to lose. How did she handle losing? Is it tough to lose?

I replied, I guess it's tough to lose anything. But she's rededicated herself to her career and her job and taking care of kids in the emergency room. That's what she does.

He said, Yeah, and there was a tone in his voice that sounded like a sneer. He said, That must've been really tough. To lose. To be a loser.

The conversation concluded shortly after that, with the president saying he thought I would do a good job and that he had a lot of faith in me.

The whole Russia team was still in the room, so they had heard my half of it. I told them the other half—the things the president said. I also wrote a memo about the conversation that very day. I wrote memos about my interactions with the president for the same reason that Comey wrote memos about his own interactions. I wanted a contemporaneous record of conversations about fraught and difficult matters, which in this specific instance was also a conversation with a person who cannot be trusted. I wrote contemporaneous memos not just about my interactions with Trump but also about my interactions with the attorney general, with the deputy attorney general, and with the vice president and some of his aides. These memos were not exhaustive records of the conversations, but summaries of important points.

Foremost in my mind, as I was writing these personal accounts, was the repeated notice, or warning—first from the attorney general and then from the president himself—that an interim director might be installed. From the moment I learned of Comey's firing, I fully expected that I, too, would be fired, or removed from my position and reassigned somewhere else. Any minute, any hour, any day now, I thought, I'll be turned out of this office.

My daughter, who was thirteen years old at the time, would joke about this with me. That whole first week in the acting director's chair, when I came home at night, she would say, Did you get fired today, Dad? Not today, honey, I would answer—but tomorrow's a new day! This kind of gallows humor had sustained me for years both at work and at home. And joking about my tenuous position helped me accomplish something important. I was trying to be open with my kids about important issues affecting our life together, so that if the worst possible scenario occurred, they would not be taken by surprise. When the director got fired without warning, both of my children were very upset, especially my son, who had spent time around Jim Comey and looked up to him. My son was shaken and upset by the way Comey had been summarily dismissed. So

I felt that I had to be candid with them about the possibility that something like that could happen to me, too. I would tell them, I don't know how the current situation will be resolved. I am the acting director now, but this could all end at any moment. We're going to hang in, and ride it out, and see what happens.

In the days following Comey's firing, the core of my concern about being replaced was a fear of what might happen to the Russia case. A special counsel had not yet been appointed. The FBI pursued multiple facets of the Russia case. But the Senate Intelligence Committee had begun its own Russia investigation. And immediately there were conflicts among these investigations.

The Senate committee investigators wanted to start interviewing people, including some of the witnesses in the Bureau's cases. If the Senate investigators leaned too far forward and interviewed people under oath, those statements could create problems for the FBI investigation if we wanted to interview the same subjects. The Bureau needed to do some high-level deconfliction work, and we had not been getting much help in that regard from the Department of Justice.

As soon as I became acting director, I convened a series of meetings about the Russia investigation—including the meeting that was interrupted by the call from the president—in which I directed an overall review of every aspect. Was the work on solid ground? Should it continue? Were there any individuals that we'd identified on whom we should consider opening new cases? If I was going to be removed, I wanted the Russia investigation to be on the surest possible footing. I wanted to draw an indelible line around it, to protect it so that whoever came after me could not just ignore it or make it go away. That's what we had been working on when the president called.

Praying for Rain

As the president requested, I went back to the White House that after-noon. When I arrived, at 2 P.M., the bodyguard Keith Schiller came down again and greeted me like I was his buddy, like someone he sees every day—Hey, what's going on? He took me to the Oval Office, where the scene was almost identical to the one I had walked into the previous night. Trump was behind the *Resolute* desk in the same posture I'd seen before, sitting on the edge of his chair, leaning forward. He lifted one arm and jutted it out, five fingers splayed, directing me to take a seat in one of the little wooden chairs. Reince Priebus and Don McGahn were there.

The president launched back into his speech about what a great deci-sion it was to fire Jim Comey, how happy it had made people, how won-derful it was that the director was gone, because so many people did not like Comey, even hated him—the president actually used the word "hate" to describe people's general feelings about Director Comey. He baited me again, looking for me to say, Yes, sir, you're right. Everyone's happy at the FBI. He was very pleased to see people telling the media that they did not like Director Comey, and he asked if I had seen that, too.

I told him I had not seen that. I did not tell him what I in fact had seen: the Hoover building as a site of dejection. I said, Well, sir, I don't know, I guess it's possible, as I told you before, but most people seem shocked and surprised by what happened. They will rebound. We will move on. Right now people are just trying to figure things out.

Later, when I reviewed this exchange and this whole conversation in my memory, I would ask myself, Should I have been more confrontational? As absurd as this unfolding situation was, it's hard to overstate the sig-nificance, for a career government employee, of having conversations with the president of the United States. Even when it's Donald Trump, it is still *President* Trump. So the reflex, the automatic response I felt from the deepest part of myself, was to be respectful and responsive. At what point is it appropriate to answer the president with a flat no? At what point is it appropriate to say to the president, Your perception is disconnected from reality?

At the time, I felt—because he was pressing me aggressively to capitulate to the force of his opinion—that I was holding my ground simply by not waving a white flag and agreeing. Maybe I should have said outright: No, no, no—everything you want to believe is wrong. But I said what I said.

Among all his odd claims, one stood out as being especially dubious. He said, as he had said during our phone conversation earlier that day, We've had so many FBI people calling us, sending us messages to say they're so glad the director is gone.

Who would do that? Who in the Bureau would send a message to the White House about something of this nature? It was not beyond the realm of the possible—there had been so many leaks in the months building up to this point. But for anyone in the Bureau to make or maintain contact with people in the White House would be unambiguously inappropriate—an absolute violation of the White House contacts policy. But the president kept saying it was happening.

Almost as a leading question, he said again that there was great dislike for Director Comey in the FBI, and he asked if I thought people were glad he was gone.

I said, Some people were frustrated with last summer's outcome on the Clinton case—it's possible that some of those people are glad. Other than that, I've seen no evidence that people are happy about the director being fired.

The president changed the subject. He said that he wanted to come to FBI headquarters to see people and excite them and show them how much he loves the FBI. He asked if I thought he should come. I said, Sir, you should come to the FBI whenever you want, you are always welcome. I was trying to think of a way to take some of the immediacy out of his proposal—to emphasize that we were just down the street, no need to hurry. He pressed me to answer whether I thought it was a good idea for him to come, and I said it was always a good idea to visit his people at the FBI. I was trying to communicate that the door was always open, so that he wouldn't feel that he had to crash through it right away, because I knew what a disaster it could turn out to be if he wanted to come to the Hoover building in the near future. He pressed even further, asking specifically, Do you think it would be a good idea for me to come down now? I said, Sure.

He looked at Don McGahn, and I realized what was happening. They were trying to paint me into a corner. The president said, Don, what do you think? Do you think I should go down to the FBI and speak to the people?

McGahn was sitting in one of the wooden chairs to my right. Making eye contact with Trump, he said, in a very pat and very prepared way, If the acting director of the FBI is telling you he thinks it is a good idea for you to come visit the FBI, then you should do it. Then McGahn turned and looked at me. And Trump looked at me and asked, Is that what you're telling me? Do you think it is a good idea?

It was a bizarre performance.

In this moment, I felt something like I'd felt in 1998 when I sent Big Felix in to meet with Dimitri Gufield. The same kind of thing was happening again now, here, in the Oval Office. Dimitri needed Felix to endorse his protection scheme. *This is a dangerous business, and it's a bad neighborhood, and you know, if you want, I can protect you from that. If you want my protection. I can protect you. Do you want my protection?* The president and his men were trying to work me the way a criminal brigade would operate. *I'll be your krysha.* The president wanted to be able to come out of this meeting and say, The acting director of the FBI invited me to speak at headquarters. The president and those around him wanted me to endorse the story they planned to tell about Comey's firing—even more, wanted me to tell their story for them.

The president and Don McGahn were both looking at me, the president's question hanging in the air: Did I think it was a good idea for him to visit the FBI?

I said it would be fine. I had no real choice. This was not worth the ultimate sacrifice.

Moving on, the president doubled down on a favorite theme—how much the FBI people loved him and supported him. He again quantified his voting tally among the FBI workforce. He said, again, At least 80 percent of the FBI voted for me.

How could I, or anyone, possibly know that? The FBI does not take candidate preference polls. That would be prohibited. For almost all federal employees, it is also prohibited to ask subordinates whom they voted for. Then the president asked me, Who did you vote for?

No superior had posed such a question during my time in public life. Not sure how to answer, I dodged—gave a total nonanswer. An idiotic answer: told him I always played it right down the middle. I heard myself saying this, and I kicked myself—kicked hard—and I continue to kick myself about it.

He gave me a sideways look, a little nod, like, What was that?

The president went on to talk about logistics and timing, and whether it would be better to come and speak to the FBI on Thursday or Friday. Today was Wednesday. I pointed out that a speech in the outdoor courtyard of the building would hold the largest crowd. I also knew it was supposed to rain on Friday, which could cause logistical problems for an outdoor event and probably force it to be canceled. I did not mention those problems. We agreed the visit would take place on Friday. We decided that his staff would talk to our staff about coordinating a joint message. He said he wanted me to promote the visit internally as much as I could—he wanted a big crowd. Make sure that courtyard is full, he told me. Praying for rain, I shook his hand, and I was dismissed.

Back at the Hoover building, I told my assistant to reach out to the White House about the possible event, and I said that if it couldn't work, that was fine with me. We conveyed to the White House all the things that needed to happen to arrange an immediate presidential speech at the FBI, and I think everybody involved decided it was more than anyone could do that week. The president soon had other things on his mind. North Korea conducted a missile test. There was fallout from his private Oval Office meeting with the Russian ambassador and foreign minister, in which he had disclosed classified information. And the president was still preoccupied with Jim Comey, warning in a tweet that Comey had better hope that "there are no 'tapes' of our conversations before he starts leaking to the press"—probably an empty threat. For whatever reason, the visit to the FBI never happened.

Worldwide Threat

When I left the Oval Office, I went straight to a prep session at the Bureau. Jim Comey had been preparing for two weeks to testify at the Senate Intelligence Committee's Worldwide Threats Hearing—an annual event where the director of national intelligence and the heads of the FBI, CIA, National Security Agency, and Defense Intelligence Agency share their assessments of the most urgent threats to U.S. national security and answer questions from senators about those threats. Preparation for the hearing typically involves a number of lengthy background sessions with staff and a review of hundreds of pages of briefing material; it also requires drafting an official statement for the record. This year the FBI's investigation of interference by Russia into the conduct of American elections, both recent and future, would be foremost on many people's minds. Even at this early stage, before the appointment of a special counsel, the evidence for Russian interference—widespread hacking of people and organizations; widespread manipulation of social media—was voluminous. And that's just the evidence already known to the public. Even before the election, the Office of the Director of National Intelligence and the Department of Homeland Security had jointly stated that they were "confident" that attempts to "interfere with the US election process" were being "directed" by the Russian government.

Ever since becoming acting director—in other words, for less than forty-eight hours—I had wondered whether I should cancel my participation in the Worldwide Threats Hearing or go ahead with it. In the end I decided that it was important to go. I believed I had to live up to every responsibility Comey had shouldered, every commitment he had made, in order, first, to send the right signal to the men and women of the Bureau, and, second, to send the right signal to everybody else. The message was that the FBI would miss nothing in this transition. There would be no dropped balls. We remained open for business.

So when I left the Oval Office, I went straight back to a prep session that night. I had been to a lot of these meetings for Comey and Mueller—when I was involved in the prepping. Usually I had been the guy sitting at the right hand of the director, listening to everyone else's contributions and trying to distill it all into better formulations.

Chiming in when you have a shapely little idea, I quickly discovered, is very different from sitting at the head of the table while a dozen people to your right and left argue the pros and cons of issue after issue, firing ideas and comments at you nonstop—all of which you have to take in while also assessing how those answers will be interpreted and processed by members of Congress, the president, and the media. I had never fully appreciated the complexity of that task. After two and a half hours of this, my tank was full. I had to get some sleep.

Thursday morning I came in early. I did not go to the morning briefs.

I sat alone in my office and tried to figure out what to say. I knew the senators would ask about morale at the FBI: some version of the questions the president had asked me three times now—questions about what was happening inside the Bureau, how the workforce had responded to Comey's firing—and I had to have a ready answer. But I still did not know how to do that in a way that was both honest and deft. While considering how to navigate the obvious tensions, I decided that now was a moment when being direct was far more important than being deft. I called Jill, told her what I planned, and warned her to get ready for the reaction. I checked the decision with two other trusted associates, and then I got in the car to go to the Capitol.

Reporters yelled questions as I arrived at the hearing, and with the other intelligence heads I was herded into an anteroom. Dan Coats, the director of national intelligence, thanked me for coming. I sensed relief among the group that I had shown up, since there would likely be a lot of FBI-related questions. A staff member gave us the order of march. We filed through a darkened passage behind the dais where the senators sit, rounded the right corner, and arrived at the long table where all of us would sit, facing the committee members. The space between our table and the dais was packed with photographers, the low whirr of camera shutters clicking, and when we sat down and pulled our papers out of our bags, the cameras were right there, on the other side of the table, less than a foot from our faces. I had no idea where I was supposed to look, whether I was supposed to acknowledge the camera somehow—smiling would be wrong, that I knew—or to ignore everything and try to do what I would do if I were by myself, just sitting at a table. A small thing, but a notable moment of lack of preparation. Somebody should tell anybody who testifies at a committee meeting like this: Be ready for dozens of cameras right up in your face.

It was Senator Martin Heinrich, a Democrat from New Mexico, who asked the question I had been expecting. He mentioned news reports that

Director Comey had "lost the confidence of rank-and-file FBI employees." He asked if, in my opinion, that was accurate. I said, "No, sir, that is not accurate. I can tell you, sir, that I worked very, very closely with Director Comey," and I went on to answer the question—this time—without hesitation. I said, "I can tell you that I hold Director Comey in the absolute highest regard. I have the highest respect for his considerable abilities and his integrity, and it has been the greatest privilege and honor in my professional life to work with him. I can tell you also that Director Comey enjoyed broad support within the FBI and still does until this day. We are a large organization; we are 36,500 people across this country, across this globe. We have a diversity of opinions about many things, but I can confidently tell you that the majority—the vast majority of FBI employees enjoyed a deep and positive connection to Director Comey."

It Wasn't His Idea

One of the regularly scheduled meetings with the attorney general, deputy attorney general, and some of their staff fell on the next day, a Friday. In these meetings—to review the President's Daily Brief materials—when the most senior participants had especially sensitive things to discuss among a smaller group, one of us would say, Can you stick around afterward? This routine briefing on May 12 was my first as acting director. After the meeting, I asked Rod Rosenstein if he could stay behind, so he did. It was just him and me.

I wanted to talk with him about the budding conflict between the FBI and the Senate Intelligence Committee over the Russia case. I was concerned that the committee's requests to interview personnel and review materials were going to cause problems for our own investigation and future prospects for prosecution. I wanted to lay down some procedural

ground rules. Among other things, I wanted the committee to agree that
they wouldn't talk to witnesses until after the FBI had interviewed them.
I also wanted them to agree that they wouldn't make recordings or recorded statements of witness testimony—too many people going over the
same ground with witnesses can result in discrepancies and can often have
the effect of muddying the facts rather than clarifying them. The FBI,
the Justice Department, and congressional committees can work well together when the rules are understood and all parties act in good faith;
the whole enterprise can fall apart in confusion if any element is out of
whack. Because the terms I sought were prosecutorial equities, I felt the
deputy should negotiate them on the Bureau's behalf.

Immediately, Rod saw the need that I was pointing out, and he said,
Yes, absolutely, you should refer all those questions to us. But I had come
to this conversation wanting more than a specific answer to this one specific request. I wanted a broader affirmation that the Department of Justice would be more actively involved. My basic message was, I need you
to protect the process here.

After speaking to those points, Rod shifted his gaze. As he leaned back
in his chair, I could see that he was not looking directly at me. His eyes
were focused on a point in space a few yards beyond and behind, toward
the door. He was a little glassy-eyed. He started talking about the firing
of Jim Comey. There was emotion in his voice. He was obviously upset.

He said he could not believe what had happened. He said he was
shocked that the White House was making it look as if Jim's firing had
been his idea. He said it wasn't his idea. The president had ordered him to
write the memo justifying the firing. Judging from later press accounts,
Rod said much the same thing to others.

The jolt of this news, even in a week of constant jolts, was extreme. I
could not believe what I was hearing. I did not know why he was telling
me this. He seemed to be in such distress. I thought he simply did not
know quite what to do. There was a long quiet moment. Then I said, Are

you sleeping at night? No, he said, he was not getting much sleep. Is your family okay? I asked. He said there were news trucks in front of his house.

He was grasping for a way to describe the nature of his situation. The conversation involved a fair amount of silence. One remark stands out in my memory. He said, There's no one that I can talk to about this. There's no one here that I can trust.

He said that he had been thinking about appointing a special counsel to oversee the investigation. He asked for my thoughts about whether we needed a special counsel. I said I thought it would help the credibility of the investigation. He told me he thought of Jim Comey as not just a friend but also a mentor, someone he looked up to. This was hard for me to hear from the guy who had just fired my boss. And, incredibly, he then said, The one person I would like to talk to about this situation is Jim Comey.

I went back to my office in a state of—I am starting to wish that there were more synonyms for shock. I didn't know how to think about what had just happened. I felt as if he had been asking me for advice, and I had not really given him advice. No substantive counsel. I thought about his isolation and the difficulties of his situation. I made an appointment to go back and see him that afternoon.

I returned to see Rosenstein by myself. I thanked him for seeing me. I told him that the decision to designate a special counsel was entirely his, and I said I didn't think I'd given him the benefit of my best thoughts on the issue, and I would like to do that now, for whatever it was worth. This is the gist of what I said to him: I feel strongly that the investigation would be best served by having a special counsel. I've been thinking about the Clinton email case and how we got twisted in knots over how to announce a result that did not include bringing charges against anyone. Because the same thing might happen with the Russia case, it raises the question of how the FBI could possibly announce such a result to a world that has become so intensely focused on the question of collusion. Had we appointed a special counsel in the Clinton case to begin with, we might not be in the present situation. Director Comey would not have had to make the decisions he felt he had to make, which ultimately—according to your memo, Rod—led to his termination. I see a high likelihood of history repeating itself as we move forward. Unless or until you make the decision to appoint a special counsel, the FBI will be subjected to withering criticism from the Hill. The mere act of enduring that criticism could destroy the credibility of both the Justice Department and the FBI.

He was very engaged. He was not yet convinced. He pointed out that he was, essentially, the only politically confirmed official at Justice involved in the Russia investigations—Jeff Sessions, after all, had had to recuse himself because of his role in the campaign and (as would soon be revealed) because of his meetings with Russian officials during that time. Rosenstein also wanted to be around to influence the selection of the next FBI director.

I told him I understood his concern. But, I said, if we've appointed a special counsel who will take this investigation wherever it needs to go, then everything else will take care of itself. Ultimately, the White House is going to choose the new FBI director on its own terms; that decision was wholly in the administration's control. The priority had to be doing the right thing for the Russia case.

We talked a lot. He again spoke of his memo that had been used to justify Director Comey's firing. He said he could tell as early as January, from his first conversations with the attorney general, that Jim Comey would be fired.

By the end of the meeting, he said he would continue to consider appointing a special counsel, but he did not see this as an urgent matter— if a special counsel was needed, Rosenstein did not think the appointment had to happen quickly.

Drawing a Line

On Saturday afternoon, May 13, Jeff Sessions and Rod Rosenstein interviewed me for the position of FBI director. It was a cordial meeting, and the questions were the ones you'd expect. Example: What do you think is the biggest challenge to the FBI right now? Easy, I said. Technology. Not in terms of any particular case or type of threat. I believed we had the experience and the capability to meet operational threats in counterterrorism, counterintelligence, and all other realms. But in the long term, we were going to be mightily challenged by changes in technology—from encryption to interpreting increasingly large data sets. And I said that if we don't get better at identifying, acquiring, and delivering technological solutions to our workforce as an organization, we are not going to be able to keep the country as safe as possible. I don't think that's the answer they expected, and it was not an answer that engaged them in this meeting. But it is the answer that I'm still very confident about.

At one point, an aide brought an iPhone to the attorney general. On the iPhone screen was a picture from 2015 of me and my family at a swim meet where my kids were competing. We were all wearing T-shirts that said DR. JILL MCCABE FOR STATE SENATE. The morning that picture had been taken, the T-shirts had arrived in the mail, and we put them on, and one of our friends took a family photo. Then the friend posted the photo to Facebook. Then the right-wing media took the photo and falsely claimed that I had gone out canvassing for my wife's campaign.

So in my interview to be FBI director, instead of having a full discussion of the challenges to American law enforcement, I had to explain in detail to the attorney general why a family snapshot was not the damning political artifact that it had been made to appear to be—while the attorney general looked skeptically at me, as if he didn't believe what I was saying.

The whole conversation felt like a charade. In the end I said, Honestly, if I could be so bold as to give you my best advice as to what I think you should do here—I think you should look hard and well to find the best candidate from outside the FBI to come in and be the next director. I think you should try to get that person on board as fast as you possibly can, and as deputy director I will try to help that person get up to speed as quickly as possible. But to be candid, I will become eligible for my retirement in March 2018, and it is my intention to retire at that time and go into the private sector.

Through the weekend, though, the issue of the special counsel was apparently gnawing at Rosenstein. On Sunday morning he called me on my cell phone. Using coded language, he said that if I had the opportunity to speak with Jim Comey, he would be very interested to hear what Comey thought about the question of appointing a special counsel. I said that I would have to think about this.

I was doubtful that seeking Comey's advice and relaying it in this manner would be ethical under the circumstances. It also seemed unwise on its face. That afternoon, I convened a conference call with some of my senior staff to discuss whether to seek Jim Comey's opinion on the special-counsel issue. We all concluded that I should not. He was no longer an FBI employee. It would be inappropriate to discuss investigative issues with him. It was also just a bad idea. Comey was a party to the matter Rosenstein was dealing with—and regardless of one's admiration for Jim, there was no getting around the fact that his thoughts on this topic would be inherently conflicted. Seeking advice on how to handle the situation—as Rosenstein seemed to want to do—would pull him immediately into dangerous waters. Rod never asked me about this again.

On Monday the fifteenth, I met again with the Russia team. From January until Comey was fired, we had been having discussions with him about how to handle the topic of whether the president was under investigation. Jim Baker said, Even though we don't have a case open on the president, we do have a case open to see whether his campaign coordi-nated with the Russians in a way that would have been illegal or improper; and as the leader of his campaign, by definition some of his activity and behavior would be within the scope of the investigation. Baker thought it was jesuitical—basically, too cute by half—to say the president was not under investigation. But Comey chose to give the president the reassur-ance that, at that moment, he himself was not.

It is important to remember that opening a case does not mean that a crime has been committed. And the FBI is rightly circumspect in its statements. That said, as analysts and scholars have discussed at length, there arguably could have been grounds for a case against the president, on two fronts. The first was obstruction of justice. The events of the preceding few days were significant. The president's possible connection to obstruction was no longer limited to his having been the leader of a campaign, some of whose members may have crossed a line in various ways. Now the president himself had fired the director. Prior to that, on at least two occasions, the president had asked the director to drop the inquiry regarding Mike Flynn. He had also repeatedly referred publicly to the investigation in a demeaning and dismissive way. He had called it "a witch hunt." And on May 11, in an interview with Lester Holt of NBC News, the president had explicitly connected his decision to fire Jim Comey to what he called "this Russia thing"—seemingly abandoning the idea that it had been Rod Rosenstein's idea, and that the cause in-volved the handling of the email case. These facts could well combine to form an "articulable factual basis"—the predication needed to open a full investigation—that the federal crime of obstruction of justice might have occurred. They could be interpreted as implying that the director had been fired in an effort to obstruct the Russia investigation, and specifi-cally the investigation of Mike Flynn.

On the collusion side, all those same facts could raise suspicion that the president might have been aware of, and supportive of, his campaign's many interactions with the Russian government and people connected closely to it, specifically in hacking the emails of the Democratic National Committee and using the DNC emails to harm Hillary Clinton as a candidate.

In theory, could the attorney general also have been a target of investigation? His denial, during his confirmation hearings, that he had ever met with anybody from Russia about the 2016 campaign was widely questioned at the time. Then the FBI received a letter from Senator Patrick Leahy, of Vermont, and Senator Al Franken, of Minnesota, noting reports that Sessions met with the Russian ambassador to the U.S. at least twice during the 2016 elections, including one meeting that took place during the Republican National Convention. The senators were concerned that Sessions's testimony during confirmation hearings "could be construed as perjury," and they asked us to look into what actually happened—the reported events that seemed to contradict the confirmation testimony Sessions had given. Then the two senators sent two follow-up letters during the following two months asking for updates on the matter.

Traditionally, the Bureau does not open perjury cases on people based on statements made in confirmation hearings unless Congress asks us to look into a particular statement by a particular person. The FBI does not want to be turned into the confirmation police. We trust that the process has its own integrity. Senators can and should ask probative questions that will reveal obfuscation or dishonesty. It could be a different story if Congress were to ask the FBI to look into the circumstances around what actually happened, as opposed to what someone testified to.

If—hypothetically—the FBI had information about events suggesting that a cabinet nominee's testimony had been untrue, and Congress asked us to look into it, a case on that person could be opened. Even to consider such a move would require consultation with the Justice Department, because a case like that would be a SIM—a sensitive investigative matter, requiring special handling according to the attorney general guidelines.

If the FBI found itself in circumstances like these, where the facts and our obligations under the guidelines were clear, and we chose not to open a case because it might involve government officials in the highest ranks, the Bureau would be guilty of dereliction of duty.

'A Strategy for Disruption'

On Monday, May 15, I went back to Justice to inform Rod Rosenstein of where we stood with the Russia investigation. In his office, I renewed my strong request that we should appoint a special counsel to pursue the Russia investigation. The pressure was on to move quickly. He didn't argue with what I was proposing, and he also did not yet endorse it.

Jim Comey, when he briefed the leadership on the Hill about the Russia case, assured them that we would keep them updated as to significant developments. I was due to provide another briefing, and the possible appointment of a special counsel would count as a significant development. Rosenstein said, Well, I'm going with you. Great, I said, I'd love to have you. But you'd better be ready, because if you're there, they're going to ask if you're going to appoint a special counsel—and some of them are not going to take no for an answer. He thought about that but did not pronounce a decision. His chief of staff, Jim Crowell, was making arguments similar to mine.

Having been in his job for only three weeks, Rod may not by this point have developed a reflexive understanding of how frequently, as an intelligence organization, the FBI had to make its way to the Hill, and what kinds of things we briefed the various intelligence committees on. When we were involved in any momentous or controversial matters, we would go up and brief the congressional leadership, the group called the Gang of Eight: the majority and minority leaders of the House, the majority and minority leaders of the Senate, and the chairs and the ranking members of the House and Senate Intelligence Committees. That group is typically pretty secure.

As I saw it, one key reason for briefing the Hill was this: By putting the deputy attorney general on notice and informing Congress of the Bureau's actions, we would be drawing an indelible line around the cases we had opened—the four known publicly and any others that may have gone forward.

In this meeting, Rod spoke again, and in more detail, about his experience of writing the memo that the president used to justify Comey's firing. On May 8, Rod said, he went to the White House. Don McGahn told him the president wanted to fire the director. The president had written a termination letter—long and rambling, as later press accounts discussed. By the time Rod walked out of the Oval Office that day, he had been enlisted to write a memo to justify Comey's firing. This memo accompanied the revised letter that the president sent to Comey.

As Rod recounted to me his memories of that meeting, he became very animated. He talked fast, he gestured a lot, he got up and walked around, he was a flight of ideas. He continued talking in this way about his experience of Comey's firing on May 9. The false story that had taken shape in press reports—the notion that the whole thing had been Rod's idea—was eating away at him.

He wondered aloud if there was some way to collect explicit evidence of the president's apparent motivations and put it unequivocally on the record. No option for doing so seemed feasible. In any case, the president already had publicly made the connection between Comey's firing and "this Russia thing," with his comments to Lester Holt.

That's where we left it on Monday. The clock was ticking. I thought I would get fired any minute. Somebody was going to knock on my door and say, Pack your bags, you're moving to Anchorage. We urgently needed a special counsel, but there was only so much I could do about that. I had to do what I could do, as fast as I could do it.

On Tuesday I went back to Justice for another meeting with Rod and some of his staff. Lisa Page came with me, to take notes. I couldn't track this conversation and transact it as I needed to and also make a record of it. When we sat down in his office, I pressed again for the appointment of a special counsel. I said, You have to do this. We're going to go to Congress—tomorrow, I hope—and I'm going to lay the scope of our investigation out for the Gang of Eight, and some of them are going to come after you with reasonable demands that we need a special counsel appointed quickly. The attorney general has recused himself. It's a mess. We need somebody independent to oversee this.

Rod was still not fully convinced. He said the same things he said the week before: What happens with the director's job? Jim Crowell weighed in heavily on my side of the argument. Rod's attention flew all over. It appeared to me that he was at the end of his rope. The stress of these issues, and his role in this whole situation, seemed to be overwhelming. In the middle of this meeting, he took a phone call. It was Don McGahn, calling to ask him to arrange for me to go back to the White House, to interview for the director's job. So we set that up for the next day.

In this same meeting Rod talked about interviews with candidates for director. Then he flipped back to talking about possible candidates for the special counsel job. It was hard to track whether he was talking about candidates for one job or for the other. One minute, he said Mueller had been asked to interview for the position of FBI director; Mueller had gone in for an interview with Trump, and left his phone there, and then the phone had to be retrieved. Then he said John Kelly was another candidate for FBI director.

I said I didn't understand what qualified Kelly as a prospect. Kelly had no law-enforcement or legal background of any kind. And why would he

leave his cabinet-level position as secretary of the Department of Homeland Security to become director of the FBI? Rod said, No, he wouldn't
leave DHS. He would just run both. I said, You've got to be kidding.
Those are two massive jobs. Each one is a huge challenge for any human
being. For one person to do both would be impossible. Rod said, This is
a strategy for disruption. It is not a serious attempt to find the right FBI
director. It is a strategy for disruption.

That night, Rod provisionally agreed to meet with the Gang of Eight
the next day. He wanted to do it as late in the day as possible. And before
I left his office, Rod also gave me the president's original draft letter firing Comey, which he had kept after his May 8 White House meeting.
I read it, I took it back to the Hoover building, sealed it in an envelope,
signed the seal, and put it in my safe.

The Gang of Two Dozen

By the afternoon of May 17, Rosenstein had confirmed his agreement to
hold a briefing for the Gang of Eight about the Russia investigation. He
had also made the decision to appoint a special counsel and taken steps
to do so. The FBI team had already set up the briefing, for five o'clock
that day, so it was a good thing he was on board. At the Capitol, on the
House side, they walked me down to the SCIF, in a basement floor. Some
of the Russia team was waiting for me there. The senators and congressmen
started straggling in, each with one or two aides—mostly staff directors—
and then Rod showed up with a couple of his people. Now that the Gang
of Eight was a crowd of two dozen in the room, I thought, the chance of
this not getting back to the president was basically zero. Then Devin
Nunes walked in, and the chance was less than zero.

Nunes, a congressman from California and the chairman of the House
Intelligence Committee, had publicly stepped away from that commit-

tee's Russia investigation. In April, just before the House Ethics Committee announced it was investigating Nunes for speaking with the media about classified information relating to the Trump campaign and Russia, Nunes effectively recused himself—although he did not use the word "recuse." Nunes was suspected of having surreptitiously been given intelligence by presidential aides during a nighttime rendezvous at the White House, information that he then publicized. Look who's here, I said to Rod. Rosenstein understood. He went to talk to Nunes, pulled him aside. Came back, told me, Nunes is staying, he says he's not recused from this, he refuses to leave.

I looked at Rod. Rod said, At the end of the day it's his recusal, it's his choice, I can't enforce it. We can't kick him out of the room.

Rod and I sat at the end of the long conference table in the middle of the room. Chuck Schumer, the Democratic senator from New York, was to my right, and Mitch McConnell, the Republican senator from Kentucky and the Senate majority leader, was to my left. I took out the outline I had prepared. As a rule, I don't work off talking points, I brief off the top of my head. Not this time.

To start the briefing I went back to July 2016, when we began investigating the possibility of collusion between members of the Trump campaign and the Russian government. We opened cases on four individuals. The question determining those actions was simple: Which individuals associated with the campaign had had significant or historical ties to Russia?

One was Carter Page, a foreign policy adviser to the campaign; he was known to have met with with Russian foreign-intelligence officers in New York, and he had recently been to Russia. Another foreign policy adviser, George Papadopoulos, had told a foreign diplomat that the Russians had offered to help Trump's campaign by providing information on Hillary Clinton. Michael Flynn, the campaign's senior foreign policy adviser and, later, for a brief period, the president's national security adviser, was known to have had multiple, high-level contacts with the Russian government and he had been seated next to Vladimir Putin at a Moscow gala dinner in late 2015. Paul Manafort was known to have had business dealings of many kinds, all of them on the shady side, with Ukrainians and Russians.

After reminding the committee of how this investigation began, I told them of additional steps we had taken. No one interrupted. No one pushed back. The mood in the room was sober. Schumer had been nodding his head and looking at me very directly throughout the brief. On McConnell's side of the table, I sensed a great deal of resignation.

At this point Rod took over the briefing and announced that he had appointed a special counsel to pursue the Russia investigation, and that the special counsel was Robert Mueller. The Gang of Eight had a lot of questions for him. What was the scope of the inquiry? Who oversees the special counsel? How could the special counsel get fired? No one was gunning to fire the special counsel, they just wanted to understand the Justice Department rules around the appointment. Rod answered every question, and then we were done. In and out in half an hour.

Nunes had stayed and listened throughout the entire meeting. Within the next few days, aides to Representative Mike Conaway, the acting chair of the House Intelligence Committee after Nunes stepped aside, contacted the Justice Department to ask if we would give the brief again, to Conaway alone. As it was explained to me, the aide said, after the Gang of Eight briefing, Nunes realized he probably should not have been there. Conaway would handle all committee business pertaining to this matter. So Conaway came to the command center at Justice, and Rod and I ran through the whole thing for him again. He took the news the same way the rest had seemed to take it. As a reality to accept.

When I came out of the Capitol in the early evening of May 17, it felt like crossing a finish line. It felt as if I'd been sprinting since the night of May 9. Now, finally, I could stop sprinting. If I got nothing else done as acting director, I had done, now, the one thing I needed to do. The Russia investigation was on solid ground. Everybody who needed to know about it knew about it. If the investigation ever got wiped away, that would involve forces beyond my control. It could not be struck from the record. All the steps we took were fully documented. If anyone tried to close it down, it could not be done in secret.

I came home and stood by the island in the kitchen, drinking a beer. The family wound down from all the things we had done that day. My own future, I knew, was probably set now. I was correct about that. In late July, the president would begin using Twitter to continue the barrage of false and scathing statements about me and my wife.

Later, when things got tough, on the days when I went down the rabbit hole, Jill would remind me of that night with the family in the kitchen. Center me and bring me back: Remember what you did and why you did it, she would say. You played your role, you did your job, your kids know it. That's what matters.

8

Real Americans

Interview

The day I briefed the Gang of Eight about the Russia investigation—Wednesday, May 17—I also had another appointment. Just before that meeting on the Hill, I had gone back to the White House for my job interview for the position of FBI director.

Inside the West Wing I made my way to the small reception area outside the Oval Office. The door was open. To the left of the door was a desk where Hope Hicks, who was then the White House communications director, was sitting. Covering the whole of the front of the desk was a poster-sized display—a map of the 2016 electoral college results. In the space where all outside visitors would wait to see the president, the main decorative element was this proof of the president's victory.

As I stood there in front of her, I could see into the Oval Office. The president was at his desk, having a loud conversation with a crowd of staffers including Reince Priebus and press secretary Sean Spicer. It almost sounded like a shouting match. A television was turned on, and the news headlines were about Comey and the FBI. The scene recalled the one I'd encountered in Pence's office. People in the room emitted bleats of exasperation: Who leaked this? How did that story get out?

It didn't seem right to be standing there, overhearing this. I looked at Hope Hicks and asked, Do you want me to go somewhere else? She answered, Oh, he's very busy. She seemed to think that I was impatient about getting in to see the president. To clarify, I said, I understand that he's busy, and I'm happy to wait until he's ready. But would you like for me to wait someplace else? I gestured to the open door with my eyes, so she would understand. She said, No, no, no, you're fine right there.

The phone rang, and she answered it. I heard her talking. She stuck her head into the Oval Office and spoke to the president: Sir, It's Senator Grassley on the phone for you. Charles Grassley, a senator from Iowa and the chairman of the Senate Judiciary Committee, had become one of the president's primary attack dogs against the FBI and the Justice Department. For months he had been writing critical letters to the Department of Justice, fanning the flames of false rumors about me. In one letter he called for my exclusion from any aspect of the investigation into Russian engagement with the Trump campaign, citing my "partisan Democratic ties"—a line that I could only laugh at, having been a registered Republican for the whole of my adult life. Now Grassley was calling the president just before my interview. A few moments earlier, I might have had a one-in-ten-million chance at this job. The odds now slimmed. The whole fact of being here felt ridiculous.

A line of people filed out of the Oval Office. Sean Spicer looked me up and down as he passed by, silent and yet somehow sarcastic. Gave no greeting. If there had been a cartoon thought bubble above his head, it would have said, What are *you* doing here?

I went in. The furniture was arranged the same way it always seemed to be: little schoolboy chairs in a semicircle in front of the desk. The president behind the desk. The sit-down wave of his hand. Reince Priebus.

Don McGahn. Rod Rosenstein was supposed to be there but wasn't. Attorney General Sessions was there, impassive. The president said, I was talking to Senator Grassley, and boy, he's no fan of yours. Trying to make a joke, I said, Yes, I was aware of that. After Grassley's fourteenth letter criticizing me, I drew the conclusion that he and I were not going to be friends.

For some reason, the president immediately began to talk about his electoral college results in the state of North Carolina. Percentages. Numbers. His commentary on this went on for a while. Not sure how to respond, I did not respond. Just held eye contact, nodded to signal comprehension, waited for the topic to exhaust itself. Eventually he began to repeat his claim that most people in the FBI had voted for him, because people in the FBI loved him. I noticed that the percentage of love was creeping up—now it was 90 percent. I took the topic as an opening.

I said, Mr. President, when we talked last time, you asked me a question, and I did not give you a straight answer. So if it's okay, I'd like to go back to that and tell you what I've been thinking. A little puzzled, his expression said, Sure, why not?

I said, Last time we met, you asked me who I voted for, and I didn't really answer the question. So I wanted to explain to you that I did not vote in the 2016 election. I have considered myself a Republican my whole life, and I have always voted for the Republican candidate for president, except in 2016. Owing to the nature of investigations that I was involved in during the campaign season, I thought it would be inappropriate for me to cast a vote. Although it's the first time I've ever missed voting in a presidential election, at the time I felt it was the right thing for me to stay out of this one.

No one in the room said a word. The president squinted. I couldn't tell if he was angry. The look certainly didn't convey approval or comprehension. For a second, he held my gaze. Then he moved on.

He said, So we're looking for a new director now, and here you are.

You're interviewing. Isn't this great? Isn't this terrific for you? You're interviewing for the director's job. How do you feel about that?

I said, I'm an FBI agent, and I would like to think that any FBI agent would be honored by the opportunity to interview for the position of director. I never imagined doing this, but I'm very happy to be considered. I love the organization, and becoming director would be the ultimate way to serve. We've only had one former agent as director, Louis Freeh.

Yeah, he said. Well, it's great, and I don't know if you're going to get it, but if you do, that's great, and if you don't, you'll just go back to being a happy FBI guy, right?

I said, Yes, of course, I'm a career professional.

Repetitions of redundancy: He told me I was doing a terrific job, he talked again about people he was interviewing—Joseph Lieberman, other FBI agents. To wrap up, he said, This has been great. This is great for you, all this attention has been great. And who knows? You might get it.

There was a lot of that—a lot of dangling. Look, it could happen. . . . As if he were going to select the new director by spinning a wheel. This was my job interview in its totality. He had barely asked a question.

"A Great Day for Democracy"

When the first tweet came—July 25, 2017—I was already hanging by a thread. I'd been acting director for six weeks. I was trying to figure out this job day by day, trying to do the right thing, keep everybody's spirits up, stay focused, keep the organization focused, do everything I possibly could to be consistent in my messaging and stay on target and keep people working.

And then this missile fired—"Problem is that the acting head of the FBI & the person in charge of the Hillary investigation, Andrew McCabe, got $700,000 from H for wife!"

I think I heard it on the news. I didn't have Twitter on my phone. Following Twitter was not a part of my life. The tweet hit me on a lot of different levels, not the least of which was it's just embarrassing to be called out by the president of the United States. To be referred to by clear implication as corrupt. To have my wife be referred to by clear implication as corrupt. It was shocking. Donald Trump had done it before, during the campaign, and now was at it again, as president.

I went into work, committed to staying upbeat and pushing forward, whether one-on-one with people at headquarters or in speeches to field offices, at a moment when the firing of the director had rocked the whole organization. Now I had this feeling that everyone I talked to probably had that tweet in the back of their minds.

Soon there would be more tweets. The next morning, as I was getting ready to leave the house, Jim Baker reached me by phone. He said, I was just calling to see if you're okay. I was confused. Said I was fine, and why was he asking? He said, Oh, I just saw the president's tweets this morning.

I looked them up—"Why didn't A.G. Sessions replace Acting FBI Director Andrew McCabe, a Comey friend who was in charge of Clinton investigation . . ." / ". . . big dollars ($700,000) for his wife's political run from Hillary Clinton and her representatives. Drain the Swamp!" Again, I was baffled about how to react. The president's statement contained no facts. It was not an argument—it was innuendo. What should I do? How could I acknowledge this in a way that wouldn't give it more significance or lend it some further credence? In the office that day we had an executive-leadership team meeting. I started the meeting by saying, I haven't seen the news today—haven't had a chance to check the paper. Anything happening? There was some awkward laughter, and then we moved on.

Two days later, on July 28, the inspector general's office contacted me. The assistant IG said I had to come and talk to him that day, that it was urgent that I speak with them immediately. The IG was investigating

Midyear, and I assumed there would be questions about my involvement in the case. I made it clear that without my lawyer present, I did not want to speak about an investigation in which I was a subject. The assistant IG said the meeting would not be an interview. He and his colleagues had something they needed to bring to my attention. In their office, I was shown the now infamous text messages between Peter Strzok and Lisa Page. IG staff and attorneys began to ask me questions about the meaning of those messages, which I had never before seen—I had not even been aware that they existed, much less that Strzok and Page had been romantically involved. They hammered me with questions about the texts that Strzok and Page exchanged, questions I could not have answered unless I'd been a mind reader—What did I think this one meant? What did I think the two of them were thinking when they wrote some of these things? Then the IG staff started asking about specific references in Page's texts, and whether she was referring to other cases. I objected. I told them they were wandering into the territory that, as they knew, we were not going to discuss at this meeting. They pressed, asking if I knew whether Page had been authorized to talk to reporters. Two of them began speaking together, asking overlapping questions, pointing to numerous references in different texts. I was disconnecting from the questioning, trying to shut this conversation down. I said I was not aware of any authorization, but in fact I wasn't following their questions. My mind was elsewhere: The information I'd just been given about those text messages represented an emergency, and I needed to deal with the consequences immediately.

I had a general sense, that day, of things coming unglued. President Trump gave a speech in New York, in which he called gang members "animals" and encouraged law-enforcement officers to use force freely when handling suspects. Chuck Rosenberg, Director Comey's former chief of staff, who now served as acting head of the Drug Enforcement Agency, called me. He was taken aback by the president's statement, and we discussed how to respond. Rosenberg issued a public statement strongly affirming core law-enforcement values of integrity, respect, compassion, and the rule of law. I spent the afternoon and evening with my senior staff trying to assess and control the damage that might be done by the texts between Strzok and Page, and trying to figure out where to reassign Strzok, who had been working for Mueller's special-counsel investigation, but who for obvious reasons we had to remove from that team. I was angry about the poor judgment that Strzok and Page had shown, and I was saddened to consider the disparagement they would now be subjected to. Strzok was a gifted investigator. Page was a gifted lawyer. I respected and trusted them both.

After that weekend, Christopher Wray became the new FBI director and I returned to the job of deputy director. The same day, I contacted the IG's office to add some clarity to the things I said in the chaotic interview of the prior week. I provided additional information about Page and her role in responding to the *Wall Street Journal* inquiries, and I suggested that they speak to Michael Kortan, who was also involved. I wasn't trying to hide anything—there was nothing to hide. As deputy director, I could authorize colleagues to speak to the press and push back on inaccurate stories that were harmful to the FBI. I corrected the record—I wanted the IG to have an accurate understanding of the facts. These sorts of corrections are common in any type of interview, especially when it covers topics the witness was not told about in advance. Witnesses recall things after the interview is over, when the heat of the moment has passed, and they have had time to reflect on the questions they have been asked. I made similar corrections in discussions with the FBI's inspection division later in the month when I realized they had apparently heard and written down something other than I knew to be the case. I thought that settled the matter. But some time after, the inspector general began investigating the statements I made in the July 28 interview. Having corrected the record without delay, I trusted that the process would confirm that I had done my best to answer the questions accurately—and when I realized I needed to clarify and correct what I had said, I did so voluntarily, without being prompted.

Through the fall, the president's anger seemed difficult to contain. He threatened North Korea with "fire and fury," then followed up with a threat to "totally destroy" the country. When neo-Nazis and white supremacists held a rally in Charlottesville, Virginia, and one of them killed a protester and injured a score of others, he made a brutally offensive statement condemning violence "on many sides . . . on many sides"—as if there was moral equivalence between those who were fomenting racial hatred and violence and those who were opposing it. He retweeted anti-Muslim propaganda that had been posted by a convicted criminal leader of a British far-right organization. Then as now, the president's heedless bullying and intolerance of variance—intolerance of any perception not his own—has been nurturing a strain of insanity in public dialogue that has been long in development, a pathology that became only more virulent when it migrated to the internet.

A person such as the president can on impulse and with minimal effort inject any sort of falsehood into public conversation through digital media and call his own lie a correction of "fake news." There are so many news outlets now, and the competition for clicks is so intense, that any sufficiently outrageous statement made online by anyone with even the faintest patina of authority, and sometimes even without it, will be talked about, shared, and reported on, regardless of whether it has a basis in fact. How do you progress as a culture if you set out to destroy any common agreement as to what constitutes a fact? You can't have conversations. You can't have debates. You can't come to conclusions. At the same time, calling out the transgressor has a way of giving more oxygen to the lie. Now it's a news story, and the lie is being mentioned not just in some website that publishes unattributable gossip but in every reputable newspaper in the country.

I have not been looking to start a personal fight with the president. When somebody insults your wife, your instinctive reaction is to want to lash out in response. When you are the acting director, or deputy director, of the FBI, and the person doing the insulting is the chief executive of the United States, your options have guardrails. I read the president's tweets, but I had an organization to run. A country to help protect. I had to remain independent, neutral, professional, positive, on target. I had to compartmentalize my emotions.

Crises taught me how to compartmentalize. Example: the Boston Marathon bombing—watching the video evidence, reviewing videos again and again of people dying, people being mutilated and maimed. I had the primal human response that anyone would have. But I know how to build walls around that response and had to build them then in order to stay focused on finding the bombers. Compared to experiences like that one, getting tweeted about by Donald Trump does not count as a crisis. I do not even know how to think about the fact that the person with time on his hands to tweet about me and my wife is the president of the United States.

At home, it was more difficult to move on. The situation was especially hard on Jill. At times, she has felt responsible for everything that has happened to me and even to the FBI—as if it all somehow grew from the kernel of her choice to run for the Virginia state senate. Of course, that's not true. Had Jill not run for office, Donald Trump would have found something else bad to say. He did not go after me because Jill ran for office. He went after me because the FBI opened the Russia case, which led to the appointment of a special counsel. He went after the FBI, and continues to do so, because its work has led to more than thirty indictments—with more likely to come—of individuals associated with Russian interference in the 2016 election. Those investigations raise questions about the legitimacy of his presence in the White House—questions that prompt fear.

Fear is why the president still has a map of his electoral college victory hanging outside the door to the Oval Office. Fear is why the president makes every person who goes into his office pass by a display meant to assert his right to sit behind the *Resolute* desk. Fear is why he asks people to pledge personal loyalty.

After December 19, 2017, it was impossible for the president or any of his supporters to believe that I might pledge personal loyalty to him—if there had been any doubt before. That was the day when my testimony to the House Permanent Select Committee on Intelligence made it clear that I would corroborate Jim Comey's version of the events surrounding his firing and the president's attempts to stop the investigation of Michael Flynn. Before I gave this testimony, the inspector general's report on Midyear had been expected to be made public the following spring, and the investigation of my statements was expected to come out later. After I gave this testimony, the inspector general informed one of my staff members that the report on me would be coming out first—and earlier than expected.

The president's tweets resumed within a few days of my testimony. It was like being the target of a schoolyard bully who slaps you around, lets up for a while until you think maybe it's over, then shows up again, saying, No, no—it's not over. You didn't think I'd forget Christmas, did you? The whole family was at home getting ready for the holidays when I was sent a screenshot of his latest tweet: "FBI Deputy Director Andrew McCabe is racing the clock to retire with full benefits. 90 days to go?!!!"

It was a very effective way to terrorize my family. All through Christmas and New Year's, the thought would buzz inside my head: He's focused on this. Can I just get to my birthday—the date of my retirement, long planned—before I get fired?

In January 2018, after conferring with the IG, Chris Wray called me in to a one-on-one meeting on a Sunday night and demanded that I leave the position of deputy director—but also asked that I announce I was stepping aside voluntarily. I refused to make what I considered to be a false statement and instead went out on leave, intending for this to last until my retirement.

"A Report of Investigation of Certain Allegations Relating to Former FBI Deputy Director Andrew McCabe," which was concluded in February 2018 though not released by the inspector general until April, determined that I "lacked candor on four separate occasions." This report was used as a pretext for dismissal. The attorney general ordered my firing on March 16—twenty-six hours before my planned retirement. I received word, as Comey had, by watching the TV news. The president marked the moment with a tweet: "Andrew McCabe FIRED, a great day for the hard working men and women of the FBI - A great day for Democracy. Sanctimonious James Comey was his boss and made McCabe look like a choirboy. He knew all about the lies and corruption going on at the highest levels of the FBI!"

I do not want to get down in the mud with the president. I do feel that I have an obligation to stand up and say, You can't do this. You can't just continue to attack people with an endless string of baseless lies. No one should be able to do that. The president of the United States especially should not. Analyzing or breaking down the specifics of what he's said on Twitter is a fool's errand. And I understand that it is meaningless to be called a liar by the most prolific liar I have ever encountered.

But I will say this. Donald Trump would not know the men and women of the FBI if he ran over them with the presidential limo, and he has shown the citizens of this country that he does not know what democracy means. He demonstrates no understanding or appreciation of our form of government. He takes no action to protect it. Has any president done more to undermine democracy than this one? His "I hereby demand" tweet in May 2018, ordering Department of Justice investigations of the investigators who are investigating him—I can barely believe that I just wrote that phrase—is a clear example. His demand for documents identifying confidential informants does harm to the men and women of the FBI on a fundamental level. It undermines their ability to build the trust that allows law-enforcement investigations to take place, in ways that, I want to believe, he does not comprehend. To think that he could recognize what constitutes a good thing for the men and women of the FBI does not deserve comment.

As for my own firing and the ostensible reasons behind it, the demands and risks of an ongoing legal process put tight constraints on what I can say, although I would like to say much more. I am filing a suit that challenges my firing and the IG's process and findings, and the unprecedented way DOJ handled my termination. I will let that action speak for itself.

Righting the Ship

On May 20, 2018, on Twitter, the president called for "real Americans" to "start getting tough" on what he calls "this Scam"—the reference was to the special counsel and the Russia probe, and the basis of the accusation was nothing more substantial than fiction and malice. This was a frightening statement, which has larger implications. I want to spell out those implications here.

Since the 2016 election, it has become commonplace to note how polarized the country has become. Disagreements that fracture public life have grown to the point where people on either side of the political divide can no longer even agree on what the facts are. People accept as fact only the information they get from their own selected news outlets. When you reach the point where your own group sees itself as representing the true believers, the only good people or the only "real Americans," then everyone else by definition must be seen as wrong, bad, fake. The president of the United States is actively pushing the citizens of this country in that direction. He exhorts his supporters to think of themselves as true Americans, and to consider anyone who disagrees with them as being treasonous, like criminals—people who should be in jail, as he has explicitly urged. The president tells one group of citizens: You are the good ones. No one else is equal to you. All the others are not as significant, not as important. They should not have the same rights. They should be treated as less-than. They are alien. They should be stricken. That is the language used by totalitarian regimes and fundamentalist religions to generate shock troops of core believers and sow the seeds of extremism. It would be impossible to overstate my concern at the president's rhetoric and behavior. I hope that others, including people close to him, are as alarmed by it as I am. But even if they are, I have seen in him no evidence of any capacity for introspection, self-criticism, or good-faith resolve. He will never back off that sort of rhetoric.

I would like to imagine a future in which we have righted the ship. The more horrendous things become, the more—I hope—it will increase the odds that America can swing back in the other direction. I hope that Americans will return to faith in one of our country's best traditions: answering the call of duty. Answering the call of duty is a tradition of both personal and professional excellence. And entire institutions, also, can embody and answer the call of duty. The FBI was built to do just that. It's the quality that made me want to be an FBI agent instead of a lawyer.

It's the same thing that compelled the FBI to change after 9/11. It wasn't just that we were being told we had to change. We knew we had to prevent the next attack. We had to answer that call. It's the same reason that Director Mueller took on the responsibility of the HIG from President Obama, despite his reluctance to get involved in an interagency feud. It's the reason Jim Comey took a bullet for the Justice Department in the Clinton email investigation—especially after the attorney general's conversation on that tarmac with former president Clinton. He knew it was a no-win situation, but he did it because he thought it was the best thing for the country. Finally, answering the call of duty was why I took the actions I did in the days after Jim Comey's firing—why I protected the Russia case by pressing for a special counsel to be appointed. I suspected that someday it would cost me my job. But I also knew that it was the right thing to do.

The purpose of the FBI is not to support one side. The purpose of the FBI is to protect the American people and uphold the Constitution. I know that the motto sounds corny, but I will say it a thousand times. That is really what we are trying to do. I'm not naïve—I know that nobody works in a vacuum. The FBI depends on Congress for funding and for oversight. Oversight is a good thing: We ought to be overseen by someone who is not us. The FBI also depends on the White House for support and direction and policy guidance. But at the end of the day, we have got to do our work independently and apolitically. That has become very hard, and it is time for more Americans to know that this difficulty of the Bureau's—this effort by Congress and, now, the White House to politicize everything—could cost our country dearly.

In order for the FBI to continue to fulfill its mission, it needs to attract the best and brightest. We don't need just former police officers, military officers, and attorneys. We also need computer scientists, we need biologists, we need statisticians. We need engineers. We need people who represent America's full spectrum of backgrounds and intellectual gifts. As the political atmosphere of our time continues to poison the intelligence community with politically motivated attacks, my fear is that people who are trying to decide whether to take a high-paying career in the private sector or to embrace a tough, maybe dangerous, and demanding career in the public sector are going to turn their backs on public service. We have got to start cherishing public service in a way that's going to continue to attract the people we need.

I look back on more than two decades of service to the Bureau with a sense of how much has changed and also of how durable the fundamentals have proved to be. My first major case as a newly sworn-in special agent concerned organized crime from Russia. And the ultimate Russian criminal organization—the Russian government itself—created the last significant issue I faced as acting director: interference in U.S. elections, the mechanism of our democracy, which resulted in the appointment of a special counsel to investigate this assault on this country's core values. People often think of values as fragile—and they certainly can be—but values grow in might when embodied in relationships, the basis of all social institutions: families, schools, churches, civic organizations. The U.S. government embodies values, too. The glaring exception to that rule, for now, is the presidency of Donald Trump, whose only value is self-seeking. But our government is vast, and it operates on many levels. The military, for instance, is a reservoir of civic values. So is local government. My vocation has been to work proudly in another bastion of legitimate values, the FBI. The FBI's core values—rigorous obedience to the Constitution, fairness, respect for those we protect, compassion, uncompromising personal integrity and institutional integrity, exemplary leadership, accountability, and embracing diversity—take their form and power not only from guidelines and procedures but through an animating culture, something that exists in the soul.

Hundreds of thousands of people in government devote their lives to the work of the United States of America. Millions upon millions of ordinary citizens serve their communities and make up the backbone of institutions of every kind. All of these people, in ways large and small, stand up for what they believe in—it's an abiding characteristic of our nation. If ever we lost that capacity, we'd be lost. But that capacity is something that real Americans will never lose.

Acknowledgments

This book describes the experience of having worked with the talented, dedicated, patriotic men and women of the FBI. For every person named on these pages there are scores more who led me, taught me, inspired me, protected me, and helped me become one of you. You are always in my thoughts. Your bravery and perseverance in the face of adversity is the true meaning of public service. God bless you and be safe.

I would not have been able to make this journey without the love and support of my family. Jill, George, and Maggie—you helped me ignore the lies and stay focused on doing the right thing, regardless of the cost. You reminded me what is truly important in life. Ellen, George, and Patrick McCabe—your guidance and protection turned me into a lawman. Susan, David, Jeff, and Kim McFarland and Charles Willis—you have always been in my corner. Gail Boren—you keep the family glued together. And Jeremiah—you show us all that sometimes, it's just better to take a rest.

Every ship needs a calm port in a storm. Karen and Fred—your hospitality and generosity gave us the safe place we needed to ignore the headlines and get this work done. You are truly supportive friends, and I am forever grateful.

All agents love to tell stories. But twenty-one years of memories don't turn themselves into a book without the help of a great writing and editing team, Michael Joseph Gross and Cullen Murphy. Thank you to Carole Ludwig for expert transcriptions and to Ben Kalin for thorough fact-checking. To Todd Shuster, David Granger, Sarah Levitt, and the team at Aevitas—thanks for putting me on this path. To George Witte, Sara Thwaite, Tracey Guest, and the whole team at St. Martin's Press—thanks for embracing this project with enthusiasm and bringing it to life.

Tough times make you appreciate the people who stand with you. Michael Bromwich, Melissa Schwartz, David Snyder, and David Schertler: thanks for believing in me and fighting for me. To Ed Puccio and the team at CEP, thanks for your consistent support of Jill and me. And to all the wonderful people, some I know and many I don't, who sent their thoughts, words, and support when I needed them most—I can never explain how much that meant to my family and me. Thank you.

Finally, thank you to each and every person who musters the dignity, the strength, and the courage to stand up for what he or she believes in. Acts of bravery and conscience are the lifeblood of a society committed to democracy and justice, decency and fairness. Standing up is more important now than ever.

Index